1966 WORLD CHAMPIONS

GEOFF HURST

WORLD CHAMPIONS

Also by Sir Geoff Hurst

1966 And All That

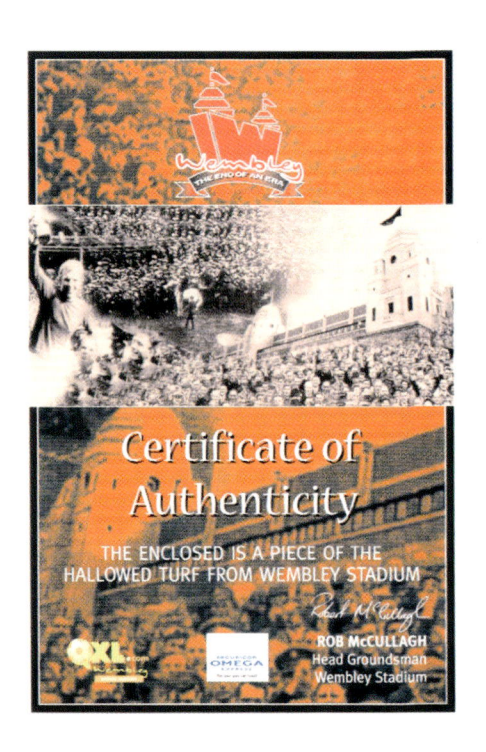

Certificate of Authenticity verifying the Wembley turf used in the manufacture of the endpapers of this book.

1966
WORLD CHAMPIONS

Relive the glorious
summer with
those who were there

GEOFF HURST

with Michael Hart

headline

Copyright © 2006 Sir Geoff Hurst

The right of Sir Geoff Hurst to be identified as the Author of the Work has been asserted by him in accordance with the Copyright, Designs and Patents Act 1988.

First published in 2006
by HEADLINE BOOK PUBLISHING

1

Apart from any use permitted under UK copyright law, this publication may only be reproduced, stored, or transmitted, in any form, or by any means, with prior permission in writing of the publishers or, in the case of reprographic production, in accordance with the terms of licences issued by the Copyright Licensing Agency.

Every effort has been made to fulfil requirements with regard to reproducing copyright material. The author and publisher will be glad to rectify any omissions at the earliest opportunity.

A CIP catalogue record for this title is available from the British Library

ISBN 0 7553 1414 X

Text design by Dan Newman/Perfect Bound Ltd

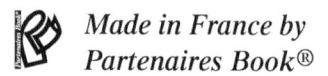

Made in France by Partenaires Book®

Headline's policy is to use papers that are natural, renewable and recyclable products and made from wood grown in sustainable forests. The logging and manufacturing processes are expected to conform to the environmental regulations of the country of origin.

HEADLINE BOOK PUBLISHING
A division of Hodder Headline
338 Euston Road
London NW1 3BH

www.headline.co.uk
www.hodderheadline.com

For any commercial enquiry for Sir Geoff Hurst and/or certain members of the 1966 team, please email: enquiries@football1966.com

Dedicated to the memory of Alf, a great manager, and Bobby, a great captain

Contents

Foreword by Sven-Goran Eriksson   8
1. **The way it was**   10
2. **Stalag Lilleshall**   24
3. **On tour**   40
4. **Bobby, Nobby, Jack and the boys**   56
5. **What was it all about, Alfie?**   84
6. **The first round**   112
7. **Argentina**   134
8. **Portugal**   152
9. **Match number 32 – the final tie**   170
10. **The party**   208
11. **Whatever happened to?**   228

Statistics   250

Acknowledgements   256

Picture credits   256

Foreword

by Sven-Goran Eriksson

Wembley 1966...fans on the pitch...and Sir Geoff Hurst's hat-trick. Those images are ingrained in the minds of every football fan, certainly in England and also around the world. That World Cup final remains one of the most famous ever and is the high point that every England team has tried to emulate for the last 40 years. How wonderful it would be if we could repeat it in Germany in 2006.

Scoring once in a World Cup final is an incredible achievement, a defining moment in any player's career, but scoring a hat-trick is truly extraordinary. This remarkable feat has never been repeated and maybe never will be. It is the stuff of dreams.

I can remember watching the game on television in Sweden. Everyone in Sweden followed English football back then, just as they do today, so there was a lot of interest in the match. I was about 18 years old and doing my military service. I don't remember exactly where I was, but I can recall the hat-trick very clearly – the header, the famous shot that came down from the crossbar and then the tremendous volley in the dying moments of the game.

What many people may forget is that Sir Geoff was quite new to the England team when the 1966 World Cup began. He was not picked for the group games because England also had Jimmy Greaves, who was an outstanding goalscorer. The door opened for Sir Geoff when Greaves was injured. I suppose, in some ways, Sir Geoff was in the right place at the right time but, like all great players, when he got his chance he seized it with both hands. He scored the winning goal against Argentina in the quarter-finals, kept his place in the semi-finals and then came that famous day on Saturday, 30 July 1966.

It made him a national hero and he went on to have a fantastically successful career with both West Ham and England, winning 49 caps for his country and scoring 24 goals.

Sir Geoff Hurst has earned his place in football folklore and deserves the gratitude of everyone who loves the game.

GEOFF HURST

1
The way it was

Christmas Day 1965 dawned cold and damp. In the grey suburban sprawl of Chadwell Heath, no trains ran along the Liverpool Street mainline track beside West Ham's training ground, and it was strangely quiet.

We were due to play Aston Villa on 27 December but the weather forecast suggested ice might jeopardise the fixture list. In the end, 32 Football League games were postponed and two were abandoned, including our match at Villa Park. We thought that might turn out to be the case as we ploughed through our training routines on muddy pitches that Christmas morning. No one complained, though. In those days, everyone from railway staff to shopkeepers had the day off but training on Christmas Day was all part of being a professional footballer. The bonus for us came in the summer when we might have seven or eight weeks to laze around. After training that morning, Martin Peters and I discussed sharing a family holiday in Cornwall.

10 WORLD CHAMPIONS

GEOFF HURST

New Year 1966 started gloomily, and the weather reflected the mood of the country. The big breweries put up the cost of a pint of beer by one penny to 1s 8d

Previous spread: *30 January 1965. The cortege at the state funeral of Sir Winston Churchill makes its way down Whitehall.*

Above: *A first in 1965. Kenneth Tynan utters the 'F' word on British TV on the programme BBC3.*

Opposite: *Great Train robber Ronnie Biggs, one of the 15 members of the gang which held up the Royal Mail's Glasgow-London train on 8 August 1963. He escaped from Wandsworth prison in 1965 after only 15 months behind bars.*

The season was due to end on Saturday, 7 May. The only other consideration when determining our holiday dates was the World Cup, which was scheduled for 11–30 July. We wanted to be certain that, wherever we were during those three weeks, it was somewhere near a TV set.

The World Cup was not to be missed, especially if you were a West Ham player. After all, England would be led by our club captain, Bobby Moore, and there was a very good chance that another team-mate, Johnny 'Budgie' Byrne, would also been in the squad.

Also, having grown up around Essex and East London, most of us could claim friendship with the sharp-shooting Cockney who most people thought could win the trophy for England, the incomparable Jimmy Greaves – assuming, of course, that Jimmy would be fit for the World Cup. A few weeks before Christmas he went down with hepatitis, a debilitating illness that was to cost him three months of the season. Jim's condition, and the implications it had for England, kept the newspapers in headlines for days at the end of 1965. His illness was really big news.

It had not been a particularly good year for news of any sort, starting as it did with the death and state funeral of Sir Winston Churchill. The war had been over for 20 years but for my generation of youngsters he remained a national hero.

It had certainly been a violent year. India and Pakistan went to war over Kashmir and the Americans became ever more deeply involved in the conflict in Vietnam. Civil riots erupted in Los Angeles, the Moors murders shocked the nation and Great Train robber Ronnie Biggs escaped from Wandsworth prison. The 'F' word was used on TV for the first time but football traditionalists were more disturbed by the

> *It had not been a particularly good year for news of any sort*

GEOFF HURST

Below: *Sir Stanley Rous, FIFA president and former secretary of the FA, choosing the ball to be used for the tournament.*

Opposite left: *Mary Quant arriving at Buckingham Palace to receive her OBE in '66.*

Opposite right: *Twiggy. The Face of 1966.*

introduction of substitutes – Charlton's Keith Peacock was the first. Then many people were delighted when the peerless Stanley Matthews became soccer's first knight.

New Year 1966 started gloomily, and the weather reflected the mood of the country. The big breweries put up the cost of a pint of beer by one penny to 1s 8d – about eight pence in today's money – and West Ham were beaten 3–0 by Nottingham Forest at Upton Park on New Year's Day.

I couldn't wait for the close season. Our plans for a couple of weeks' holiday on a beach in Cornwall were progressing nicely and the party had grown. Ronnie and Dawn Boyce, Peter and Doreen Brabrook and all their children were joining Martin and me and our families. I had no idea that as the cold winter turned to spring and summer, those plans would be in jeopardy.

Even though I was looking forward to getting away from London for a while, there is no doubt it was the city of the moment, despite rising prices and belligerent trade unions. *Time* magazine had declared London to be a 'swinging city' and the heart of a new culture as exemplified by the Beatles and the queen of fashion, Mary Quant.

Carnaby Street was the place to be seen and Twiggy, the six-stone Cockney waif on the cover of *Vogue*, was the model to be seen with. 'Day Tripper' by the Beatles spent five weeks at number one in the pop charts in the New Year as the social revolution introduced us to the mini-skirt and the new concepts of the pill and pot. Mystified old folks, my mum and dad among them, clung desperately to fast-eroding traditions and standards. Life would never be quite the same again.

The first hint of a significant change in my own life came on a frosty morning over the New Year holiday. Because of the icy pitches, the West Ham players were training indoors at the roller-skating rink in Forest Gate. We were playing five-a-side football when the manager, the late Ron Greenwood, sauntered over to me.

'I've just had a message from the FA,' he said. 'You've been called into the England squad for the game against Poland.'

> The first hint of a significant change in my own life came on a frosty morning over the New Year holiday

> **The World Cup was just six months away and I hardly dared believe that I might get picked for that**

I had four England Under-23 caps but didn't think I was close to the senior side. England were due to meet Poland on 5 January at Goodison Park and I felt privileged to be involved for the first time. The fact that I didn't play in the 1–1 draw did nothing to dilute my enthusiasm. The World Cup was just six months away and I hardly dared believe that I might get picked for that.

The day after England played Poland, Sir Stanley Rous, a former Watford schoolmaster and referee who had risen to become the President of FIFA, presided at the World Cup draw in London. The 16 competing nations were divided into four groups of four and England were drawn in Group One with Uruguay, France and Mexico.

The matches were to be played at Wembley and London's old White City Stadium and at the grounds of Sheffield Wednesday, Aston Villa, Manchester United, Everton, Middlesbrough and Sunderland.

All the host stadiums had been modernised in the build-up period, but seating accommodation remained in short supply. For instance, although the Wembley capacity was 97,000, only 45,000 of those fans

The World Cup draw has just been completed in London in January. F.I.F.A. President Sir Stanley Rous is seated in the middle, with Harry Cavan (N. Ireland) on his left and Secretary Dr. Helmut Kaeser on his right.

could be seated. Old Trafford held 64,000, offering 18,340 seats. The Villa Park capacity was 54,000 with just 12,000 seats. Sunderland had 5,870 seats in a 63,000 capacity stadium and so installed 9,000 temporary seats.

Renovating their stadiums was an expensive business for the clubs – it had cost Middlesbrough more to paint their ground in 1964 than it had to erect it sixty years earlier – so the Government agreed to help, giving £500,000 towards ground improvements and running the tournament. The Football Association put in £150,000. Around 2.4 million tickets were printed for the 32 matches and a sell-out at every ground would mean total receipts of £1.75 million with a further £300,000 from TV and radio fees. These were big numbers in those days!

In March, just four days after it was announced that the sale of tickets had topped £1 million, Sir Stanley and the rest of the population must have choked on their breakfast cereal as they read that the World Cup had been stolen. Yes, stolen! The solid gold Jules Rimet Trophy, named after the French lawyer who was FIFA president from 1921 to 1954, was just 12 inches high, weighed nine pounds and would be completely hidden if placed inside the FA Cup.

I was at home when I heard the news on the radio and I remember thinking, 'Why would anyone steal it?' You couldn't sell it because it

Above: *The official programme for the World Cup captures the 'excitement' of the draw!*

Opposite: *The Fab Four on 23 June 1966, just about to leave London for their last ever world tour, taking in Germany, Japan, the Philippines and the USA. They played their last UK concert, a 15-minute set for the* New Musical Express *Poll Winners' concert, a few weeks earlier, on 1 May.*

UK No. 1 album on 1 January 1966: *Rubber Soul* by the Beatles. No. 1 for nine weeks

GEOFF HURST

17

Above: *A kickabout with my mates John Sissons, Les Allen and Ronnie Boyce. The World Cup was looming and I could only hope I would be involved.*

I made my debut in a match of indifferent quality. The best I can say is that I made no mistakes

was far too well known. If you melted it down, what would it be worth? I rang Martin Peters and we had a chuckle about it. At training the next day, Bobby Moore wondered whether it would be ransomed by the robbers.

The trophy was insured for £30,000 at the time it was 'lifted' from a stamp exhibition in Central Hall, Westminster, and was missing for eight days. Then a black-and-white mongrel dog named Pickles found it in a garden in Beulah Hill, South London. In the interim period, the FA chairman, Joe Mears, disclosed that he had indeed been asked to pay a £15,000 ransom for its return. Pickles and his owner, a Thames lighterman, had saved the nation from embarrassment and became overnight heroes. Pickles was given celebrity treatment by the newspapers and the owner picked up a £6,000 reward, but the thief was never caught.

What would have happened had the trophy not been discovered? Well, Brazil had won the Jules Rimet Trophy twice already and were tipped by many to win it a third time in England. Under the competition rules they would then keep it. I remember Joao Havelange, President of the Brazilian Sports Federation and the man who succeeded Sir Stanley as FIFA President, saying that, if Brazil won for a third time, they would immediately donate another trophy. They wanted to name it The Winston Churchill Cup, 'in memory of the greatest man of the twentieth

DAILY SKETCH

Monday, March 21, 1966 — Price Fourpence — *** — WEATHER: Dry and sunny

Go for happy go luxury HILLMAN SUPER IMP

...and go for SUPER IMP reliability See Page 10

World Cup. 9lb., 12in. tall.

Thin man steals trophy during church service

ENGLAND LOSES THE WORLD CUP

That's the cup, that was—a policeman guards the empty case last night.

By PETER BURDEN and GEORGE GORDON

POLICE searched last night for a slim man who, they believe, stole soccer's solid gold World Cup from a display cabinet in Central Hall, Westminster.

The trophy, one foot high and weighing 9lb., was insured for £30,000. Melted down, the gold would be worth about £2,000.

Last night Scotland Yard issued this description of the man they think stole it—

Age, late 30s; height, about 5ft. 10in.; sallow complexion, thin lips, black hair; face may be scarred.

THE CUP—a symbolic winged figure—was to have been awarded to the winners of the world soccer championship to be decided in Britain next July.

It was brought to London by delegates from Brazil, the present holders.

THE THEFT of the cup—star item in a stamp exhibition called "Sport with Stamps"—took place between 11 a.m. and noon while a Methodist service was being held in another part of the hall.

LOCKED

Last night Chief Detective Inspector Little of Scotland Yard, leading the investigation, addressed the evening congregation and asked if anyone had seen anything unusual in the morning.

Earlier he learnt that security guards were in the exhibition, area behind locked doors, when the cup vanished.

A senior officer said: "We prefer not to say how many men were on duty because there are other things on exhibition. We are not just concerned with the cup. It wouldn't be right to disclose security details."

The exhibition, he ➡ Back Page

TWO-PAGE RACING SPECIAL!

IT'S The Flat! And Gimcrack of the Daily Sketch heralds it with a 20-1 winner! He gave Abbotsbury Abbot at Sedgefield on Saturday.

And he gave 712 winners (55 winning naps) on the Flat last season.

Turn to Pages 16 and 17 for Britain's best Service.

Study the Top Writers in Gimcrack (John Rickman), Norman Pegg and Joe Canty. And note a Sketch exclusive...

WINNERS BY COMPUTER

Make your racing pay this season with the **Racing Sketch**

'Hallelujah' songs barred

A PROGRAMME of "protest" songs in an ITV religious series was axed last night—because of the Election.

The show, "Hallelujah," included one song called "Three Cheers for UDI," which contained references to Mr. Wilson.

ABC Television, which presents the series, substituted another show seen last year.

Sydney Carter, who introduces the show, said: "It was considered too controversial to go out at the moment."

There was another TV Election ban yesterday—an American producer and a BBC TV camera crew were forbidden from all further Labour campaign meetings.

The decision follows a clash with Mr. George Brown during a speech at Edinburgh on Saturday. It ended with the cameramen walking out.

Mr. Brown told the crew to "stop fooling around"

when they spotlighted a heckler and clustered around to film him.

A Labour Party spokesman said last night: "They totally disrupted the meeting as everybody stood up and turned round to see what was going on.

"Attention was so concentrated on the hecklers that it was impossible for Mr. Brown to continue."

Mr. Brown reported to Transport House that the

American was in the balcony directing operations "like a man on a 'Ben Hur' film set."

It is alleged that Mr. Joseph Strick, the documentary producer, switched his lighting so that Mr. Brown was suddenly plunged into near darkness on the platform while the television lights picked out the hecklers. The banned crew are from the documentary section of the BBC's current affairs department.

All busy mums deserve an automatic washing machine

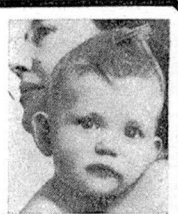

And now they can have one for the price of a twin-tub

The Imperial Superautomatic—just the thing for busy mums! Imperial does all the wash from start to finish, and gives you much more time for your family. It's more automatic than leading machines of twice the price. Yet it costs as little as some twin-tubs!

Compare Imperial's features with any other machine: Automatic pre-wash; 9 lb. load; stainless steel drum; special two-way washing action; 5 fresh water rinses; spin dries and switches off automatically; can be set to boil; works from any cold tap... no plumbing required.

Yet it costs only 79 gns. or easy terms!

Fully guaranteed for 12 months, with worry-free insurance and nation-wide after sales service. Generous part-exchange on your old machine.

FREE! Don't delay! Post coupon for exciting colour brochure and 'Guide to Washing Machines'. Available in Scotland and N. Ireland.

Please post me, without obligation, my FREE colour brochure.

Name
Address
Town

To: "Free Brochures", 261/5 Gray's Inn Rd. London, W.C.1. Tel: BRU 7994

Imperial

Continuous daily demonstrations in our showrooms—Thursdays till 8 p.m.

century,' said Havelange. So a new trophy may have been named in honour of Britain's wartime Prime Minister had Pickles not intervened.

I thought that was a wonderful idea, but although Brazil won the tournament for the third time in 1970, and therefore kept the Jules Rimet Trophy, a new Cup in honour of Churchill never materialised. The trophy was stolen again, in Rio in 1983, and this time was never recovered.

The tournament was just four months away when Sir Alf Ramsey called me into the England squad for the second time. West Germany were the opposition, Wembley the venue. This time I was in Alf's starting line-up, unaware of course that the Germans would play such a significant role in my career.

I made my debut in a match of indifferent quality. Nobby Stiles, curiously wearing the No. 9 shirt, scored the only goal. My own contribution was nothing special. The best I can say is that I made no mistakes.

Would I get another chance? The answer came in April when Alf retained my services in the team that played Scotland at Hampden Park. When I scored the first of England's four goals with a right-foot shot from the edge of the penalty area, I discovered what it felt like to silence 123,000 screaming Scots. It felt good!

For the first time, I began to think that I might have a realistic chance of getting into the World Cup squad. It was obvious, assuming

I began to think that I might have a realistic chance of getting into the World Cup squad

20 WORLD CHAMPIONS

> Ah yes, I remember it well - Saturday July 30th when England won the World Cup for the only time... I remember that the kindergarten gave all of us children the day off to watch the match. Unfortunately, fringe reception in Ireland was very fuzzy and I went to bed that evening convinced that Germany had won!
>
> Terry Wogan

Opposite top: *World Cup Willie pops into FA headquarters to make sure preparations for the tournament are well in hand.*

Opposite bottom: *World Cup hero Pickles takes his new-found celebrity status in his stride.*

Below: *The Beach Boys' masterpiece,* Pet Sounds, *entered the album chart on 9 July 1966 and peaked at No. 2.*

he was fit, that Jimmy Greaves would be in the starting line-up, and Roger Hunt was ahead of me in the pecking order. I didn't mind. Just being in the squad would be the greatest honour of my career.

Roger's form that season had been sensational. His 30 goals in 37 matches helped Liverpool win the First Division title for the seventh time, equalling Arsenal's then record. Against West Ham at Upton Park, he hit three in three minutes as Liverpool beat us 5–1.

The great Bill Shankly had put together a fabulous Liverpool team, and that season it had all the hallmarks of an emerging dynasty. They assumed the leadership in November and raced away with the title, using just 14 players.

They were unlucky not to win the European Cup Winners' Cup, as well. Their opponents in the final at Hampden Park were Borussia Dortmund, who'd beaten us, the holders, in the semi-final. Roger missed a great chance to clinch the match when it was 1–1. It was a costly miss because the Germans scored in extra time, winning 2–1.

In the European Cup – the forerunner of the Champions League – Partisan Belgrade surprised everyone with their semi-final win over Manchester United, whose exhilarating 5–1 victory over Benfica in Lisbon in the previous

GEOFF HURST

TIME

THE WEEKLY NEWSMAGAZINE

ATLANTIC EDITION — **APRIL 15, 1966**

LONDON: The Swinging City

round ranked among the great English club achievements of the decade.

The prospect of a Manchester United–Real Madrid final had excited the purists in the game but, instead, Real faced Partisan in Brussels. Their captain, Francisco Gento, was 32 and the only survivor of the peerless Real side of the fifties that won five European Cups in consecutive seasons. When Real beat Partisan 2–1 in the final, it signalled the end of an era. It was Gento's eighth European Cup final and the sixth time he'd finished on the winning side – records that still remain unchallenged. A small, powerful winger, Gento retired in 1971, having helped Real to win 12 Spanish titles. 'He was one of the fastest players I saw,' Jimmy Greaves told me.

A few days before the European Cup final, Sir Alf Ramsey named his provisional party of 40 players for World Cup duty. I was in his squad, and so was Martin Peters, who had still to make his international debut.

Suddenly, the World Cup had a different significance for both of us. I don't think either of us seriously thought we'd make the final 22 but, just in case, we checked the Cornwall dates again. Would our holiday have to be moved? Or cancelled? Perhaps we wouldn't be watching Bobby Moore on TV after all. Just maybe, we would be there with him.

> *I don't think either of us seriously thought we'd make the final 22. Might our holiday have to be moved? Or cancelled?*

Below: *'Bestie' scoring his second in the remarkable victory over Benfica.*

GEOFF HURST

23

2
Stalag Lilleshall

It was typical of Sir Alf Ramsey's caution and thoroughness that he announced England's provisional World Cup squad of 40 players before he was required to do so by FIFA rules. The world governing body stipulated that the names had to be with them by the end of May. There was a second deadline – 3 July, eight days before the tournament began – for each nation to advise FIFA of their final list of 22 players.

Alf named his original 40 in mid-April. He was at war with some of the big clubs – notably Leeds United – over the release of players and he wanted them to know which of their players were likely to be used by England in the weeks ahead. He also wanted the nation to know his plans, so that if the clubs withdrew players, the public would know who was to blame.

That season, Leeds, Liverpool, Manchester United, Chelsea and West Ham were all involved in the latter stages of the three big European competitions. On top of that, Leeds and Liverpool were battling it out at the top of the old First Division and Manchester United and Chelsea were both through to the semi-finals of the FA Cup. The other semi-finalists, Everton and Sheffield Wednesday, also had players involved in the squad.

WORLD CHAMPIONS

GEOFF HURST

Previous spread: *Jubilant Everton celebrate their fantastic victory in the '66 FA Cup final. That's Ray Wilson's head being grabbed by Brian Harris. The others are Jimmy Gabriel, Alex Scott, Mike Trebilcock and Alex Young.*

Above: *The West Ham Three who made Sir Alf's initial 40. Myself, Bobby Moore and Martin Peters.*

Opposite: *Johnny 'Budgie' Byrne about to score against Burnley in 1964.*

Not all club managers were as sympathetic as West Ham's Ron Greenwood to the selection problems facing the England manager. I remember, years later, Ron actually leaving Bobby Moore and me out of the West Ham team so that we would be fresh for a big England match in the European Championship qualifying programme. You can't imagine club managers doing that today.

Liverpool had seven players named in Alf's 40 – Tommy Smith, Chris Lawler, Gordon Milne, Peter Thompson, Ian Callaghan, Gerry Byrne and Roger Hunt.

Chelsea had five – Peter Bonetti, Marvin Hinton, John Hollins, Barry Bridges and Peter Osgood.

Everton had four – Gordon West, Ray Wilson, Derek Temple and Fred Pickering.

Leeds had three – Jack Charlton, Paul Reaney and Norman Hunter.

Manchester United had three – Nobby Stiles, Bobby Charlton and John Connelly.

West Ham had three – Bobby Moore, Martin Peters and me.

So, more than half the squad came from six of the clubs with most to play for at the end of that season. The seventh, Sheffield Wednesday, beaten 3–2 by Everton in a classic FA Cup final on 14 May (Everton were 2–0 down and came back with three goals in fifteen second-half minutes), also supplied one player – goalkeeper Ron Springett.

The rest of the 40 were Tony Waiters, Jimmy Armfield and Alan Ball (Blackpool), Jimmy Greaves and Terry Venables (Tottenham), Gordon Banks (Leicester City), George Cohen (Fulham), Keith Newton (Blackburn), Ron Flowers (Wolves), Terry Paine (Southampton), George Eastham (Arsenal), John Kaye (West Bromwich Albion), Joe Baker (Nottingham Forest) and Gordon Harris (Burnley).

Many of the squad had no experience of senior international football. Osgood (who died so tragically earlier this year), Kaye, Smith, Bonetti, Hinton, Peters, Callaghan, Hollins, Reaney and West hadn't played for the England side. Some of them never would. But the big talking point in the newspapers focused on who'd been left out. The most notable absentee was my West Ham team-mate Johnny 'Budgie' Byrne. He was an enormously talented player with 11 England caps and seven goals to his name. I was disappointed for him because I owed a lot of my early success at West Ham to the partnership he and I developed.

No one doubted his talent, but he was an incessant talker and joker off the pitch – that's why we called him 'Budgie'

GEOFF HURST

27

Below: *Cilla Black enjoyed three Top 10 hits in '66: 'Love's Just a Broken Heart', 'Alfie' and 'Don't Answer Me'.*

Opposite: *Chairman Mao's* Little Red Book *is first published in English in 1966. Here, in Tiananmen Square in November 1966, Red Guards recite in unison from Chairman Mao's works.*

He was the star and I was the straight man, doing the donkey-work. I didn't mind that because I learned so much from him. Playing alongside him was one of the best things that could have happened to me. I really envied, for instance, the way he could cushion a pass with his chest and have the ball at his feet, ready to play, in fractions of a second. It was something I tried to copy.

No one doubted his talent, but he was an incessant talker and joker off the pitch – that's why we called him 'Budgie' – and I'm not sure he was quite Alf's cup of tea in the dressing room. Of course, he was disappointed when he learned he wasn't in the 40, but his World Cup wasn't quite over, although there was no place for him in the team Alf selected to play Yugoslavia at Wembley on 4 May. This was England's last international home game before the finals of the World Cup began. Alf had planned the fixture list meticulously. During the 1965–66 season, we played 12 international matches before the World Cup. Sven-Goran Eriksson's team played ten prior to the 2002 World Cup. Glenn Hoddle's team played nine leading up to the finals in 1998.

Perhaps impressed by the wing play of Scotland's little Jimmy Johnstone at Hampden Park a month earlier, Alf called up two wingers – Southampton's Terry Paine and Chelsea's Bobby Tambling, who had not even been in the provisional 40. Both played well in England's 2–0 win, and so did Jimmy Greaves, who had been recalled to the team after his long illness.

Although originally committed to wingers, Alf was in the process of abandoning this traditional concept in favour of a 4-3-3 system, which, ultimately, he modified to 4-4-2. I think Alf retreated from deploying conventional wingers simply because he felt that those in England's squad were not good enough for the challenges ahead.

WORLD CHAMPIONS

On 6 May, Alf announced another squad. This time he nominated the 28 players he wanted for 18 days' World Cup training at Lilleshall. I was in the party, honoured and relieved

He acknowledged the value of good wingers in getting behind defences but, for him, defensive duties such as tackling, tracking back and covering were at least as important. I've always believed that the 2–0 win over Spain in Madrid in December 1965 was a significant stage in the evolution of Alf's team. He picked a side without conventional wingers and they lined up in the 4-3-3 formation. Nine of the World Cup-winning team played that day. Only Martin Peters and I, both uncapped at the time, were missing.

The fate of the wingers, though, was still in the balance with the World Cup just two months away. Peter Thompson, Ian Callaghan, Terry Paine, John Connelly and now Bobby Tambling were all in the frame.

Above: *25 of the 27 who made it to Lilleshall. Missing are Ray Wilson and Bobby Tambling. Ray was still nursing his bad back. Not sure where Bobby is. Perhaps he did escape for a while. Standing l-r: J. Connelly, G. Milne, B. Moore, I. Callaghan, J. Charlton, P. Bonetti, G. Banks, R. Flowers, R. Charlton, J. Armfield, N. Stiles, L. Cocker, W. McGuinness, N. Hunter, H. Shepherdson, G. Byrne, G. Cohen, R. Springett; sitting l-r: P. Thompson, J. Byrne, G. Eastham, myself, M. Peters, K. Newton, A. Ball, T. Paine, J. Greaves, R. Hunt.*

Then, on 6 May, two days after we'd beaten Yugoslavia, Alf announced another squad. This time he nominated the 28 players he wanted for 18 days' World Cup training at Lilleshall. I was in the party, honoured and relieved. So was Martin.

The 28, from whom Alf would select his final 22, included three late replacements for injured players – Bobby Tambling for Barry Bridges, Everton's Brian Labone for Marvin Hinton and 'Budgie' Byrne, reinstated in place of Fred Pickering.

The irreverent 'Budgie' was so excited you couldn't stop him talking as West Ham prepared for the final First Division match of the season, against Leicester City at Filbert Street on 9 May. Both teams were stranded in mid table, and in the eyes of most of the fans the season was already over. This was reflected by the attendance figure that day – just 16,066.

WORLD CHAMPIONS

Bobby Moore, the iconic leader at the very heart of England's World Cup bid, had been left out of the West Ham side. He had looked very ordinary two days earlier when West Ham lost 1–0 at Stoke, and he was in dispute with the club over a new contract. Defeat in the semi-final of the Cup Winners' Cup meant that, for the first time in three years, the club ended the season on a flat note. 'Mooro', as Bobby Moore was known, was also concerned about his position in the England side because Norman Hunter of Leeds was emerging as a genuine contender for a place in the back four. A lot of talk was circulating about the England captain moving to a bigger club. Tottenham were known to want him. The papers said that the club were asking £80,000 for him, which would have been the bargain of the decade as far as I was concerned.

We lost 2–1 to Leicester – a jubilant 'Budgie' scored our goal – and a few days later Martin and I and the rest of the gang, with children in

Below: *Our 'Enery might not have won the title but he put up a hell of a fight against the magnificent Cassius Clay.*

WORLD CUP

JULY 11 to 30
1966
ENGLAND

Above: Sir Alf chatting with Bobby Moore and Harold Shepherdson.

tow, drove to Cornwall for our summer holiday. It had been touch and go but we'd managed to fit it in. My wife Judith and Martin's wife Kathy were delighted. We'd fiddled with the dates a little to ensure that we were back in time to rejoin the England squad at Lilleshall.

One of the things I remember about that holiday was finding a TV set one evening to watch Cassius Clay retain the world heavyweight title by beating London's very own Henry Cooper in front of a 46,000 crowd at Highbury Stadium on 21 May. Henry was doing well until his eyebrow split. The referee stopped the fight in round six. Clay, later to embrace Islam and become Muhammad Ali, was in the process of becoming the most famous man on the planet.

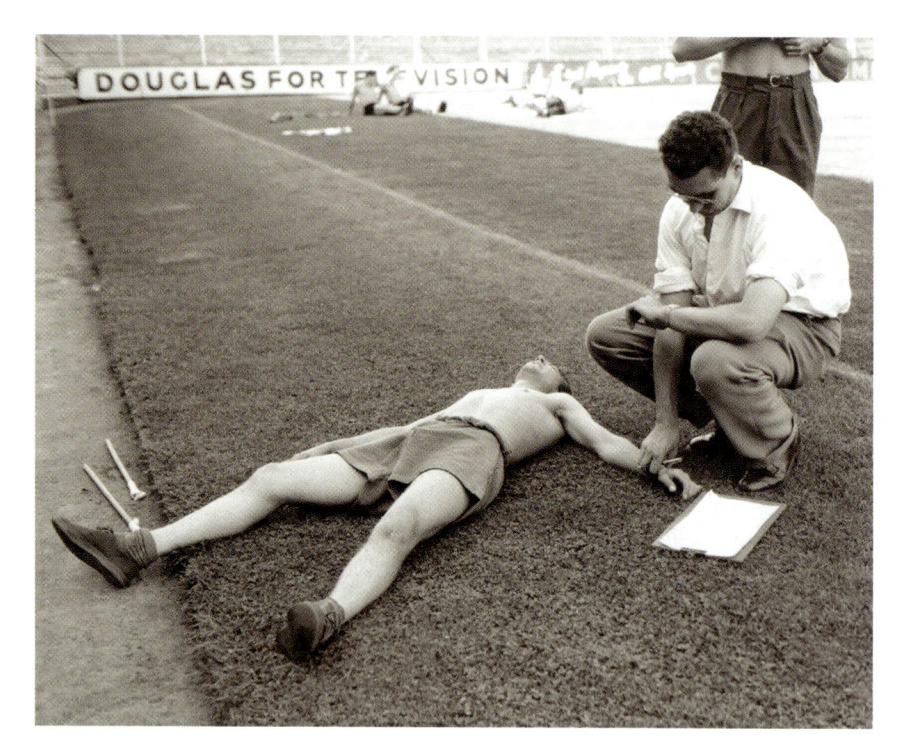

Alf had ordered us to report back on 6 June, a little more than a month before the World Cup was due to start. Of the 28 selected, 27 turned up. Ironically, Brian Labone, in the squad because Marvin Hinton was injured, also had to withdraw because of injury. Five of the remaining 27 would be told by 3 July that they had not made it into Alf's 22 and would therefore play no part in the World Cup finals. No one knew which five would be axed so all of us threw ourselves into 18 days of training with vigour and optimism. No one wanted to be told by Alf, 'Sorry, but I don't have room for you.'

A vast imposing country estate in Shropshire, once the home of the Duke of Sutherland, Lilleshall was a wonderful place to prepare for the World Cup, but not everyone agreed with me. Plenty of 'Stalag Lilleshall' jokes were flying around as Alf and his trusty lieutenants, coach Les Cocker and physiotherapist Harold 'Shep' Shepherdson, laid down the ground rules. They boiled down to, 'You are here to work. If you don't like it, go home.'

Alf listed all the things we couldn't do. If you leave the estate, he said, don't bother coming back. If you sneak out for a pint, don't come back. Anyone who doesn't like the rules, go home now. I could sense Jack Charlton's unease as he listened to Alf describe the regime that we would be subjected to in the coming days. We joked about forming an escape committee. Jack insisted on being part of the break-out if it carried the promise of a drink. Somehow, Alf got to hear about it and called us together.

'Anyone who pops out for a pint is finished with the World Cup, with me and with the England squad for good,' he said.

That was the end of the break-out jokes. Even Jack observed the rules for the duration of our stay. He tried Alf's patience from time to time, but there was mutual respect. They didn't speak often because whenever Jack addressed Alf his answer was invariably, 'No, Jack!'

Alf didn't need to like his players to work with them. What was important was that they respected each other. At 10.30 each evening Alf would walk into the TV lounge where the players gathered after dinner to remind us it was time for bed. One evening we were watching

> *I could sense Jack Charlton's unease as he listened to Alf describe the regime that we would be subjected to in the coming days*

Tom Jones with Albert Finney in the starring role. It was good fun and the lads were enjoying it when Alf declared, 'Good night, gentlemen.' That was enough. Very often we were at the critical stage in a movie but everyone got up and went to their rooms. Alf was always strict about things like that. During his time as England manager in the years following the World Cup, I missed the ending of *Butch Cassidy and the Sundance Kid* three times. It wasn't until 1990 that I realised they both got shot!

Occasionally, you'd hear Les or 'Shep' walking along the corridors outside the players' bedrooms. Sometimes they'd knock and ask if you wanted plasters or bandages for the morning training session, or they'd ask if you wanted a sleeping pill. We knew that the real reason for the nightly tour was to check that we were all in our rooms.

Alf's staff was pitifully small compared with the back-up that Sven-Goran Eriksson receives today. Sven has a support staff of about a dozen, including three outfield coaches, a goalkeeping coach, a team doctor, physiotherapist, three masseurs and kit managers.

In 1966 Alf had Les and 'Shep' and the former Manchester United and England half-back Wilf McGuinness, who briefly followed Sir Matt Busby as manager at Old Trafford. The only other member of staff with whom we had regular contact was Dr Alan Bass, an immensely likeable Harley Street consultant and the Arsenal team doctor. He was known as 'Alfie' after Alfie Bass, a TV actor of the time.

One of Alf's first tasks when he succeeded Walter Winterbottom was to appoint a team doctor. England had survived without one for years until the 1962 World Cup when one of the squad, Peter Swan, was given dangerously mistaken treatment and almost died in Vina del Mar. A simple stomach upset was wrongly diagnosed.

A practical, methodical man, Alf wanted to build his regime

Below: *Wilf McGuinness when he was at Manchester United.*

Opposite: *Alan Bass demonstrates how to take the pulse of a Crystal Palace trainee in the days before he became the first England team doctor.*

UK No.1 single on 1 January 1966: 'Day Tripper/We Can Work It Out' by the Beatles. No.1 for five weeks

on strong foundations. Quite rightly, he considered a team doctor essential.

Dr Bass was enormously popular with the players. We found him very easy to talk to, and I know he was a reassuring figure for Nobby Stiles, whose wife Kay was expecting a baby any day. When she suggested that he should come home for the birth, Nobby replied, 'Are you joking?' The competition for places in the team was so intense that he knew if he left, even with Alf's blessing, he could return to find his place in the pecking order had gone to another player.

It was every player's ambition to be involved in the starting 11 against Uruguay on 11 July. This is what fuelled practically everything we did as a squad. Each day consisted of full training in the morning, lunch, games in the afternoon, baths, tea, TV and bed.

The training matches were realistic enough for Jack and Nobby nearly to come to blows one day. Their row, which had been festering for days, demonstrated to me the intensity of the preparation programme.

WORLD CHAMPIONS

Alf had to intervene when it threatened to get out of hand. Perhaps sensing the need for a little relaxation, he decided that we could have a drink in the TV lounge one evening. This was the only time he relaxed the no-alcohol rule while we were there.

The taut, claustrophobic atmosphere that generated tension also fostered the bonding process, helping to create the team spirit that would be so important in the weeks ahead. Alf was pushing us to the limit physically and watching closely to see which of us had the mental ability to cope.

As far as I was concerned, he was all-powerful and I believe that one of the things that made his job possible was the willingness of the players to accept his authority without question. I'm not sure that today's coaches wield the same authority. Could you see, for instance, David Beckham or Wayne Rooney wearing enamel FA badges in their suit lapels? We were issued grey suits and smart Burberry raincoats for the World Cup and told that whenever we wore the suit at formal occasions, we had also to wear the enamel badge. The suit was just about acceptable, but the badge made you look like a school prefect.

The first time we had to wear the suit I decided not to wear the badge, and the first person I should meet? Alf, of course.

> In 1966 I was living in San Bernardino, California, and the final was shown in the middle of the night. The few friends I had persuaded to stay up and watch the match found my excitement quite incomprehensible. When the final whistle went they realised they were catching a glimpse of a culture that was completely alien to them. Grown men did not cry at all, let alone at the result of a football match.
>
> As a Liverpool supporter, I was especially pleased for Roger Hunt and tried to explain to my American friends the importance to my life of such figures as Billy Liddell, Alan A'Court, Jimmy Harrower, Albert Stubbins etc. They weren't interested. I think this may have been the moment I decided it was time to come home.
>
> John Peel

> *As far as I was concerned, he was all-powerful and I believe that one of the things that made his job possible was the willingness of the players to accept his authority without question*

> *One thing remained, of course. The shirts for the World Cup were numbered 1 to 22 and there were 27 of us. Five were still to be culled from the squad*

> I really cannot remember exactly what I was doing on Saturday 30th July 1966 - my memory is good, but not that good.
>
> What I do remember about 1966 is that I was working on the pirate ship Radio Caroline and in the January of that year the winter gales were horrendous and I almost made it back to land when Caroline ran aground on the Essex coast.
>
> Also, my recording career was going well in those days! Well, I was making records ... whether they were going well was a matter of opinion! In 1966 I recorded a song called 'Green Light'. I'm sure everyone remembers that one. No? I wonder why?
>
> In 1966 I was also voted the 10th most popular disc jockey in Britain in the 'New Musical Express' poll. Ah, those were heady days!
>
> Tony Blackburn

'Geoffrey, you're improperly dressed,' he said. 'Where's your badge?'

'Sorry, Alf,' I replied. 'I think I've lost it.'

'Not to worry,' he said, reaching into his pocket and producing another badge. 'Now pin this on – and don't lose it.'

Looking back now, I think the only real problem for Alf during that 18 day get-together was Ray Wilson's back injury. Hurt on the first day of training, Ray spent four days on his back in the room he shared with Bobby Charlton before miraculously rising from his bed on the fifth day and declaring himself 'fit for anything'. No one was going to let anything get in the way of grasping the chance of a lifetime.

By the end, we knew each other's strengths and weaknesses on and off the playing field. We were as familiar with each other as the players at any club side, which was exactly what Alf had hoped to achieve.

One thing remained, of course. The shirts for the World Cup were numbered 1 to 22 and there were 27 of us. Five were still to be culled from the squad.

On the last day, as we collected our gear before returning home for 48 hours, Alf began drifting quietly among the players, steering those he wanted to talk to into quiet corners. The five unlucky players were

Bobby Tambling, Keith Newton, Gordon Milne, Peter Thompson and 'Budgie' Byrne. The fact that 'Budgie' had pulled a hamstring during training didn't help his case. Years later, Alf told him that leaving him out of the World Cup squad had been one of his harder decisions.

For those five the dream was over. They knew that within weeks the public would probably have forgotten they were even in contention for the World Cup. Alf, typically, asked all five if they would remain in training in case an emergency arose, and all five agreed.

'Any other questions?' asked Alf. 'Budgie' raised his hand.

'Can we keep the Burberry raincoats, Alf?' he asked.

Below: *Twister was the game of 1966.*

3
On tour

With the squad, if not the starting 11, settled in his mind, Alf Ramsey led his 22 players up the steps on to the charter flight to Helsinki. A four-match European tour was the final stage in his preparation for the World Cup. Some thought it was a gruelling undertaking so close to the big kick-off but Alf had planned the tour with typical care and told us that he wanted four games of increasing difficulty to monitor our state of readiness and sharpen our fitness.

The itinerary read Finland (26 June), Norway (29 June), Denmark (3 July) and Poland (5 July). Having drawn 1–1 with the Poles at Goodison Park in January – Bobby Moore heading our goal – we all knew that the last game would be the hardest, especially as it was the fourth in the space of nine days.

During the course of the trip it became quite clear to us why Alf had cut his squad down to the stipulated 22 players long before the FIFA deadline of 3 July. He wanted to focus solely on the chosen 22 and knew it would be more of a hindrance than a help to have the extra five on tour when he already knew that they would not be involved.

GEOFF HURST

ENGLAND

22 Selected Players

1 Gordon Banks
2 George Cohen
3 Ramon Wilson
4 Norbert Stiles
5 John Charlton
6 Robert Moore
7 Alan Ball
8 James Greaves
9 Robert Charlton
10 Geoffrey Hurst
11 John Connelly

12 Ronald Springett
13 Peter Bonetti
14 James Armfield
15 Gerald Byrne
16 Martin Peters
17 Ronald Flowers
18 Norman Hunter
19 Terence Paine
20 Ian Callaghan
21 Roger Hunt
22 George Eastham

The names and numbers of the players taking part in each match will be announced over the public address system prior to the kick-off. This information should be inserted in the space provided on the relevant page for each game, covered between pages 44 and 55.

Les noms et les numéros des joueurs sélectionnés seront annoncés par moyen du haut-parleur avant le coup d'envoi de chaque match. Ces renseignements sont à ajouter à la page qui convient, c'est-à-dire entre la page 44 et la page 55.

Die Namen und Nummern der Spieler welche an jedem Spiel teilnehmen, werden per Lautsprecher vor dem Anstoss bekannt gegeben. Diese Angaben können an der hierfür für jedes Spiel vorgesehenen Stelle—Seiten 44 bis 55—eingetragen werden.

Los nombres y números de los jugadores que toman parte en cada partido serán anunciados por los altavoces antes del comienzo del partido. Esta información debe ser incluida en la casilla correspondiente en la página relativa a cada partido incluida entre las páginas 44 y 55.

Alf used 20 of his 22 players during the first two matches, and the other two, Peter Bonetti and George Eastham, were in the starting line-up for the third game, against Denmark. Two of the 22 made their international debuts on the tour – Liverpool's Ian Callaghan in the first match in Finland and Chelsea goalkeeper Bonetti against the Danes.

Ian 'Cally' Callaghan, a player of great enterprise and skill, was one of three wingers in the party along with Terry Paine of Southampton and John Connelly of Manchester United. Even at this stage, I don't think Alf was quite sure which, if any, of his wingers he would use in the first match of the tournament.

No one was really surprised when 'Cally' was named in the team to face Finland, but we were surprised when we learned that Bobby Moore had been left out. The most choked of all was Bobby himself. He had been captain for practically every match over the previous two years.

He'd missed the Yugoslavia game in May, supposedly because of his preoccupation with his contract dispute with West Ham, but this time his absence from the team in Helsinki had an effect on him. I remember him telling me sometime later, 'After that, I never again assumed I'd be in the team until Alf read out the eleven names.'

Blackpool right-back Jimmy Armfield, playing his 43rd and, as it turned out, last England game, was made captain. Norman Hunter was given 'Mooro's' place alongside his Leeds club colleague Jack Charlton in the heart of the defence.

England won 3–0, but it wasn't a classic. The heat didn't help our cause, although we were easily the more accomplished team. Ian Callaghan set up Roger Hunt's goal. Martin Peters, in his second international, and Jack Charlton both scored their first goals for England.

For Norman Hunter it had been an opportunity to stake his claim to a place in Alf's first 11. Alf can't have been all that impressed because three days later Bobby Moore was reinstated when England faced Norway in Oslo. Jimmy Greaves was also back in a team that showed nine changes from the one on duty in Helsinki. Only Bobby Charlton and Roger Hunt played in both games.

Martin Peters and I were both left out and, as if to confuse the travelling pressmen desperate to work out England's World Cup starting 11, Alf named *two* wingers – Terry Paine on the right and John Connelly on the left.

We struggled in the early stages against Norway. A poor back pass by Ron Flowers presented the Norwegians with the opening goal and probably closed the door on his 11-year international career. It was his 49th and last cap.

Previous spread: *Alf's final 22. Back row: 'Shep', Les Cocker, Hunt, Flowers, Bonetti, Springett, Banks, Moore, Greaves, Alf; middle: Armfield, Callaghan, Byrne, Eastham, myself, J. Charlton, Ball, Stiles; front: Hunter, Cohen, Paine, Wilson, R. Charlton, Peters, Connelly.*

Opposite: *As we were announced to the world in the official World Cup programme.*

> *We were surprised when we learned that Bobby Moore had been left out. The most choked of all was Bobby himself. He had been captain for practically every match over the previous two years*

GEOFF HURST

43

By. 4628 HAVNE- og KANALRUNDFARTEN København 1966

For a long time in the first half England looked in trouble but we needn't have worried

For a long time in the first half England looked in trouble but we needn't have worried. Jimmy Greaves suddenly took the game by the scruff of the neck and scored four goals to demonstrate, once again, his undisputed world class. 'Mooro' and John Connelly each scored to make the final result 6–1, but afterwards everyone was talking about the incomparable Greaves. It was the sixth occasion on which he scored three or more goals for his country in a single match.

At the time, Jim was the second most expensive player in English soccer history. Tottenham had paid Milan £99,999 to sign him. The Spurs manager Bill Nicholson refused to pay the extra pound and thus make him the first £100,000 player. Only Denis Law had cost more – £116,000 when Manchester United signed him from Torino eight months after Jim's return from Italy in November 1961.

The nation was looking for signs that Jim had recovered from that bout of hepatitis and his appetite for goals remained as sharp as ever. The four in Oslo convinced everyone that, if we were going to win the World Cup, Jim would be the man to score the goals.

Jim was ebullient in the dressing room after the match and Alf caught the mood of growing optimism among the players.

'Well done, boys,' he said. 'Tonight you may have a drink!' We had been together for nearly a month and it was only the second time he'd relaxed the alcohol ban.

44   WORLD CHAMPIONS

Sadly, two days after beating Norway, the FA chairman Joe Mears suffered a fatal heart attack in an Oslo park, aged just 61. He was also the chairman of Chelsea and had played a significant role in the preparation for the World Cup. Hosting the tournament should have been the proudest moment of his life in football administration.

Jimmy Greaves, who had started his career with Chelsea, knew him well and was upset. Mr Mears had been an officer in the Marines and was known as one of the few members of the FA Committee happy to sit and chat with players.

Jimmy had partnered Roger Hunt against Norway but when Alf named the team to face Denmark in Copenhagen on 3 July, I was chosen to play alongside Jim. Bobby Charlton, somewhat surprisingly, was left out. Alf was quite clearly looking at all his options.

Opposite: *On the pre-tournament European tour we did have some time to relax. This is a postcard that was made from a photo of us on a boat trip in Copenhagen in July.*

Below: *And Martin and I enjoying café life with the* Guardian's *football correspondent Bert Barham, Frank Bough and Brian Moore. I am clearly learning a lot from the morning paper. Has Martin just seen someone he doesn't like?*

__Much speculation about the significance of the shirt numbers filled the tiresome journey by plane, coach and rail to Chorzow in the Polish coalfields__

It was only the second time Jim and I had played together. I did my best to give him the support he needed but something wasn't quite right, although you could have said that about the entire team. Apart from Alan Ball's usual energetic contribution, it was a flat England performance. Nonetheless we won again. Jack Charlton and George Eastham scored our goals in a 2–0 win.

At lunchtime on the day of the game in Copenhagen, Alf confirmed his 22-man squad with the Football Association and they, in turn, submitted the names to FIFA along with their squad numbers. As expected, the players who were to represent England in the World Cup were:

No.	Name	Position	Club	Age
1	Gordon Banks	goalkeeper	Leicester	28
2	George Cohen	full-back	Fulham	26
3	Ray Wilson	full-back	Everton	31
4	Nobby Stiles	midfield	Manchester United	24
5	Jack Charlton	centre-back	Leeds	30
6	Bobby Moore	centre-back	West Ham	25
7	Alan Ball	midfield	Blackpool	21
8	Jimmy Greaves	striker	Tottenham	26
9	Bobby Charlton	midfield	Manchester United	28
10	Geoff Hurst	striker	West Ham	24
11	John Connelly	winger	Manchester United	27
12	Ron Springett	goalkeeper	Sheffield Wednesday	30
13	Peter Bonetti	goalkeeper	Chelsea	24
14	Jimmy Armfield	full-back	Blackpool	30
15	Gerry Byrne	full-back	Liverpool	28
16	Martin Peters	midfield	West Ham	22
17	Ron Flowers	centre-back	Wolverhampton Wanderers	31
18	Norman Hunter	centre-back	Leeds	22
19	Terry Paine	winger	Southampton	27
20	Ian Callaghan	winger	Liverpool	24
21	Roger Hunt	striker	Liverpool	27
22	George Eastham	midfield	Arsenal	29

The average age of the squad was a little more than 26. On the eve of the World Cup the least experienced in international terms were Bonetti and Callaghan with one cap each. The most experienced was Bobby Charlton with 68 caps. The average was 23 caps.

Although we'd known since leaving Lilleshall that only injury or some unforeseen catastrophe would change the make-up of the squad, it was still a relief to know that I had a shirt number. As we prepared for the last of our four warm-up matches, you could sense the growing excitement among the players.

Above: *FA and Chelsea chairman Joe Mears on the left, with Sir Stanley Rous at the Variety Club luncheon in January 1966. Sadly, just over five months later Joe Mears died while on tour with the team in Norway. He never got to enjoy the World Cup victory that he had worked so hard to make possible.*

Much speculation about the significance of the shirt numbers filled the tiresome journey by plane, coach and rail to Chorzow in the Polish coalfields. As the second and third choice goalkeepers were 12 and 13 and the reserve full-backs 14 and 15, most assumed that those numbered 1 to 11 would be Alf's first choice starting line-up against Uruguay. Since I had the No. 10 shirt, I hoped they were right.

I hadn't played well against the Danes so it was no real surprise when I was left out of the side for the final dress rehearsal against Poland on 5 July. Backed by a huge crowd of 93,000, the Poles felt they had a point to make, having failed to qualify for the finals. From England's point of view, each man was playing for his place. Despite the close proximity of the World Cup, there was no shirking or pulling out of tackles.

This time Alf sidelined all three wingers. He brought in Martin Peters on the left and played Hunt and Greaves together at the front. It turned out to be a tough match but once again we produced a sound defensive

Above: *Violence during the anti-Vietnam War riots outside the American Embassy that summer.*

Opposite: *Vietnam. The US Air Force bombs Hanoi for the first time on 29 June 1966.*

performance and Roger supplied the only goal with a powerful half-volley from 25 yards. Martin, too, was an impressive figure in midfield and Bobby Moore played with all his old authority.

Poland was still a hard-line Iron Curtain country and not a particularly comfortable place to be, so it was a relief to enjoy a steak on the charter flight home. Alf gave little away, but he was in a relaxed, mellow mood. The tour had been a success for him. Four straight wins with 12 goals scored was as good as it could possibly get in the build-up to a major tournament.

We returned to London in buoyant good humour, confident that, at the very least, England would be difficult to beat in the coming weeks. Our away record suggested that we had one of the best-organised defences in the world. We had conceded just one goal in our four tour matches and were unbeaten in a total of 12 consecutive away games prior to the World Cup. This, to my way of thinking, renders ridiculous the theory that England won the World Cup only because we played at Wembley. The truth of the matter is that we were probably a better team in away matches.

Alf allowed us to return to our families for two days before gathering on the Friday to prepare for the opening game on Monday, 11 July. He said later that his decision to allow his players to relax for two days was one of the most important elements of England's preparations.

It was a relief to unwind at home with Judith and Claire, our eldest daughter, who wasn't quite a year old. I tried to step back from the World Cup and focus on family life, but it was difficult. The World Cup dominated the media. The other nations had arrived and, when you read what they had to say, you realised that England were not the only team who thought they could win. Most of the smart money seemed to be going on Brazil.

> I was a Blue Coat at Pontins Holiday Camp, Bracklesham Bay, when the World Cup was on. I remember watching the game in the chalet belonging to the catering manager, as he was the only one on site at the time to have his own TV. After doing the welcoming duty at the main gate, I dashed over to the chalet just in time to see the game. My viewing was interrupted, however, by inconsiderate holiday makers who turned up in the afternoon to check in. I managed to see all the important parts of the game though.
>
> Roger de Courcey

I tried to step back from the World Cup and focus on family life, but it was difficult

Above, left to right: *We may have been focused on it, but the World Cup wasn't the only sport going on that summer.*

Jackie Stewart won the Monaco Grand Prix.

Billie Jean King won Wimbledon.

And Jack Nicklaus won the Open.

Before arriving in England they'd played 12 friendly matches in six weeks, winning nine and drawing three. West Germany had won five consecutive warm-up games since losing at Wembley in February and had a rising young star in Franz Beckenbauer, but the bookies rated them no higher than 20–1 shots. Portugal, too, had won five on the trot and it seemed that, alone of the big nations, Argentina's preparations had been slapdash and unimpressive.

A real sense of expectancy pervaded pubs and work places. For the man in the street it wasn't the easiest of times and the World Cup provided a distraction from more important issues. Faced with runaway inflation, the Prime Minister, Harold Wilson, had just frozen prices for 12 months, increased taxes and cut holiday currency allowances. The seamen were on strike, causing mounting congestion at the ports, and dozens of demonstrators were arrested at anti-Vietnam War protests outside the American embassy in Grosvenor Square.

On the sports front, Billie Jean King won the first of her six ladies' titles at Wimbledon, a 19-year-old American student called Jim Ryun cut the world mile record to 3 minutes 51.3 seconds and Jackie Stewart, a young Scot, won the Monaco Grand Prix. In golf, Jack Nicklaus won the first of his three British Open titles with victory at Muirfield – over

WORLD CHAMPIONS

> *A real sense of expectancy pervaded pubs and work places. For the man in the street it wasn't the easiest of times and the World Cup provided a distraction from more important issues*

four days. That was the first time the championship had been extended by an extra day. Nowadays, all the main golf tournaments are staged over that period.

The preparations for the World Cup had been largely trouble free, apart from the theft of the Jules Rimet Trophy, which was now safely under lock and key. However, as happens at every World Cup, whispers suggested that FIFA were showing favouritism to the host nation. The fact that Englishman Sir Stanley Rous was the FIFA president simply added weight to the rumours. Sir Stanley had tried to be scrupulously fair, but some of the South American nations were complaining about the European bias in the selection of tournament referees.

In those days, hard tackling and tackling from behind were still acceptable, particularly in England. Some Latin countries, who practised their own, subtler, dark arts, promoted the theory that Sir Stanley, himself a former referee, had instructed the tournament officials to turn a blind eye to robust tackling. He denied it and, personally, I don't think that was ever the case.

In the event, the match officials had significant roles to play in the unfolding drama of the World Cup. Thirty-one referees were chosen for the tournament by the FIFA referees committee from a list of 148

REFEREES FOR THE TOURNAMENT

Referees who will have charge of matches in the Final Series were chosen in Barcelona at a meeting of the FIFA Referees' Committee. There were 148 nominations from 82 FIFA member associations.

Fourteen African nations submitted the names of 24 referees; from 17 Asian associations 25 names were put forward; 31 European associations made 62 nominations; 12 North Central American and Caribbean associations recommended 22 officials; and the remaining 15 were listed by South American countries.

The principle of selecting seven referees from the organising country, and one from each competing finalist country, was maintained. It was decided to select a further nine referees from countries whose teams do not appear in the last 16.

The designation of referees and linesmen for duty at the 32 games in the Final Series, and other decisions relating to refereeing during the tournament, will be taken by Sir Stanley Rous, President of FIFA, and the following members of the Referees' Committee: Dr. M. Andrejevic (Yugoslavia), Mr. P. Escartin (Spain), Mr. N. Latyshev (U.S.S.R.), Mr. A. Lindenberg (Switzerland) and Mr. Koe Ewe Teik (Malaysia).

All the referees and linesmen will be chosen from this list:

Competing Countries

Argentine	ROBERTO GOICOECHEA	Brazil	ARMANDO MARQUES
Bulgaria	DIMITER ROUMENTCHEV	Chile	CLAUDIO VICUNA
England	KEVIN HOWLEY	England	JAMES FINNEY
England	WILLIAM CLEMENTS	England	ERNEST CRAWFORD
England	KENNETH DAGNALL	England	GEORGE McCABE
England	JOHN TAYLOR	France	PIERRE SCHWINTE
West Germany	RUDOLF KREITLEIN	Hungary	ISTVAN ZSOLT
Italy	CONCETTO LO BELLO	North Korea	CHOI DUK RYONG
Mexico	FERNANDO BUERGO ELCUAZ	Portugal	JOAQUIM FERNANDES CAMPOS
Spain	JUAN GARDEAZABAL	Switzerland	GOTTFRIED DIENST
U.S.S.R.	TOFIK BAKHRAMOV	Uruguay	JOSE MARIA CODESAL

Non-Finalist Countries

Czechoslovakia	Dr. KAROI GALBA	Northern Ireland	JOHN ADAIR
Israel	MENACHEM ASHKENASI	Peru	ARTURO YAMASAKI
Scotland	HUGH PHILLIPS	Sweden	BERTIL LOOW
United Arab Republic	ALY KANDIL	Wales	LEO CALLAGHAN
	Yugoslavia	KONSTANTIN ZECEVIC	

Reserves: KURT TSCHENSCHER (West Germany) and H. M. ANGULLIA (Singapore)

54

names nominated by 82 member associations. The principle of selecting seven referees from the organising country and one from each of the competing finalists was maintained. A further nine were chosen from countries whose teams did not qualify for the finals.

The seven English referees were William Clements, Ernest Crawford, Ken Dagnall, Jim Finney, Kevin Howley, George McCabe and John Taylor. Leo Callaghan (Wales), Hugh Phillips (Scotland) and John Adair (Northern Ireland) were among the nine referees from non-finalist countries.

What is inescapable is that 21 of the 31 referees were European. As nine of the 16 competing nations were from Europe you can judge for yourself whether the FIFA referees committee had appointed a disproportionate number of European officials.

Above: *Two days before it all kicked off. Alf looking relaxed at a press conference in Hendon Hall, our home during the three weeks of the tournament.*

None of this seemed to matter a jot to Alf Ramsey. The weekend before the opening game the squad joined him in the familiar surroundings of the Hendon Hall Hotel in north London. We had all stayed there before. It was close enough to Wembley to be convenient and secluded enough to ensure we were left alone. England invariably stayed there before Wembley games. Once the home of the great eighteenth century English actor David Garrick, its ivy-clad walls and dark, panelled corridors became our home for the duration of the tournament.

My room-mate was Martin Peters. In those days, players always shared a room and I think it was a good thing. Today they all have their own rooms when they travel with England. Typical of Alf's attention to detail, he'd insisted during the build-up period that players change rooms frequently to (a) get to know team-mates, and (b) avoid the creation of cliques. I think some England coaches have had problems with cliques in more recent years but there was no evidence of this during my seven years in Alf's squad.

We slipped back easily into the training-resting-eating routine, although now there was a little more resting. We were at least as fit as everyone else in the tournament and remained convinced that we would be difficult to beat.

I didn't know, nor did anyone else, what team Alf would pick to face Uruguay. Training on the Sunday offered few clues. That evening in our room, Martin and I discussed the options. Martin had played really well in Poland but if Alf decided to use a conventional winger, we both suspected that he would probably be the player left out. I didn't think I'd be in the starting line-up. I hadn't faced Poland in the last game and my performance in the previous match in Denmark had been woeful. Although Alf kept a tactful silence at the time, years later he told me that he'd rarely seen a worse display. He'd even wondered whether, at that late stage, he could change his party of 22! I never knew whether he was joking or serious about that.

Anyway, that night the 22 players in his squad went to bed in the Hendon Hall Hotel unaware which of them would be asked to represent England at Wembley the following evening.

```
Although I was manager at Coventry City, at the
time I had been working for the BBC during the
World Cup. On the day of the final I was not
actually part of the show so Joe Mercer and I
were given complimentary passes to watch the game.
My overriding memory is of tears trickling down
both our cheeks as Geoff hammered in the fourth
and final nail in the Germans' coffin.
   Later I managed to help a lost Mrs Ball find
her husband at the Royal Garden Hotel, ending
the day with my old chum Ron Greenwood, who did
as much as Alf Ramsey to win the World Cup in
providing the magnificent three: Hurst, Peters,
Moore.


Jimmy Hill
```

Above: *At the Bank of England training ground at Roehampton, where we travelled to most days. The rest of us are obviously very busy... watching Ron Springett and Peter Bonetti practise headers. Perhaps they were planning on coming up for corners if things got desperate in the games ahead. Jimmy is helping them out.*

Opposite: Daily Mirror, *12 March 1966.*

GEOFF HURST

4
Bobby, Nobby, Jack and the boys

Alf Ramsey had five truly world-class players in his squad of 22. It would have been unthinkable had England kicked-off the World Cup without Gordon Banks, Bobby Moore, Ray Wilson, Bobby Charlton or Jimmy Greaves. I don't think any England coach since then can claim to have been blessed with five such outstanding players providing the backbone of his team.

Even though Bobby Moore had suffered an indifferent spell of form, I think everyone in the squad realised that these five players would provide the heartbeat of the team. Gordon Banks was unchallenged as England's number-one goalkeeper. Bobby Charlton remains, for me, England's greatest ever player. Ray Wilson was simply the best left-back in the world and, when it came to scoring goals, Jimmy Greaves had no rival.

WORLD CHAMPIONS

GEOFF HURST

Above: *Banksie enjoying a glass of Pastis. No, sorry, that's the French actor Fernandel.*

Previous spread: *It's Gordon this time. Getting the better of the Lawman at Wembley in '65.*

Opposite: *Ray in October '65 playing for Everton. He's about to take on Fulham here, at Craven Cottage.*

By comparison the rest of us were fetchers and carriers but, as with any team, we were as important to the success of the unit as anyone else. Alf spent four years modifying the unit but, as history shows, he still hadn't got it quite right on the first day of the World Cup.

For him, the technical ability to do the job was only part of the requirement. He also looked closely at the personalities of his players. He liked solid, undemonstrative characters, who wouldn't be intimidated by a hostile atmosphere. He also looked for players who would maintain dressing-room harmony and enhance team spirit. Disruptive individuals were quickly identified and weeded out.

Four of the five world-class players appeared in all six World Cup ties. The exception was Greaves and, but for his injury against France, I'm sure he would have played in all six games too.

Four other players appeared in all six games – right-back George Cohen, centre-half Jack Charlton, midfield player Nobby Stiles and striker Roger Hunt. Seven others played – Martin Peters (five games), Alan Ball (four), Jimmy Greaves (three), me (three), John Connelly (one), Terry Paine (one) and Ian Callaghan (one).

In my opinion, there was not a single weak link in Alf's 22-man squad. Some were more accomplished than others, but no one would have let the team down. What I remember most clearly of the two months we spent together was not just getting to know them all as personalities but appreciating just how good they were as footballers.

Some players you appreciate fully only when you train with them on a regular basis. Gordon Banks was one. I'd played against him many times and was, of course, aware of his reputation but I didn't really know how good he was until I started shooting at him in training. His positional sense was exceptional and, after a while, I realised that I had to try to out-think him because most of the shots I hit instinctively he saved. He was a master of positioning and angles, and his judgement rarely failed him. Unlike some of his contemporaries, his shot-stopping style was functional rather than spectacular. Courage he had in abundance. He viewed broken bones and concussion as an occupational hazard.

I played alongside Gordon for six years in the England side and I can't recall a single serious mistake in that time. His save from Pele in the 1970 World Cup is widely recognised as one of the great examples of the goalkeeper's art. His sudden absence from the quarter-final against

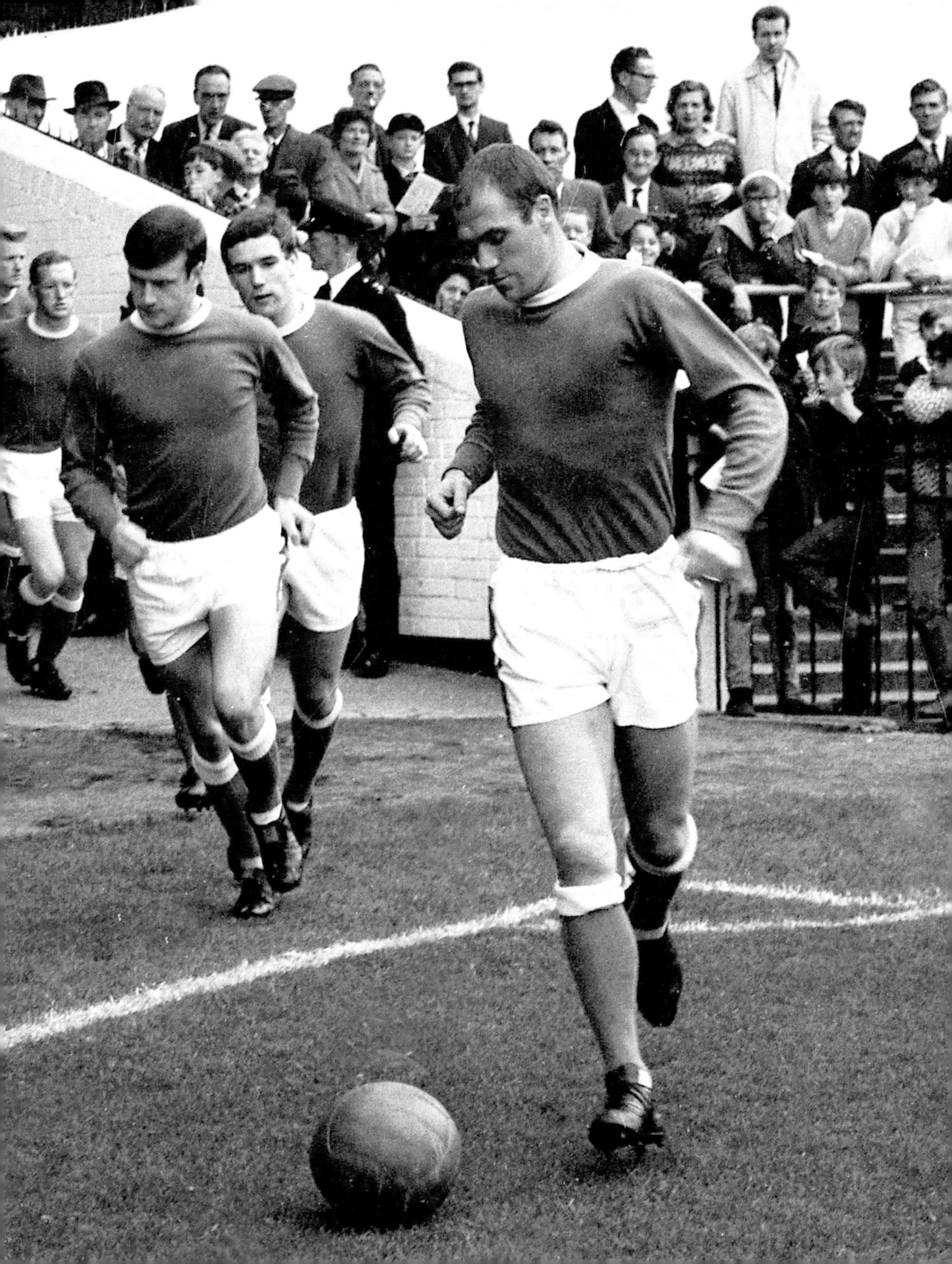

Above: *George at Fulham in March '65, thwarting Leeds' Terry Cooper and making sure his keeper has the ball safely in his hands.*

Opposite: *George's boss – Tommy Trinder.*

West Germany a week later, due to food poisoning, perfectly illustrated his value to the team. His understudy, Peter Bonetti, was a very good goalkeeper but the boys in the team knew that Gordon was *the* best and his absence might therefore be critical, and so it proved – but that was four years later.

Modest and unflappable, he was known to the lads as 'Fernandel' because he looked very much like a soulful French comedian of that name. His calming influence helped set the tone in the dressing room.

It was typical of 'Banksie' that he was always ready to share any plaudits with the four men in front of him. He knew that England had an outstanding back four in which George Cohen on the right and Ray Wilson on the left provided the balance.

WORLD CHAMPIONS

George was a west London boy from Kensington who spent his entire career with Fulham. At the time they were a bit of a music-hall joke, largely because of the irreverence of their much-loved chairman Tommy Trinder. That didn't stop them becoming the first club to pay a £100-per-week salary following the removal of the maximum wage in 1961. The lucky recipient was the late Johnny Haynes.

John had won the last of his 56 England caps by the time George made his international debut in 1964. George quickly became England's regular right-back and was unchallenged until 1968. He used to make thunderous forays along the right flank for both Fulham and England. His crossing wasn't so good though, and the locals at Craven Cottage claimed that with the wind in the right direction he could easily put one of his long passes into the River Thames! More importantly, his tackling and positional sense were excellent. Few wingers got past him because he was quick, fit and as strong as a bull.

George and Ray Wilson had a natural affinity on the field despite their backgrounds and personalities being very different. A laconic northerner from Derbyshire with a wicked sense of humour, Ray was the oldest of the World Cup team. At 31, he was six months older than Jack Charlton in the summer of 1966, and together they used to love taking the mickey out of the southern boys.

One night at Lilleshall, Alf arranged a private screening of a film for us, a 'whodunnit'. We'd looked forward to it all day and eventually filed into the little cinema room like a lot of excited schoolchildren. The lights went out, the titles came up and from the back of the room Ray shouted, 'We've seen this one, Jack, haven't we? Dalby's the murderer.' Jimmy Greaves, who could give as good as he got when it came to banter, suggested that we feed Ray to the peacocks that lived on the estate!

Everyone in the squad recognised that Ray was the complete fullback. He could attack and defend with equal competence. His tackling was precise and his distribution accurate and I'll always be grateful to him for starting the move that led to my winning goal against Argentina.

He was one of the most experienced players in the team having made his England debut in 1960. In total he played 63 times for England in a

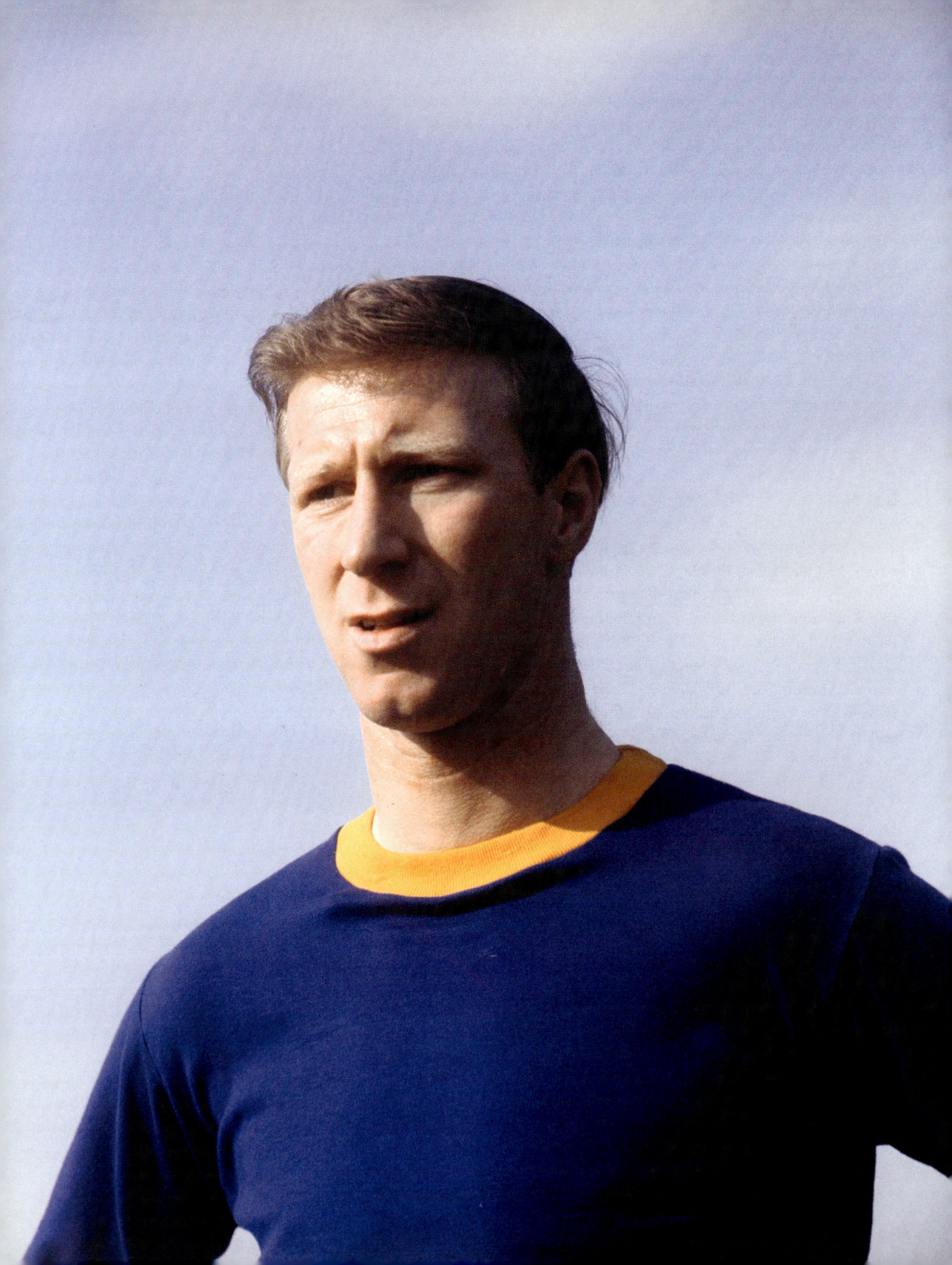

Opposite: *Jack at Leeds in '65.*

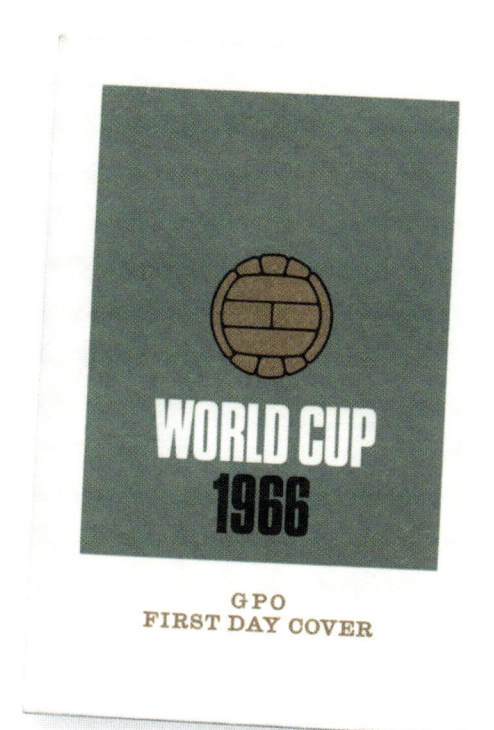

career that embraced Huddersfield, Everton and Oldham. Twenty-eight of those games were in the same team as George, and the consistency of the pair has prompted many to rate them as England's best full-back partnership of all time.

Ray was one of the dressing-room jokers and Jack Charlton loved his impish humour. They had a natural rapport and would stick together if there were ever any argument. Alan Ball, who loved to tease Jack – and still does – would often hold up an item of Jack's clothing and ask in a loud voice, 'Do they still wear these in Yorkshire, Jack?'

Ray, supporting his mate, would butt in, 'Nowt wrong with that! They're just jealous, Jack!'

Sometimes the lads would be rocking with laughter at Jack's expense but everyone knew how important he was to our success. In his own way, he was as critical to the team as his brother Bobby.

Jack knew he was nowhere near his younger brother in terms of technical proficiency, but his forte was the ability to stop others of Bobby's talent inflicting damage on us. One of the things I most admired about him was his honesty. He wouldn't kid himself or anyone else about his own ability, but he was a genuinely tough guy in a tough team at Leeds United. I played against him many times and still have memories – and scars. He wasn't vicious, but you knew when you'd been tackled by Jack Charlton.

He also had a long memory. Anyone who was silly enough to hurt or upset him would eventually pay the price and crumple in a heap.

> *He wasn't vicious, but you knew when you'd been tackled by Jack Charlton*

Opposite: *Mooro. Quite simply England's greatest captain.*

Above: *And the man who made it possible for Bobby to play in the tournament. Our manager at Upton Park, Ron Greenwood, arriving here on his first day in charge in 1961. Sadly, Ron died in February 2006 as I was writing this book.*

It might take him six months or a year, but Jack would always get his revenge.

It was this competitive nature that, Alf believed, made him the perfect partner for Bobby Moore. One half of the centre-back combination was a technician who read the game wonderfully well, while the other half was an uncompromising, mobile stopper who, at 6ft 2in, was outstanding in the air.

This defensive combination illustrated Alf's obsession with creating the perfectly balanced team. He felt that the balance was essential. He knew, for instance, that when Ray Wilson charged forward on the left flank, George Cohen would hold back. When George went forward on the right, Ray would hold his defensive position. Similarly, Alf valued the way Jack was always around to cover for Bobby. If the captain pushed forward, as he often did, Jack would diligently cover his back.

I remember Jack, who was nearly 30 when he made his England debut, asking Alf why he continued to pick him.

'I don't always pick the best players, Jack,' replied Alf. 'I have a pattern in my mind and you fit the pattern. I pick you because you won't trust Bobby Moore.'

Jack played for England until 1970. He made one appearance in the World Cup in Mexico and, on the plane home, decided that it was time to retire from international football. He said to the manager, 'I think I've had enough, Alf.' Before he could say anything else, Alf replied, 'I totally agree.'

A couple of statistics sum up Jack's value to England. In his 35 games, England lost just twice and kept 22 clean sheets. He took the same tough, winning mentality with him into management and had

GEOFF HURST

Below: *Dusty Springfield reached No. 1 in the singles chart on 31 March 1966 with 'You Don't Have to Say You Love Me'. She had two other Top 10 hits in the year, 'Going Back' and 'All I See is You'.*

another fabulous career. I think Jack would have made a good England manager but when we were all young and playing together I think most of us would have assumed that the cool and authoritative Bobby Moore had more of the right qualities for a management job at that level.

'Mooro' was an outstanding leader on the pitch but his management career never really took off, although he did try with Oxford City and Southend United. Perhaps he wasn't cut out for management or dealing with players from the lower echelons of the game. Nothing, though, will ever dilute my memory of him climbing the 39 steps to the royal box in the old Wembley Stadium, wiping the mud from his hands before accepting the Jules Rimet Trophy from the Queen.

The image of Bobby holding aloft the World Cup is etched indelibly in the minds of generations of football fans. For him, it was the ultimate achievement in a wonderful career – and he was just 25.

Bobby was England's greatest captain and probably England's greatest defender, but it could have been so different for him that summer. For a start, his ongoing dispute with West Ham meant that from 30 June, when his contract expired, he was not registered with any club. Only players registered with clubs affiliated to the Football Association were eligible to play for England. This meant, of course, that he could not play in the World Cup in July.

Although he was in no hurry to sign a new contract with West Ham, Bobby's position was a cause of growing concern for Alf. So he invited the West Ham manager Ron Greenwood to the

> The day West Ham - whoops - sorry, England won the World Cup I was a teenager already playing in bands and living in a bed-sit in Earls Court. As the big day of the final at Wembley finally came, I was feeling in limbo so decided to make the pilgrimage back to the East End to a safe 'Hammer Haven' - my father's house.
>
> The match kicked off and we lived every second of it, Mum included. I don't think we sat down once and when Geoff Hurst scored his third goal the council flat shook as we danced and sang. It was brilliant!
>
> That night I took my parents to a pub in Bermondsey where I was playing and the celebrations carried on till around three in the morning.
>
> *David Essex*

Hendon Hall Hotel. Ron and Bobby were ushered into a private room and told they had 60 seconds to reach an agreement, which they did. Bobby signed a temporary contract covering the month of July, so once again he was eligible to play for England.

Unfortunately, this protracted dispute had gnawed at Bobby for some time and was undermining his form. That's why Alf had looked at other options. Norman Hunter, Leeds United's accomplished left-footed defender, played three games for England in the build-up period that spring, but he lacked Bobby's command and ability to read the game. Although quicker and more aggressive, he didn't have Bobby's timing, composure, experience or passing range. As it turned out, Bobby played magnificently in the tournament. He was, quite simply, the best defender in the world.

Bobby was indisputably a star, and not just in the football context. He was a sporting hero but his blond good looks made him popular beyond the confines of the football field. At a time when television was rapidly increasing in popularity, Bobby's fame and success elevated him to celebrity status. Whatever his broader appeal may have been, though, there is no doubt that he was one of the most significant figures in English sport in the last century.

> *The image of Bobby holding aloft the World Cup is etched indelibly in the minds of generations of football fans. For him, it was the ultimate achievement in a wonderful career – and he was just 25*

Opposite: *Myself and Martin at Upton Park against Sheffield Wednesday in '65. As Alf said, Martin was a player 'ten years ahead of his time'.*

> **In my opinion, no England centre-back since Bobby has had anything like his range of skill. We always have a toast to absent friends at our reunions – 'Mooro' and Alf**

Bobby was eight months older than me and joined West Ham before I did, but in terms of the pecking order at the club he was light years ahead of me. The fan mail the players received reflected their status. The staff at the West Ham training ground used to lay out three piles of letters. The biggest pile was for Bobby Moore. The second one was for Johnny Byrne. The third pile was for the rest of us.

People loved him – and that was never more apparent than when he died of bowel cancer in February 1993. There was a profound sense of national loss. Tributes arrived from all over the world but the loss was felt most at West Ham where his family, friends, fans and the people of east London left their flowers, scarves and messages at the tall iron gates in honour of a legend.

Martin and I had known that he had a problem back in 1964 when he went into hospital and missed three months of West Ham's season. We didn't know the nature of the problem and, happily, he made a full recovery at the time.

Today, those who were privileged to play alongside him in 1966 recall him with great affection. We often talk about him and his contribution to England's success when we meet at our reunions. Inevitably, comparisons are made with modern-day players because any debate about the quality of defenders must always start with Bobby Moore. Phrases such as 'not in Mooro's class', 'couldn't lace Mooro's boots' or 'Mooro could do that with his eyes closed' are regularly used. In my opinion, no England centre-back since Bobby has had anything like his range of skill. We always have a toast to absent friends at our reunions – 'Mooro' and Alf.

I guess that, among the players, few were closer to Bobby than Martin Peters and me. The fact that the three of us had played for West Ham for four seasons before the events of the summer of 1966 bound us together in a way that remains unique in the history of British sport.

The public assumption has always been that we were the very best of friends. The truth is we were team-mates and spent a lot of time together, but I don't think you could say that we were 'best friends' because Bobby didn't have best friends. He had plenty of mates and, at the height of his fame, more hangers-on than he knew what to do with. Although he wasn't shy, he was essentially a private man and many mistakenly thought this was aloofness.

Martin was cut from similar cloth. Like 'Mooro' he'd been brought up to value the East End working-class qualities of politeness and hard work. Martin was a natural athlete, good at any sport, and of the three of us, he was the most naturally gifted footballer. He was versatile enough to play anywhere – and did. In my time at West Ham he wore all 11 shirts – yes, even goalkeeper. As an outstanding schoolboy international, all the big clubs were after him but he chose West Ham.

WORLD CHAMPIONS

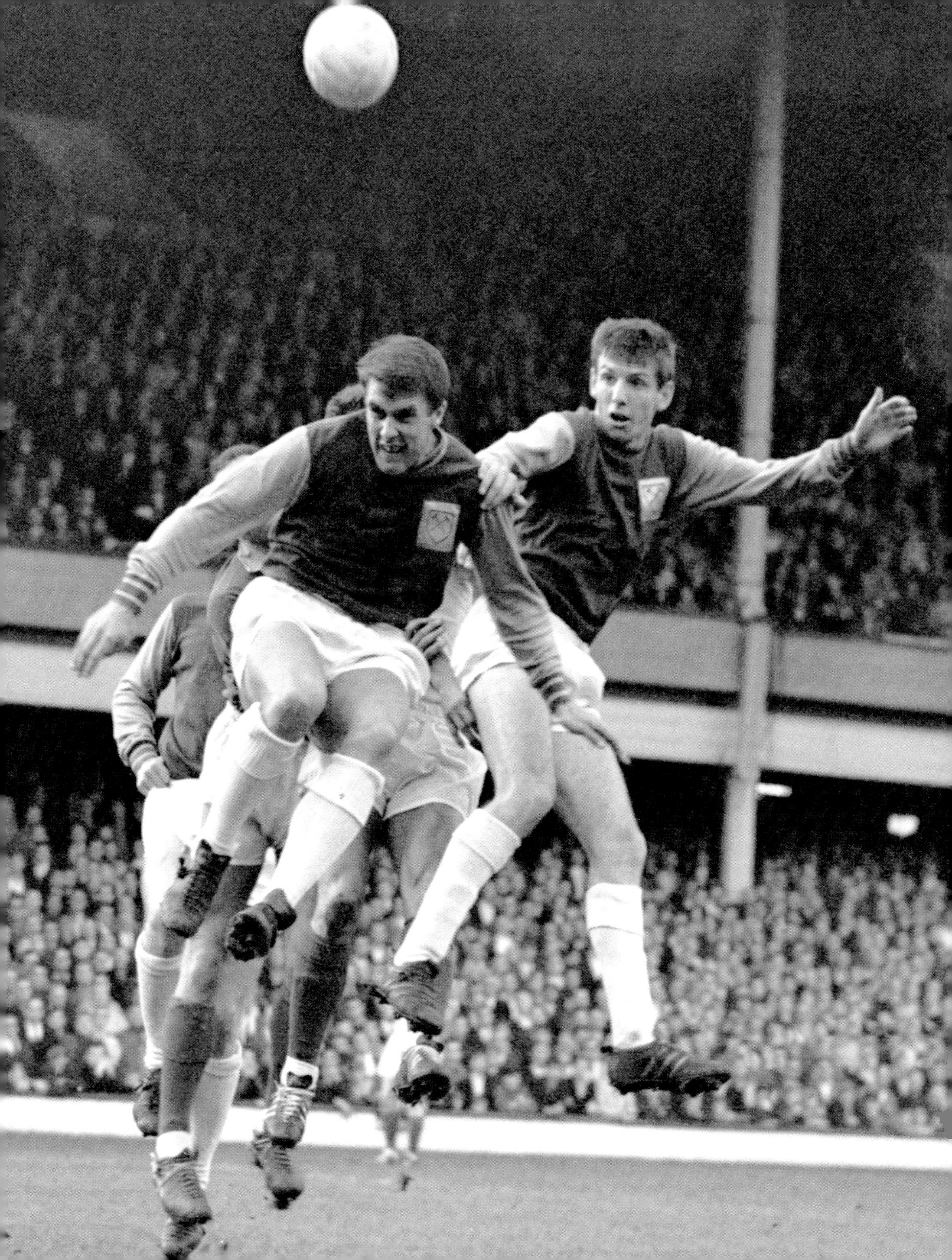

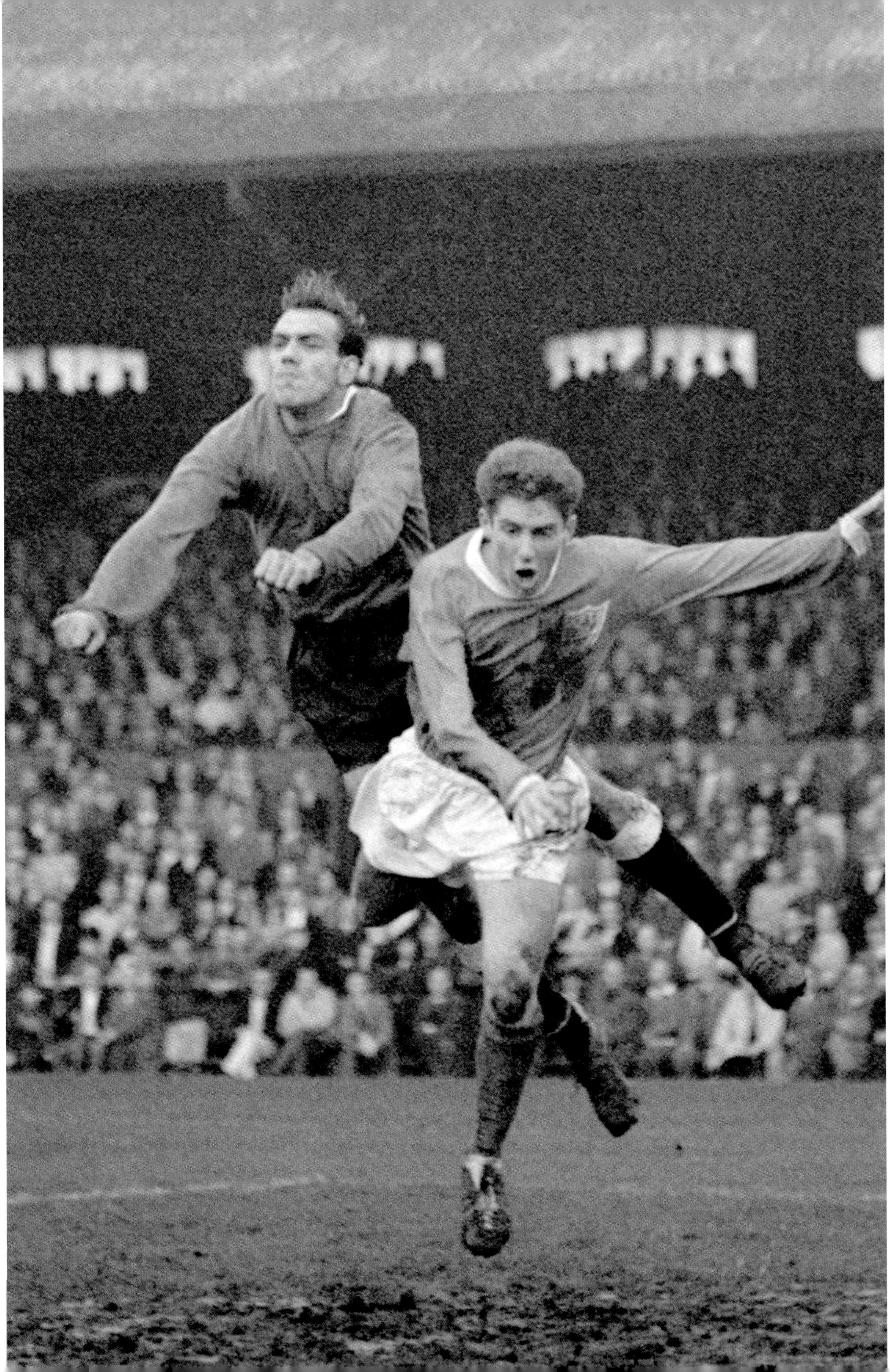

It was the right decision. Ron Greenwood was an innovative, challenging coach who was able to draw the best out of the quietly spoken young man. Initially, Alf was reluctant to select him for England, insisting that he couldn't head the ball, but in the end he famously acclaimed him as a player 'ten years ahead of his time'.

I don't think the man in the street fully appreciated the contribution Martin made, which is a shame because he was a remarkable player who gave great service to West Ham, Tottenham and Norwich City. He left West Ham in 1970 in search of a new challenge, joining Tottenham in part exchange for Jimmy Greaves in football's first £200,000 transfer, but I've always felt that it wasn't until he moved to Norwich that people began to appreciate what a truly great player he had become.

When Martin, Bobby and I played together for England we were like a family unit and, as with any family, we had little traditions unknown to outsiders. Martin and Bobby, for instance, liked to be the last to pull on their shorts in the dressing room before going out on to the field. For years I watched the pair of them, each trying to outwit the other in order to comply with their superstition.

Martin, having pulled on his shorts, would notice that Bobby had slyly removed his so that he could pull them on again. I've seen them actually hopping on to the pitch with legs tangled in shorts as they tried to outdo each other.

Although Martin and I are remembered for the goals we scored against West Germany, and Bobby, quite rightly, picked up the Player of the Tournament award, I thought our best player in the final was Alan Ball. His energy, endurance and determination were central to our victory. He ran the legs off Karl-Heinz Schnellinger, who was no seven-stone weakling.

As a youngster, Alan was told by Bolton Wanderers that he wasn't big enough to be a professional footballer. Bitterly disappointed, he vowed to prove them wrong. Having learned the basics from his dad, who was also a player and manager, he eventually served his apprenticeship with Blackpool before playing with distinction for Everton, Arsenal, Southampton and England.

He was just 20 when he made his England debut in a 1–1 draw with Yugoslavia in May 1965, and he spent the next ten years in England's midfield. Few in my memory have been blessed with greater stamina. He was a galvanising force in the team, and so passionate was his commitment that some of his encounters were bound to end in acrimony, as happened in 1973 when he was sent off against Poland.

In the 1966 final he forced and then delivered the corner that led to England's second goal and set up the third with his cross to me from the right flank. His energy in the 30 minutes of extra time gave us the edge over the Germans. As I struck the fourth goal at the end of the match, I looked across to see if I had any support. I did. It was Alan Ball.

I thought our best player in the final was Alan Ball. His energy, endurance and determination were central to our victory

Opposite: *Alan taking on Fulham keeper Tony Macedo in November '65.*

Opposite: *Nobby playing for Manchester United in '65.*

> In 1966 I had been in 'Coronation Street' for 200 years - and I was quite slim then! On Saturday July 30th I had some friends round, as I had a big colour TV, and we had take-away Chinese and champagne. What a day!
>
> *William Roache*

> **No player was as efficient at winning the ball as Nobby. He considered losing a tackle to be a personal affront and, consequently, some of his tackles were only just legal**

Alan and Nobby Stiles were responsible for ensuring that we chased every lost cause. In many ways they were the soul of the team. They made sure everyone pulled their weight. Alf was fond of both of them because he admired their attitude and the way they followed his instructions.

One day after training, as we all sauntered off the pitch, Alf called them both to one side.

'Have either of you got a dog?' he asked. Alan said that he had. 'You know how when you throw a ball, your dog chases after it?' continued Alf. 'Well that's what I want you both to do for Bobby Charlton. I want you to chase the ball, win it and give it to him.'

No player was as efficient at winning the ball as Nobby. He considered losing a tackle to be a personal affront and, consequently, some of his tackles were only just legal. He was a terrific competitor and he didn't appreciate shirkers. He once screamed unrepeatable abuse at me because he felt I was slacking. Nobby was warm and amiable off the pitch, but a toothless, fearsome figure on it.

Nobby was a far better player than people realised, although his great strength was his ability to mark. He had the satisfaction of nullifying Eusebio, the tournament's leading goalscorer, in the semi-final.

Alf gave Nobby the holding role in midfield. He protected the area in front of the back four with bulldog defiance in all six matches in the tournament. He and 'Bally' had a great understanding, on and off the field. They roomed together throughout the tournament and each morning Nobby got up at seven to go to church. Alf never knew and Alan told no one.

It was partly because of Nobby's diligence in midfield that his Manchester United club-mate Bobby Charlton was able to claim the freedom of the pitch. Bobby was unquestionably the finest footballer in the team but he would be the first to acknowledge the debt he owed to

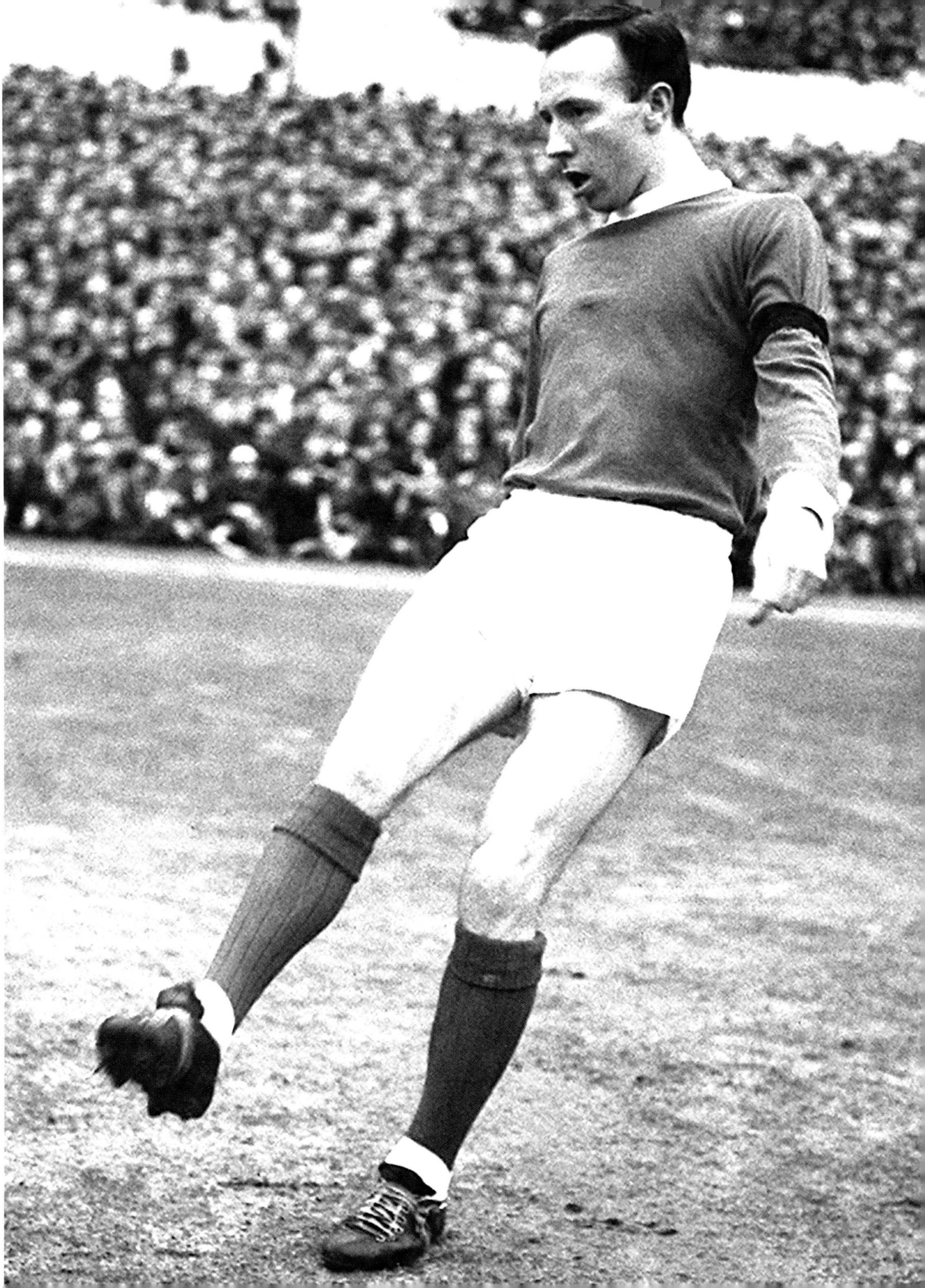

Above: *Bobby playing for United in the FA Cup final five months before the horrors of Munich.*

Opposite: *And Bobby in May '66. England's Greatest Ever.*

Nobby, with whom he won the League Championship, the European Cup and the World Cup.

What makes the Bobby Charlton story all the more remarkable is the fact that he survived the Munich air crash in February 1958 when so many young Manchester United team-mates, including Duncan Edwards, Tommy Taylor and Roger Byrne, perished. He was thrown from the plane, still strapped to his seat.

Less than three months after that terrible experience he made his debut for England against Scotland at Hampden Park alongside Tom Finney and Billy Wright. He was 20. He volleyed a stunning goal in a 4–0 win and, a month later, hit two more as England beat Portugal 2–1. After that, he just went on scoring goals, for both England and United.

One of manager Matt Busby's original 'Babes' – he won the FA Youth Cup in consecutive seasons 1954–56 – Bobby could score goals better than most. Others may have scored more, but few scored more spectacular goals. Who can forget the run and shot of classic simplicity against Mexico in 1966 or his second against Portugal, driven home with awesome power?

His total of 49 goals in a 106-cap career spanning 12 years gave him a record he still holds as England's top marksman. A quarter of a century later, Gary Lineker threatened the record, finishing his career with 48 goals in 80 appearances, but he was essentially a finisher who worked exclusively in the penalty box.

Bobby Charlton worked across the width and depth of the field and scored goals from anywhere. He could play on the wing. He could play at the front as a centre-forward or in a deeper role, attacking from midfield. It was here, at the heart of the game, that I always felt he was most effective. I think that it was as an organiser, full of power, running and spontaneity, that Alf considered him most valuable.

The role Alf gave him alongside Nobby in the middle of the field required great stamina and Bobby had plenty of that. He didn't waste energy but used it intelligently at decisive moments. Bobby Charlton in full cry, swerving past defenders with what remained of his hair straggling behind him, is another of the sights of 1966 I will never forget.

UK No. 1 single on the day the World Cup opened: 'Sunny Afternoon' by the Kinks. No. 1 for two weeks

Above: *Roger was at the height of his powers in '66. He's being challenged by Leeds' Norman Hunter here in the 1965 FA Cup final. I am sure he will have felt that.*

Opposite: *The goal-scoring legend. Jimmy playing for Spurs in 1962 and ghosting past Leicester's Frank McLintock and Len Chalmers. No mean feat.*

He already had 68 caps when the tournament began so his experience, his modest demeanour and his status around the world qualified him perfectly for the role of squad spokesman – particularly when we felt the need to approach the manager. Bobby was on safe ground because we all knew that Alf would never drop him.

When we were issued with our regulation grey flannel suits during the build-up period, Bobby was chosen to ask Alf if, on less formal occasions, we could dress casually. 'No!' said Alf.

During the tournament when we were travelling almost daily from the team hotel in Hendon to the Bank of England training ground at Roehampton in south-west London, the players became increasingly bored with the three hours spent in the motor coach. Bobby was deputed to approach Alf and suggest to him that we moved to a training ground closer to the hotel. Bobby waited for the right moment and one day, when the team bus was stuck in traffic on the way to Roehampton, he went to the front of the coach and put the proposal to Alf.

WORLD CHAMPIONS

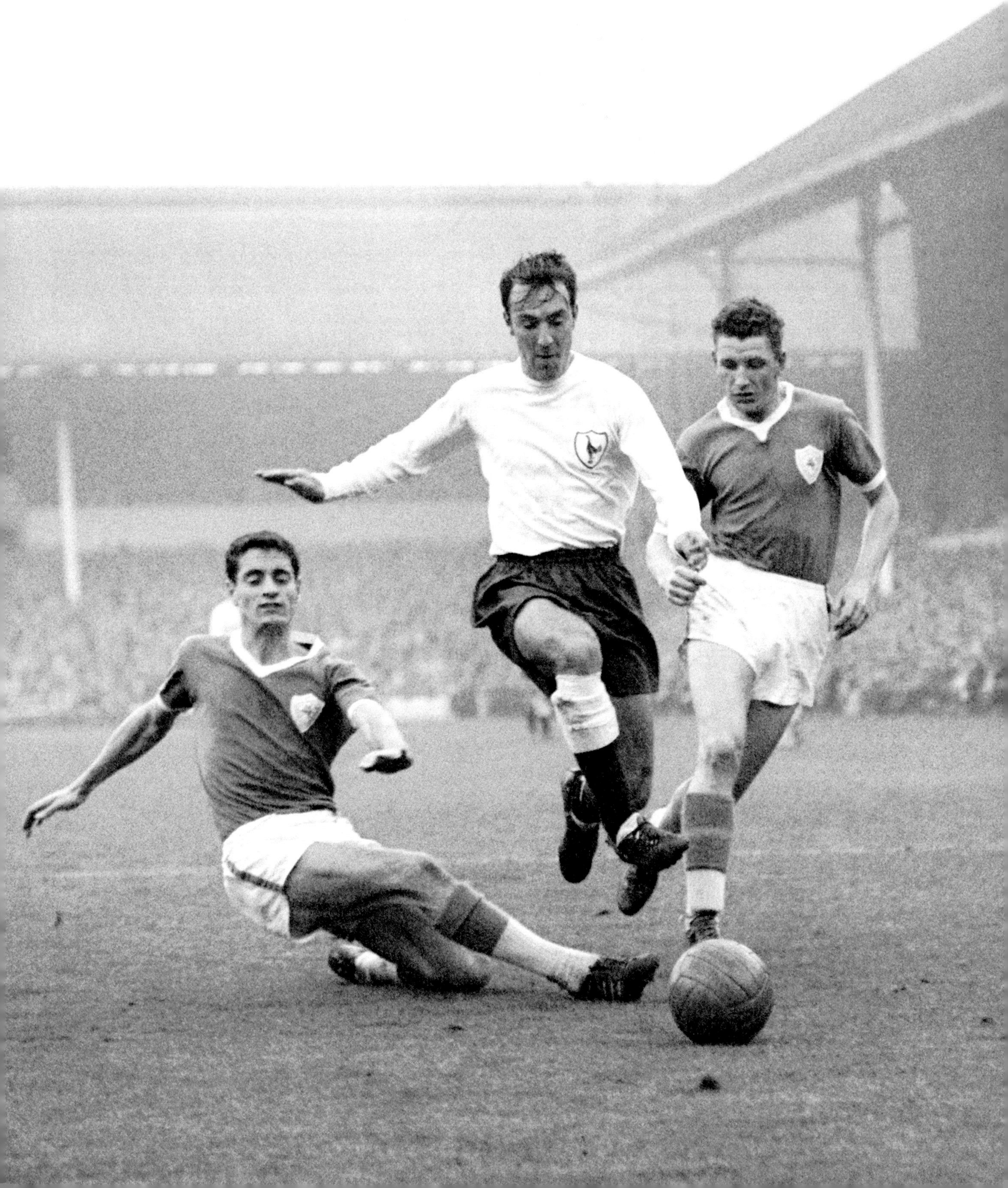

WORLD CHAMPIONS

'I'll give it some consideration,' said Alf. Before Bobby had returned to his seat, Alf turned and called down the bus, 'I've considered it and we'll stay as we are.'

One of the most important figures in England's epic triumph that summer was the unsung hero of '66, my strike partner Roger Hunt. He was vastly more experienced that I was, having made his England debut in 1962, scoring in a 3–1 win over Austria. He appeared fitfully over the next couple of seasons while he established an impressive goalscoring reputation with Liverpool.

Finally, in 1964, after scoring four in a 10–0 win over the United States, Alf recognised his formidable strengths. He was in the squad to stay because of his work ethic, his team spirit and his goal record.

When I was called into the team for the quarter-final with Argentina, Roger and I had played just three matches together, so I leaned heavily on his greater experience. There was nothing spectacular about his game but he was a prodigious worker. The fans loved him at Anfield and always called him 'Sir Roger'.

He was at the peak of his powers that summer, having contributed 27 goals to Liverpool's championship-winning season and helped

Above: *John getting his cross over for United against Spurs in '65.*

Opposite: *Terry playing for Southampton in December '63. Pity they forgot to lay any grass.*

GEOFF HURST

Above: *Ian in 1963, lining up for Liverpool against Spurs. Ultimately, Alf's decision to play without wingers reduced him to a single appearance in the tournament.*

them to the final of the European Cup Winners' Cup. He was typical of the players who appealed to the legendary Liverpool manager Bill Shankly, who laid the foundations for decades of success by combining the creative skills of the Scots with the strength and determination of the English.

Roger was hard, fast and direct, a battering ram of a player and I would never have scored the goals I did without his support and running. He adapted to an entirely different system of play with England because at Liverpool he'd always played with wingers.

The fact that Roger played in all six matches in the tournament tells you how highly he was valued by Alf. He responded with three goals – one against Mexico and both in the 2–0 win over France. In our striking partnership at the time, he was the senior man. I was simply in the right place at the right time when Jimmy was injured.

Jimmy and Roger played together in the opening three games. Had Jimmy not been injured, I think he would have played in the following three games, too, and my life might have been very different. Not everyone agrees with my assessment. Many years later, for instance, Alf revealed that he had been on the point of leaving Jimmy out of the

THE MAN FROM U.N.C.L.E.

ANNUAL

UNITED NETWORK COMMAND FOR LAW AND ENFORCEMENT

Authorised edition starring Robert Vaughn as Napoleon Solo and David McCallum as Illya Kuryakin

Above: *Bob Dylan's* Blonde on Blonde *entered the UK album charts on 20 August 1966, reaching No. 3. A few weeks before its chart entry, on 17 May, Dylan and his band were playing a gig at Manchester's Free Town Hall and after an acoustic first half, Dylan turned electric, prompting the infamous shout of 'Judas' from the audience.*

team anyway. He hadn't shown his best form, nor had he scored, in the first three games. His injury may have spared Alf a difficult decision but, had he been fit, he would have been in my team. He was a player who could turn a match for you with one flash of brilliance.

A badly gashed shin collected against the French was to cost Jimmy his place in the team for the rest of the tournament. He was fit again before the final and, with his goalscoring pedigree, he had every right to expect a recall. He said at the time that he couldn't imagine himself not playing. In fact, no one could imagine him not playing.

Although I'd taken his place, I believed that there was a very good chance Alf would leave me out and bring him back for the final, but he didn't. He selected me to play and left Jim out. I think Jimmy's disenchantment with football began that day.

He played just three more games for England and then, in a mood of growing frustration, presented Alf with an ultimatum. He told the manager that he wanted to be selected for England's starting 11 on a regular basis or be left out of the squad altogether. Alf, not a man to take kindly to such an ultimatum, told Jim that his England career was over.

Three other members of the squad who appeared in the tournament were the three wingers. John Connelly, of Manchester United, played in the opening match against Uruguay but was replaced by Southampton's Terry Paine for the second game, against Mexico. Alf made just one change for the third game, against France, Liverpool's Ian Callaghan replacing Paine.

Clearly, none of them did quite enough to convince the manager because in the quarter-final against Argentina they were all left on the bench and none appeared in the tournament again. So, more by circumstance than design, Alf switched to something more like 4-4-2 – and introduced his 'wingless wonders' to the world.

WORLD CHAMPIONS

> *I believed that there was a very good chance Alf would leave me out and bring him back for the final, but he didn't. He selected me to play and left Jim out*

In July and August 1966 I was spending most weekends in Blackpool doing a Sunday night variety show with Tony Hancock. Arriving on Saturday morning, I would check in and then go to the ABC theatre where the show was televised.

Not being daft, I made particular friends with the girl dancers. As usual they were the best company in any show and I enjoyed sitting, gossiping and laughing, and disposing of endless cups of tea. In addition, they had acquired an excellent colour television set.

On the afternoon of the final, I found I wasn't the only one aware of this. The room was filled with people from all parts of the theatre, stagehands to stars.

As the match drew to a close, it was getting on for time when we should have been preparing for the Saturday matinee show - but nobody moved. Who could have?

In those days I had an odd superstition about Ken Wolstenholme. Whenever I was watching live football on TV and he was commentating, towards the end he would inevitably say, 'Well, the 90 minutes are up on my watch!', whereupon the side I was NOT supporting would inevitably score.

So it was that in the last five minutes of that great game I was surrounded by people yelling 'Come on England!' while I was screaming 'Don't mention your watch!' God bless him, he didn't. But we all know what he did say.

I don't think the matinee started quite on time that day but somehow nobody seemed to mind. Blackpool that night was the closest thing to VE day I have ever seen!

John Junkin

5
What was it all about, Alfie?

When you take the district line from the City of London out towards the vast residential sprawl of Essex you pass through an area that has probably produced more outstanding footballers than any other in the UK.

The people of east London have always taken pride in the fact that some of football's greatest names were once kids in the locality. Then, in 1966, a far wider audience suddenly recognised what the Cockneys had known for a long time.

The world associated the East End with Dickensian squalor, Jack the Ripper, the dockyards and the Blitz until Alf Ramsey, himself a product of Dagenham, unveiled to a global audience the rich seam of football talent that had coursed through the back streets for more than half a century. In the years since 1966 it has become a standing joke among the locals that West Ham won the World Cup for England. This is, of course, an exaggeration.

WORLD CHAMPIONS

GEOFF HURST

Above: *Michael Caine seduces Shelley Winters in the 1966 smash* Alfie.

Previous spread: *Alf a few months after the war ended, having signed for Southampton.*

What is a fact is that four key participants in England's World Cup bid that summer were all born in east London within about five miles of each other – a distance covered by six stops on the district line. Martin Peters was born in Plaistow, Jimmy Greaves in East Ham, Bobby Moore in Barking and Alf in Becontree. In between Plaistow and East Ham is Upton Park where you alight for West Ham, a club that continues to be the focal point for the emotional loyalties of thousands of East Enders.

Although I was born in a suburb of Manchester, I was six when the family moved to Essex and as a young apprentice at West Ham, I became aware of the special sense of community among the working-class residents in that part of London.

In the build-up, Jimmy Greaves was widely acknowledged as the man whose goals could win the tournament for England. The son of a tube-train driver, he was born in February 1940 but, at just six weeks old, the family were bombed out by the Luftwaffe and uprooted to Dagenham. Like Martin, Bobby and me, he spent part of his career at West Ham.

86 WORLD CHAMPIONS

GEOFF HURST

87

WORLD CHAMPIONS

Alf, born to a hay and straw dealer at Becontree Heath, Dagenham, in January 1920, was one of the first of a long and impressive line of footballers to emerge from what was one of the poorest areas of the capital city. Apart from my World Cup colleagues, George Male, Terry Venables, Trevor Brooking, Frank Lampard and Tony Adams, to name just a few, all came from the east London area. Today, the tradition is maintained by another group of England players – David Beckham, Frank Lampard junior, Sol Campbell, John Terry, Ledley King, Ashley Cole and Joe Cole.

I think it's remarkable that east London has continued to produce a high number of top-quality players at a time when the decline in development in other parts of the country has forced many of the big Premiership clubs to go abroad in search of talented youngsters. I suspect Alf Ramsey would be puzzled – maybe even irritated – by the number of foreign players now in our domestic game. In his day, kids played for their local junior team and hoped to be spotted by the local Football League club.

Opposite: Cathy Come Home, *Ken Loach's ground-breaking drama about a young couple who become homeless, was first broadcast on BBC2 on 16 November 1966. Cathy Ward was played by Carol White. The show led directly to the creation of the charity Shelter.*

Below: *21 July 1966: 15 young women cram into an Austin Mini, breaking the world record.*

Opposite: *Spurs manager Arthur Rowe explaining tactics in 1950. He had a huge influence on the way Alf thought about the game.*

> I shall never forget the 1966 World Cup final, firstly because England won it, and secondly because I didn't see even a millisecond of live action.
>
> I remember very well what I was doing - I was a deckchair attendant on Swanage beach. As an impecunious university student, this was the best I could do to make ends meet during the vacation. I remember plodding around in my mangy white coat with my machine, desperately sidling up to the beach hut owners to get the latest from those who had radios. A deeply frustrating experience all round, redeemed only by the euphoria of our final triumph.
>
> David Mellor

> *Those who saw Alf play tell me that he worked devilishly hard to maximise his potential. In that sense he was a bit like me as a player. He wasn't a natural, but he was willing to learn*

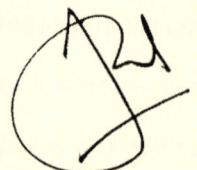

Alf played for his school at Becontree Heath, then Dagenham Schoolboys. No offer came to join West Ham or anyone else, so he became an errand boy at the age of 14. It was while playing for a local Dagenham team called Five Elms that Alf was spotted by a scout from Portsmouth and encouraged to sign as an amateur.

He didn't play a single game for Portsmouth, partly because of the war. Then in 1940, when he was playing for the Duke of Cornwall's Light Infantry, his battalion lost 10–0 to Southampton, who were sufficiently impressed with Alf's stoical resistance to offer him a regular game if he joined them as an amateur.

So, when the army could spare him, Alf played for Southampton and, when the war ended in 1945, they offered him a professional contract at £8 per week. He played a total of 90 consecutive games for Southampton between 1946 and 1949 as an inside-forward, centre-half and finally at right-back, where he established himself.

In December 1948 he won his first England cap in a 6–0 victory over Switzerland at Highbury. Alf was absolutely thrilled to be asked to play alongside the gods of the game – Finney, Matthews, Wright and Mannion. At this time, remember, England were considered *the* world power in football and had never been beaten on home soil by a team from outside the UK.

GEOFF HURST

WORLD CHAMPIONS

Those who saw Alf play tell me that he worked devilishly hard to maximise his potential. In that sense he was a bit like me as a player. He wasn't a natural, but he was willing to learn. He lived and breathed football and when Southampton sold him to Spurs for £21,000 in May 1949 he came under the wing of the man who was to introduce him to the finer tactical points of the game.

The Spurs manager, Arthur Rowe, was a master tactician who had developed a short passing game played at high speed. This 'push and run' style suited Alf, who was proud of his fitness and had the wit to spot openings and the skill to deliver accurate passes.

With Alf and another future managerial great, Bill Nicholson, in the team, Spurs won the Second Division championship in some style in 1950. The following season, Rowe's tactics baffled the élite of the First Division and they won the League Championship for the first time, with Alf missing two games only. In fact, in three seasons he missed just five matches.

The other coach to have a significant influence on Alf was Walter Winterbottom, a scholarly bespectacled figure who spent 16 years as England's national coach yet never once selected the team – until the appointment of Alf as manager, that was a task left to the superior minds of the FA selection committee. But Walter left behind a lasting legacy in the form of a nationwide coaching network.

A qualified PE teacher and wartime wing commander in the RAF, he presided over two of the lowest moments in England's history – and Alf was right there in the thick of it on both occasions.

Nicknamed 'The General' at Spurs because of his growing authority and status in the team, Alf was well established as England's right-back when Walter took the team to the 1950 World Cup in Brazil. It was the first time England had deigned to enter the tournament and, as the mother nation of the game, they were considered joint favourites for the title along with Brazil.

Watching Walter struggling to cope at that World Cup made a big impression on Alf and, years later, he would recall the pressure that the national coach had been under.

While the selection of the team was left to the travelling FA chairman, Arthur Drewery, a fish merchant from Grimsby, Walter had to take the training, organise medical treatment, accommodation, travel and financial matters and, at one stage, even cook for the team.

The team Drewery selected, with Alf at right-back, beat the part-timers of Chile 2–0 in Rio in the opening match. It was not an impressive England display and Walter urged the sole selector to recall Stanley Matthews for the next match, against the United States.

The FA selector refused and insisted that England fielded an unchanged team. Whether Matthews' inclusion would have made a

Opposite: *The other great influence on Alf's career – Walter Winterbottom, England manager from 1946 to 1962.*

> *While the selection of the team was left to the FA chairman, Arthur Drewery, a fish merchant from Grimsby, Walter had to take the training, organise medical treatment, travel and financial matters and, at one stage, even cook for the team*

Below: *Key moments in Alf's career. Here he is playing for England in the infamous defeat by the USA in the 1950 World Cup in Brazil.*

Opposite: *And scoring a penalty in the 6–3 thrashing by Hungary in 1953. This was Alf's last game for England and it left a massive impression on him.*

difference we will never know, but the fact is that without him England suffered one of the most humiliating defeats in the nation's football history.

On a bumpy pitch in the little mining town of Belo Horizonte, the American part-timers, who had been out partying the previous evening, beat mighty England 1–0. The formality had turned into a fiasco and England's World Cup progress was in serious jeopardy.

To qualify, England had now to beat Spain. The last time the two nations had met England had won 7–1 but not this time. Spain won 1–0 and as the game drew to a close 90,000 Brazilians in the Maracana Stadium took out white handkerchiefs and waved them at the English players.

Alf would say years later that the trip to Brazil that summer taught him the dangers of complacent preparation and of underestimating even the most modest opposition.

Although the World Cup in those days was far less significant than now, Walter Winterbottom claimed afterwards that the tournament in Brazil had put England's position in the world in sharp perspective. Typically, Alf still believed that the traditional English virtues of strength and discipline, when properly applied, would invariably triumph over the flair of South American or continental teams. Many felt the same but, in truth, the jingoistic belief that England were still great now rested solely on the unbeaten Wembley record and here Alf was about to find his faith tested to the full once again.

Hungary, who had not entered the 1950 World Cup, were the 1952 Olympic champions and when they visited Wembley in November 1953 they were halfway through a six-year spell during which time they lost just once.

The 'Mighty Magyars' were one of the great teams of the last century and had three truly outstanding attacking players in Ference Puskas, Nandor Hidegkuti and Sandor Kocsis. Unforgettably, they beat England 6–3 – the first defeat at Wembley against foreign opposition.

> *Alf still believed that the traditional English virtues of strength and discipline, when properly applied, would invariably triumph*

Above: *The beginning of a managerial legend. The Ipswich team of 1961 that Alf guided to the First Division title against all the odds.*

The Hungarians gave Alf, Billy Wright, Stanley Matthews and the rest of them a real football lesson and demolished any lingering vestiges of English superiority. Ron Greenwood, a spectator at Wembley on this historic occasion, told me years later that the movement and passing of the brilliant Hungarians had highlighted just how out of date the English game was becoming.

Six men who faced Hungary that day never played for England again. Alf was one of them. It was his 32nd cap in a five-year international career.

His decline as a player coincided with that of both England and Spurs. The once great 'push and run' side at White Hart Lane suffered a major setback when Arthur Rowe's deteriorating health meant that he had to be replaced by Jimmy Anderson. The new manager's first decision was to drop several first-team players, including Alf who was 34. Age had caught up with some of them, many of whom smoked like chimneys. Smoking was not unusual among the top players in those days.

Alf occasionally had a bet on the horses, but he didn't smoke. He didn't drink much either, although he could be tempted by a pint of brown ale. He devoted much of his spare time to reading. Towards the end of his playing career he decided that he wanted to continue in the game as a manager and felt that by reading he would improve his command of the language.

For much the same reason he felt that elocution lessons would remove some of the rough edges that were the inevitable consequence of a Dagenham upbringing. It is one of the contradictions of the man that he retained a love of jellied eels while cultivating the clipped tones of a BBC newsreader because he felt that would elevate his social status.

Although clearly sensitive about his working-class origins, he was never happier than when talking about football with his players. I understand, though, how many outsiders interpreted his formality as coldness.

Alf had clearly impressed those who mattered at White Hart Lane because, after 226 first-team games, there was talk of him being offered a job on the coaching staff. Before this could materialise, Ipswich Town, just relegated after one heady season in Division Two, offered him the job as manager. So, in August 1955, Alf's career in football management took root in Suffolk where a famous local brewing family, the Cobbolds, had great plans for the little club.

The Cobbold family were Suffolk landowners who had guided the club with great benevolence since 1878. In Alf's terms, they were gentry and this merely added to his desire to be able to mix comfortably with the social élite.

Even though I have always been a truly loyal Scotland fan, I must admit that as I knew both Bobby Moore and Geoff Hurst I was somewhat biased that afternoon, and along with every other person supporting England who saw or listened to that unbelievably exciting match, cheered like crazy when Geoff produced three of those magnificent goals.

Lulu

He felt that elocution lessons would remove some of the rough edges that were the inevitable consequence of a Dagenham upbringing. It is one of the contradictions of the man that he retained a love of jellied eels while cultivating the clipped tones of a BBC newsreader

UK No. 1 single on the day of the World Cup final: 'Out of Time' by Chris Farlowe. No.1 for one week

On the training ground, he put to good use all that he had learned from Arthur Rowe and Walter Winterbottom. It took him just two seasons to steer Ipswich back to the Second Division.

He assembled an anonymous group of players and instilled in them the belief that they could compete with the best. He devised a fledgling 4-4-2 system designed to get the best out of his two strikers, Ray Crawford and Ted Phillips, and his ageing winger, Jimmy Leadbetter, who no longer had the power or pace to make attacking runs on the flanks. They responded magnificently, and in 1960–61, Crawford and Phillips shared 70 goals – a major factor in winning the Second Division championship.

Leadbetter played a full role as well. He was known as 'Sticks' because of his thin legs – he used to wear long shorts to cover his knees and sneak out of the dressing room at half-time for a cigarette. How times have changed in the game!

The astonishing rise of 'Ramsey's Rustics' was widely greeted with derision. That summer, as he prepared Ipswich for their first season in the top division, he strengthened his squad with just one signing – Falkirk's Doug Moran whose £12,000 fee exceeded the cost of the entire Ipswich team.

Compare that to Bill Nicholson, Alf's former team-mate who had just won the League and FA Cup double as manager of Tottenham with a team valued at nearly £400,000. The glamorous Spurs were favourites to retain the title and everyone expected Ipswich to go straight back down to the Second Division.

Everyone was wrong. Alf once again convinced ordinary players that, with organisation and belief, they could beat anyone, including Tottenham. They beat Spurs twice that season and Crawford and Phillips repeated their goalscoring heroics, sharing 61 goals.

In what was perhaps the last example of a small-town club overwhelming the giants of the game, little Ipswich Town won the League Championship. Their 56 point total remains the lowest on record but does not disguise the fact that Alf had once again demonstrated an extraordinary ability to coax the best out of relatively ordinary players.

One evening, as the club celebrated their unlikely success with a party at Portman Road, Alf was watching Ipswich Boys play Norwich Boys. The chairman, John Cobbold, finally found him sitting alone in the main stand and suggested he join the party.

'Not just now, Mr Chairman,' he replied. 'I'm working.'

Alf took great personal pride in the fact that his unfancied Ipswich team had emulated the feat of the Spurs side that became the first in history to win the Second and First Division titles in consecutive seasons. He, of course, had played in those teams in 1950 and 1951. Now, still in the fledgling years of a managerial career, he'd matched that success largely because of his tactics.

The strategy of football in England remained more or less unchanged and, although Alf was essentially a traditionalist, he had toyed with a new tactical idea in the hope that it would get the best from his players at Ipswich. Like everyone else, he had two wingers, but everyone else had the two wingers serving a centre-forward. Alf had two centre-forwards, Crawford and Phillips, and he withdrew his two wingers, Jimmy Leadbetter and Ray Stephenson, into deeper midfield positions. Ipswich had triumphed with that crude form of 4-4-2 and within a decade the formation came to dominate English football. It became the tactical line-up favoured by most coaches.

> *Alf once again convinced ordinary players that, with organisation and belief, they could beat anyone, including Tottenham. They beat Spurs twice that season*

> *It says something about the state of the game at the time when the manager of Burnley could turn down the chance to manage the national team in a World Cup that was to be held in England*

Bill Nicholson had recognised the threat posed by Alf's tactics. When Spurs, the defending champions, met Ipswich at White Hart Lane in a crucial match in March 1962, Nicholson proposed a change of tactics to counter Alf's line-up. His players were unhappy with the new formation and Nicholson, reluctantly, gave way. Spurs lost 3–1. Had they won the match, Spurs would have won the double again.

Nicholson at least had the satisfaction of beating Burnley 3–1 in the FA Cup final. The Burnley manager at the time was Jimmy Adamson, whom Walter Winterbottom had nominated as his successor.

After 137 matches in charge and another disappointing World Cup in Chile in 1962 – England were beaten by Argentina and Brazil – Walter felt he'd had enough of haggling with the amateurs of the FA selection committee. He quit and suggested that Jimmy Adamson should succeed him, but Jimmy didn't want to leave Burnley. He had, after all, seen exactly how the FA treated his friend Walter.

Looking back now, it says something about the state of the game at the time when the manager of Burnley could turn down the chance to manage the national team in a World Cup that was to be held in England.

Snubbed by Adamson, the FA somewhat surprisingly ignored Bill Nicholson and instead turned to the man who had won the League Championship with Ipswich Town five months earlier. In October 1962, they asked Ipswich chairman John Cobbold for permission to interview Alf.

The timing was perfect for Alf. In a sense, the FA's approach offered an escape route, because First Division rivals had by then worked out his tactics. In fact, when Bill Nicholson insisted his players change their strategy for the FA Charity Shield in August, they beat Ipswich 5–1.

By October, Ipswich were third from bottom of the table. They had little money to reinforce their squad. For Alf, the immediate future looked grim and that's why the FA offer was irresistible. He was 42.

Alf agreed to take the position as full-time England manager from the end of 1962–63. This arrangement gave him the chance to steer Ipswich through their one and only bid to lift the European Cup. They won their preliminary round match 14–1 on aggregate against Floriana of Malta and were then drawn to meet AC Milan in the first round.

This was the Milan of Maldini, Trapattoni, Altafini and Rivera. Although they lost the first leg 3–0 in Milan, Alf coaxed a superb performance from his team in the return leg at Portman Road. Their 2–1 victory was not enough to salvage the tie, but it was no disgrace to lose so gallantly to the team that went on to win the European title that season.

Alf's first contact with the England squad occurred in the dressing room prior to the European Nations Cup match against France in Paris in February 1963. It was not a good start. Alf had not picked the team and they failed to respond to his half-time rallying call and lost 5–2.

Alf knew he had a lot of work to do but, unlike his predecessor, his hands would not be tied by the whims of the FA selection committee. In his discussions with the FA chairman Graham Doggart, he had insisted that he would take the job only on the understanding that he alone would be responsible for team selection. Apart from a £4,000 a year salary – twice what Walter was earning – he wanted total control over team affairs and the FA gave it to him. After 90 years, selection by committee was over.

The professionals in the game, the people who knew him, greeted Alf's appointment with knowing nods of approval. The media, the fans and those who didn't know him were not so sure.

Alf made the point that in his time as manager of Ipswich his priority had been to devise ways of stopping better players. Coaxing the best from his own players was important, too, but he said that as the impoverished manager of a small club, he'd learned the value of subduing the star players among the opposition.

To do this successfully required planning. Alf devoted a lot of thought to team tactics. The day of the maverick winger, for instance, was over.

Above: *The Rolling Stones' single 'Paint it Black' entered the charts on 19 May 1966 and reached No. 1 a week later. They had two other Top 10 hits in the year, '19th Nervous Breakdown' and 'Have You Seen Your Mother Baby, Standing in the Shadow', and toured Europe, America, Australia and the UK.*

Radio Times (Incorporating World-Radio)
July 7, 1966. Vol. 172: No. 2226.
LONDON AND SOUTH-EAST
JULY 9—15
Radio Times
WORLD CUP NUMBER
SIXPENCE

Alf wanted players who worked for the team as a whole. He wanted a balanced, cohesive unit and he was prepared to sacrifice individual flair to get it. That had been the secret of his success at Ipswich.

The soon-to-be redundant FA selection committee picked the team for the last three matches of season 1962–63. Alf had agreed with Ipswich that he would stay with them until the end of the season, helping his successor Jackie Milburn, his old England team-mate from Newcastle, settle in to the job. Ipswich, in turn, agreed that he could take the England training sessions before each of the last three internationals that season.

The first of the three was the 5–2 defeat by the French – a significant setback because it meant that England were out of the European Nations Cup and would have no competitive football whatsoever in the three-year build-up to the 1966 World Cup.

There was little about the two matches that followed to encourage Alf. In April 1963 a crowd of 98,000 saw a very good Scotland team,

Below: *Buster Keaton died on 1 February 1966. Not as he performed this wonderful stunt.*

> *It was soon obvious the captaincy suited 'Mooro'. A quiet authority about his presence on the field made him a natural leader, but it was another year before he was given the job on a permanent basis*

Opposite: *The Charlton boys training with England at Stamford Bridge on 8 April 1965. Two days later Jack would make his England debut in the 2–2 draw with Scotland at Wembley and Bobby would score.*

reduced to ten men when Eric Caldow broke a leg, beat England 2–1 at Wembley in the Home International championship.

It has to be acknowledged, though, that the FA selection committee finally got something spectacularly right because this was the match in which the great Gordon Banks made his debut. They retained his services for a friendly international against Brazil at Wembley a month later. That game ended 1–1, Bryan Douglas providing an 85th minute equaliser to avoid another Wembley defeat.

Then Alf was on his own. The blazer brigade from the FA struck 'team selection' from the committee agenda for ever and Alf went back to Ipswich for a farewell reception at which he was presented with a bedside tea-maker as a farewell gift.

His first task was to put together a squad for three end-of-season matches in Czechoslovakia, East Germany and Switzerland. The touring party included five of the players who would face West Germany in the World Cup final three years later – Gordon Banks, Ray Wilson, Bobby Moore, Roger Hunt and Bobby Charlton.

A 4–2 victory over the Czechs in Bratislava was England's best result for a long time. Jimmy Greaves scored twice but what turned out to be most significant for Alf was the injury that robbed England of team captain Jimmy Armfield. In his absence, Alf gave the captaincy to Bobby Moore for the first time.

At the age of 22, 'Mooro' became England's youngest captain. Alf tried to reassure him by saying, 'Whatever decisions you make on the field will have my full support.'

Those in the team recall that it was soon obvious the captaincy suited 'Mooro'. A quiet authority about his presence on the field made him a natural leader, but it was another year before he was given the job on a permanent basis.

England went on to beat East Germany 2–1 in Leipzig and Switzerland 8–1 in Basle. After three straight wins from his first three games in charge, Alf returned to his Ipswich home believing that he'd at least halted England's decline.

That summer, in an interview he gave to a local newspaper, he placed his head on the block. In a couple of sentences he demonstrated his belief in English football and English footballers.

'England will win the World Cup,' he said. 'We have the ability, strength, character and, above all, players with the right temperament. Such thoughts must be put to the public, and particularly to the players, so that confidence can be built up.'

For Alf, it was the equivalent of the Gettysburg Address, a profound, unequivocal statement of intent. It put him under enormous pressure and no England manager since has been brave enough to repeat such a prediction.

GEOFF HURST

Above: *The shape of things to come. Alf sends out a team without wingers. Spain versus England, 8 December 1965. Joe Baker opens the scoring in England's 2–0 victory.*

A couple of months later, at a big formal press conference in London, he was asked if he had in fact predicted that England would win in 1966. He could hardly withdraw his statement.

'I repeat,' he said. 'England will win the World Cup.'

Years later, if we teased him about what he'd said, Alf would insist that he'd meant it. Whether he did or not, the effect his words had on the players was very positive. They told us that he believed we were good enough to win the World Cup and, slowly, we began to believe it.

As the tournament approached, few realised the full extent of the tactical quandary gripping Alf. He obviously valued wingers. He'd shown that with Ipswich, and on his first England tour that summer of 1963, Bobby Charlton and Terry Paine had played very successfully in the wide positions. It slowly became clear, though, that while he appreciated the unpredictable attacking options provided by free-spirited wingers, he placed greater value on tackling, covering and working hard to track opposing players.

Two impressive Wembley results late in 1963 suggested that Alf was steaming ahead with two wingers in a 4-2-4 formation. The 2–1 win over the Rest of the World in a match that marked the FA Centenary, followed by a thumping 8–3 win over Northern Ireland, meant that he'd won his first six matches in control.

The new mood of optimism faltered briefly when Scotland won 1–0 at Hampden Park the following spring, but confidence was restored a couple of months later with a 4–3 victory in Portugal, where Liverpool winger Peter Thompson made an encouraging debut. My West Ham team-mate Johnny Byrne scored three of the England goals.

The game in Lisbon was the first of an exhausting six-match programme that took in Dublin, New York, Rio and Sao Paulo. The squad had trained for a couple of days in London and on the eve of departure, six players broke curfew in order to visit a West End restaurant and have a few drinks. The six were Gordon Banks, Bobby Moore, Johnny Byrne, Bobby Charlton, Ray Wilson and George Eastham.

When they returned to the Hendon Hall Hotel in the early hours, they each discovered that their passports had been placed on their beds. No more was said about the matter until they arrived in Estoril. After the first training session, Alf ordered all of his players back to the changing rooms. 'Except you six,' he said. 'You know who you are.'

Alf told them that if he'd had enough players to make up a team, he'd have left the errant six at home. All six played against Portugal and all six took heed of his warning. Only two of them, Eastham and Byrne, would fail to line-up for the World Cup final two years later.

That incident confirmed Alf's unyielding attitude when it came to matters of discipline. Even the most argumentative players soon realised there was little point in irritating the manager. He would always listen to what you had to say but he would then make up his own mind. In the end, we came to admire his obstinacy.

As with any team, though, some members took a mischievous delight in irritating the boss. Jimmy Greaves was one. Around this time the Michael Caine film *Alfie* was enormously popular. Jim loved whistling the movie's theme song 'What's it all about, Alfie?' He'd often do this on the team bus and the players thought it hilarious.

Alf, old-fashioned, upright and quite the opposite of the Cockney spiv portrayed by Caine in the film, took it all in his stride. Nothing seemed to disturb him. He knew where he was going and he knew how to get there. It was this unflinching self-belief that won the loyalty of the squad and fuelled his pursuit of a new and initially unpopular tactical plan.

> *Alf, old-fashioned, upright and quite the opposite of the Cockney spiv portrayed by Caine in the film Alfie, took it all in his stride. Nothing seemed to disturb him. He knew where he was going and he knew how to get there*

Jubilant Norbert Stiles, wearing the No. 9 shirt for England for the first time, scores the winning goal for England against West Germany at Wembley in February. Goalkeeper Tilkowski had failed to hold Hunt's header and Ball is following up.

Above: *Matches against the Germans would become significant milestones in my life. This game proved to be a dress rehearsal for the World Cup final. Not that any of us knew that. For me, I was just thrilled to be playing my first game for the national team. The photo is from the official programme of the tournament.*

With Peter Thompson in full flow, England massacred the United States 10–0 in New York, but then a 5–1 defeat in Brazil and a 1–0 defeat in Argentina suggested to Alf that his tactics might need a major rethink if his team was to compete with the very best in the world and fulfil his bold prediction in 1966.

With one year left to prepare, Alf's team looked anything but potential World Cup winners. England won just five of their nine fixtures in 1965. Alf, searching for a winning formula, used 14 different attacking players in those matches – Bobby Charlton, Johnny Byrne, Barry Bridges, Jimmy Greaves, Peter Thompson, John Connelly, George Eastham, Terry Paine, Alan Ball, Mick Jones, Derek Temple, Alan Peacock, Joe Baker and Roger Hunt.

At least defensively Alf seemed to have found what he was looking for. When Jack Charlton made his debut in a 2–2 draw with Scotland at Wembley in April 1965, the World Cup defence came together for

> Saturday July 30th 1966 found me sitting in the sunshine of Estartit, Spain, alongside a heavily pregnant wife, listening to the World Cup final commentary being delivered in Spanish. If that wasn't bizarre enough in itself, my companions were mainly German tourists who, for the ensuing 120 minutes at least, forgot the frailties of a hotel which today would be answerable to the Trades Description Act. How I, an Arsenal reserve 'keeper, could time my holiday to be out of the country on this great occasion for English football must lend itself to my Scottish blood.
>
> So there we were spending the World Cup afternoon accompanied by grinding cement mixers, a bus load of Germans and a few ex-patriots. To be honest the 90 minutes plus extra time contained enough good humour - just - to outweigh the traditional rivalry of the two nations.
>
> And the Union Jacks and knotted handkerchiefs reigned supreme. A bottle of vodka was ordered (an appropriate choice with hindsight remembering the famous Russian linesman) in salute of Geoff Hurst's second goal, even though we couldn't understand the delay in the referee's decision at the time, and as our Spanish Wolstenholme completed his own version of 'they think it's all over...' one inebriated Brit actually jumped into the waterless pool. It not only completed the most bizarre football occasion of my life but the whole afternoon transformed a disastrous holiday into the realms of fantasy.
>
> Bob Wilson

With one year left to prepare, Alf's team looked anything but potential World Cup winners. England won just five of their nine fixtures in 1965. Alf, searching for a winning formula, used 14 different attacking players in those matches

the first time. Banks, Cohen, Moore, Charlton J. and Wilson were to become the permanent pillars of England's defensive strategy.

Situated immediately in front of them, breathing fire and brimstone, Nobby Stiles also made his debut that day against the Scots. Having led 2–0, England finished the match with nine men. Sadly, Johnny Byrne, one of the injured, never played for England again.

GEOFF HURST

109

Above: *We were ready for the tournament to begin, and so were the BBC team. L-r: Ken Aston, Kenneth Wolstenholme, Wally Barnes, David Coleman, Frank Bough, Alan Weeks and Arthur Ellis.*

A 3–2 defeat by Austria at Wembley in October 1965 was also significant because this was the match in which Bobby Charlton moved from the wing to a free role in midfield. As Alf retreated from deploying conventional wingers, Bobby grew spectacularly into his new roaming midfield role. With his tenacious United team-mate Stiles at his shoulder, he knew he had the freedom to burst forward into attacking positions.

One other debut of significance occurred in 1965. Alan Ball, a prickly little midfield player with Blackpool, was called into the side for the 1–1 draw with Yugoslavia in Belgrade four days after his 20th birthday. His ability to run for 90 minutes, press forward in support of the attack and then chase back to help out in defence, was an important element in the evolution of Alf's World Cup team.

The last match of 1965 was perhaps the turning point, the moment when the manager realised that he had finally found a system that maximised the talents of the available players. It was a cold December night in Madrid when he sent out a team without wingers to face Spain, who were European champions and had already qualified for the World Cup finals to be held nine months later.

Alf adopted a 4-3-3 formation with Bobby Charlton, Nobby Stiles and George Eastham in midfield. Alan Ball was supporting the front two of Roger Hunt and Joe Baker with instructions to drop back to help out in midfield when necessary.

England played brilliantly on a pitch covered in thawing snow. They won 2–0 but it could have been more. The newspapers the following day were full of praise for Alf's 'wingless wonders'. That line-up became the template for his tactics at Wembley the following summer.

Shortly after that, I got my England call up, joining the squad for the game against Poland in January 1966. Even though I didn't get on the pitch, I learned an important lesson during my first morning in training. Alf was working on set pieces and wanted a couple of players to help him demonstrate a point he was making about free kicks.

He looked at the crowd of players around him and began calling out names. I instinctively took a step backwards, anxious not to be selected on my first morning. Alf spotted me. He said nothing at the time but later, when no other players were near, he said to me quite firmly, 'I've got no use for shrinking violets. I've picked you for what I know you can do. It's now up to you.'

I later learned that Alf used the same technique to preach the same message to all the youngsters he selected. We were all given the same lecture – 'You are here because I believe you are good enough to play for your country. You will not be asked to do for me anything that you are not asked to do every week by your club.'

A month later, I was thrilled to make my debut, albeit in the rather uninspiring game against West Germany at Wembley. We won 1–0 but the fans were desperately unhappy with the quality of our performance. In the dressing room afterwards Alf said, 'That lot will be cheering their heads off if we get the same result against the Germans in the final.'

Six weeks later, after we'd beaten the Scots 4–3 in Glasgow, Martin Peters made his debut in a 2–0 win over Yugoslavia at Wembley. No one realised it at the time but Martin was the final piece in the jigsaw.

The next match at Wembley would be the World Cup's opening fixture – England v. Uruguay.

> *He looked at the crowd of players around him and began calling out names. I instinctively took a step backwards, anxious not to be selected on my first morning*

6 The first round

In the beginning, Alf Ramsey settled for a compromise. England's first match, he reckoned, would be the hardest of the three in Group One and he wanted to get his team selection right. As he kept reminding us, he didn't want the ignominy of defeat in our opening game. When he named the team he chose, as many suspected he would, the first 11 names and numbers from the squad list of 22 submitted to FIFA – with one exception, and that was me. I had shirt No. 10 but Roger Hunt, with shirt No. 21, was chosen to partner Jimmy Greaves at the front. I wasn't really surprised, nor was I disappointed.

There was no hope of getting on to the bench. Although substitutions had been introduced in friendly international matches in 1923, providing both nations agreed beforehand, FIFA refused to permit the use of substitutes in the World Cup until 1970. By then, the Football League had been using substitutes in English domestic football for five seasons.

WORLD CHAMPIONS

GEOFF HURST

JULES RIMET CUP
WORLD CHAMPIONSHIP
ENGLAND 1966 JULY 11-30

WEMBLEY · EVERTON · SHEFFIELD · SUNDERLAND · ASTON VILLA · MANCHESTER · MIDDLESBROUGH · WHITE CITY

OFFICIAL SOUVENIR PROGRAMME

PRICE 2/6

I sat behind Alf at Wembley in my grey flannel suit, proud and happy to be involved. Had you told me six months earlier that I'd be at Wembley on 11 July, 1966 as part of the England squad, I'd have fallen over laughing. I tried to keep the whole experience in perspective and was quite content to sit and watch and hope that I might get a game at some stage in the tournament.

The 11 players chosen to start the 1966 World Cup were Banks, Cohen, Moore, Charlton J., Wilson, Ball, Stiles, Charlton R., Connelly, Hunt, Greaves.

The inclusion of John Connelly, the Manchester United winger, suggested that Alf had private hopes of unhinging the Uruguayan defence despite all his public proclamations that a sound defensive display would be England's priority.

At the time, Uruguay were recognised as one of the major forces in South American football. They had a population just one quarter that of London, and had won the World Cup twice and the Olympic title twice.

The 'Celestos', as they were called because of their sky-blue shirts, had lost 2–1 at Wembley in a friendly match in 1964. Bobby Charlton had played that day and before the match he gave us an idea of what to expect from a team of talented individuals.

Previous spread: *At last. The tournament was underway. England walked out against Uruguay and I was happy to be involved, even from the stands.*

Below: *Bobby introduced the Queen to all the players before kick-off.*

THE TIMES TUESDAY JULY 12 1966

WORLD CUP
England frustrated by contracting defence
Negative pattern set for days ahead

FROM OUR FOOTBALL CORRESPONDENT
England 0, Uruguay 0

The World Cup of 1966 got off to a regal opening at Wembley stadium last night. But it was scarcely a royal night for England as Uruguay, the champions of 1930 and 1950 but no longer highly regarded in the world scale, held them to a draw.

As an entertainment it could scarcely have been worth the £85,000 taken from the pockets of a 75,000 crowd. Yet it seemed to set the pattern of what we may expect in the days ahead in this modern world game where the great thing it seems is not to lose.

The flags unfurled, the march-past over, the ceremonial speech by the Queen completed, it became more and more ominously clear within the first quarter of an hour that England were about to spend the clear summer's night bashing their heads against a powerfully knit, cleverly organized Uruguayan defensive wall—a Uruguayan side that one second could muster eight or nine men inside their penalty area and the next break out into counterattack like some expanding concertina.

True they were superb technicians and masters of the ball, these South Americans. They covered and shadow-boxed, as it were, riding and feinting against every thrust that England could produce. Every English player certainly fought and bestirred himself to the last breath—none more so than Ball, Bobby Charlton and the full backs, Wilson and Cohen, who time after time streamed down the wings trying to make the overlap that would at last create a breakthrough.

VIOLENT SHOT

Individually one could not truly fault any of them. But the breakthrough never came and all too soon, as a team, they showed their anxiety as they tried to pick their way through the contracting, congealing defence quickly gathered before them.

It was not that the Uruguayans themselves ever really looked like the victors. Only twice in the whole match can I remember them bringing a flutter inside the English penalty area. Once early on when a violent shot at long range from the edge of the area by Cortes was turned aside by Banks for a corner with a flying dive; and once early in the second half when a fine tackle by Jack Charlton put an end to a dangerous thrusting dribble by Perez.

Yet if Uruguay never looked like winning nor did England. Some, of course, may still say that they will win the war in the end; but certainly in terms of tactics they did not win this first battle in Group 1 of the tournament.

In the struggle somehow was reflected something of the larger agony that is afflicting football. We in Britain were the creators of the game, but somehow or other we must lead the pack and readjust in the future the balance between science and spectacle. All this last night might have been highly scientific. But it was certainly no spectacle. And somehow England must help to halt the drift to this defensive philosophy.

STUDY IN TACTICS

Football, indeed, seems to have found itself in impasse. At this rate it could strangle itself. Maybe it was absorbing as a study in tactics and technique. But basically for the man on the terrace last night when he got home to bed it must have seemed to him soporific and boring.

The answer perhaps lies in great artists like the Brazilians and one or two others like them, teams that can command a virtuoso or two; Pele, for instance, who can beat three, four or five men in a sudden expression of fantasy. But England for the moment, or certainly last night, did not possess such a man.

Now and then Greaves could snake past one or two; Bobby Charlton also; even Ball. But always they were outnumbered and overpowered and there it was. Yet how good it was at the beginning to have felt a part of the throb and challenge of it all.

But by half-time I felt in a state of abominable self-deception. It seemed the answer was to make the mind a careful blank, for by then the match had struck a destructive defence discord. England's anxiety became more and more apparent as they found themselves prisoners inside the penalty area and reduced to long-range shooting by Bobby Charlton, Hunt, Greaves and the rest.

BRILLIANT SAVE

If only there had been somebody, a real master, to galvanize them, but there was none. And in the end a negative match for long periods became tiresome; and ended heavily overloaded by defence.

True, there were moments in the second half when England all but snatched the single goal they needed for victory. With 25 minutes left Wilson crossed from the left, Greaves headed backwards and a left foot shot from 20 yards by Bobby Charlton was diverted by a flick from Connelly which the alert Uruguayan goalkeeper turned brilliantly round the post.

If that was near so, too, was another move with a quarter of an hour left when Greaves, for once, outpaced the defence to Ball's pass, only to see his cross picked off Connelly's head once more by the prehensile Mazurkievicz.

In the last five minutes England twice more were nearly there. Once Connelly headed a flick from Jack Charlton to the top of the Uruguayan crossbar and threw his arms up in despair. Yet the referee's whistle in that second told him that he was offside.

As the last moments unwound a fine move begun again by Jack Charlton enabled Ball once more to feed Greaves out on the right flank. Up came Charlton again, pressing for the decisive blow; his square header was back heeled inches past the post by Connelly and the last chance was gone.

MONTHS OF PLOTTING

England, after all these months, seasons even, of plotting, planning, and training, last night found themselves frustrated. Certainly they never had the ball mastery and a subtle technique of men like Rocha, Silva, or Viera. We know that already. Even more important they will have to discover some way of penetrating these massed defences.

ENGLAND.—Banks (Leicester City); Cohen (Fulham), Wilson (Everton); Stiles (Manchester United), J. Charlton (Leeds United), Moore (West Ham United) (captain); Ball (Blackpool), Greaves (Tottenham Hotspur), R. Charlton (Manchester United), Hunt (Liverpool), Connelly (Manchester United).

URUGUAY. — Mazurkievicz; Troche, Manicera, Goncalvez, Caetano, Cortes, Rocha, Perez, Ubinas, Viera, Silva.

REFEREE.—L. Zsolt (Hungary).

Greaves, Jack Charlton and Hunt move in as a corner from Connelly threatens danger to Uruguay in the opening World Cup match at Wembley last night.

Alf was particularly impressed with their clever attacking midfield player Pedro Rocha, who made and scored goals in equal number. They also had an outstanding goalkeeper in Ladislao Mazurkiewiecz. 'Let's not underestimate them,' Alf warned us in the dressing room.

It was an evening match and we were at Wembley two hours before the kick-off, which was just as well. The Hungarian referee Istvan Zsolt was unhappy to discover that seven of our players had left their identity cards at the team hotel. He had to inspect them before the start so a police motorcyclist was sent back to the Hendon Hall Hotel to collect them.

In the dressing room we could just hear the massed bands of the Grenadier Guards playing out on the pitch. This was followed by a marching display by several Guards regiments, a fanfare of trumpets, the national anthems and the flag-bearing parade by the 16 competing nations – the opening ceremony seemed to drag on and on. The players were just eager to get started.

Finally, Sir Stanley Rous invited the Queen to declare the final series of the eighth world championship officially open. The teams were presented to the Queen and Bobby Moore handed her a red, white and blue bouquet of flowers. Then, at 7.30, the referee blew his whistle, Bobby Charlton rolled the ball to Jimmy Greaves and the World Cup kicked off.

As a spectacle, the match was a non-event. Uruguay defended with prodigious energy. Their sweeper and captain Horacio Troche had an outstanding game. John Connelly's trickery failed to make an impression, and he really tried hard, on both wings. Even the great Jimmy Greaves lacked the craft to outwit an eight-man defence.

It was a typical opening game – dour and unimaginative. Tension gnawed at the players and few seemed willing to take risks. The crowd of 87,148 clapped and sang and chanted 'England, England' but you could sense their disenchantment towards the end of the game.

It finished 0–0 and as the England players trooped wearily back to the dressing room they were expecting a broadside from Alf. They were wrong. He immediately emphasised the positive aspects of the performance. He said it was a point won, rather than a point lost.

'You didn't concede a goal, either,' he said. 'Clean sheets are going to be important in this tournament.'

Below: *Jimmy in full flight. Not exactly a classic game but a point on the board and no goals against.*

WORLD CHAMPIONS

It was a great piece of man-management. Dejected as they left the pitch, the players were bubbling again as they left the dressing room. Alf had lifted spirits and confirmed his faith in our ability to win the tournament. I suspect, though, that neutral observers might have given Uruguay the edge on the day.

I have little doubt that Uruguay set out to frustrate and earn a draw. Their elderly manager Ondine Viera was asked if a draw was a satisfactory result.

'Oh yes,' he replied. 'Very satisfactory.'

What I didn't realise at the time was that you had to trawl back 28 years to find the last occasion when England had failed to score in a Wembley international. On that day in 1938 the opposition was Scotland, and they won 1–0.

Our next Group One match was five days later, against Mexico, and rather than allow us to fret over the newspaper criticism of the Uruguay stalemate, Alf took us all to Pinewood Studios the following day. We met Sean Connery, George Segal, Norman Wisdom, Britt Ekland and Yul Brynner, and watched the shooting of a scene from the forthcoming James Bond movie *You Only Live Twice*. It was another good move by Alf. He didn't want any sense of disappointment taking root in the camp.

Alf wasn't the sharpest when it came to naming contemporary pop singers and film stars, though. When Connery came into view on the set he whispered, 'Look lads, it's Seen Connery.'

Typical of his mischievous nature, Bobby Moore put his arm around Alf and said, 'Now I've shorn everything!'

Opposite: *At Pinewood Studios. Who are those blokes standing next to Jimmy and Bobby? 007 himself, 'Seen' Connery according to Alf, and Yul Brynner.*

GEOFF HURST

Opposite: *Training at Roehampton the day before we took on Mexico. Les, Alf, Shep and Ron Springett hard at it.*

It was a light-hearted day and just what we needed. The press were there, of course, and a lot of young starlets saw it as a good photo opportunity. We were invited to stay for lunch and Alf allowed us to have a small glass of wine. I suspect one or two had more than just the one. I seem to recall Ray Wilson falling from a chair with a resounding crash during filming and the scene having to be re-shot.

The following morning we were back on the training ground, concentrating on a lot of attacking set pieces. I worked hard in the hope that I might get into the team to play Mexico.

In the evening we travelled to Wembley to watch Mexico play France in the other Group One match. A draw was the best result we could hope for and it ended 1–1. France, of course, had knocked England out of the Nations Cup three years earlier but I saw nothing in either team that I thought would seriously trouble us.

Alf was delighted with the result because it meant that after the first round of matches all four nations in our group had a single point. So, despite the disappointing performance against Uruguay, we'd not lost any ground in our bid to be one of the two teams to qualify from our group for the quarter-finals.

Typically, he waited until the afternoon of the match against Mexico before revealing his line-up. He decided to retain Jimmy Greaves and Roger Hunt so there was still no place in the team for me, but he did make changes. I was delighted that Martin Peters was called up for his World Cup debut. Although no one realised it at the time, he would stay in the team for the rest of the tournament. Alan Ball was a little unlucky to be left out but Alf was still going through the process of finding the

> *Alf was delighted with the result because it meant that after the first round of matches all four nations in our group had a single point*

```
On that day I was walking over to Blackheath to
do some shopping and wondered if war had been
declared, as the whole area was deserted, as far
as the eye could see.
  The shops were quite empty, apart from the
assistant, and when I enquired where everyone
had gone I was told that the World Cup final was
being played that afternoon. The memory of the
withering look that I was given has lived with me
for 40 years.
```
Glenda Jackson

WORLD CHAMPIONS

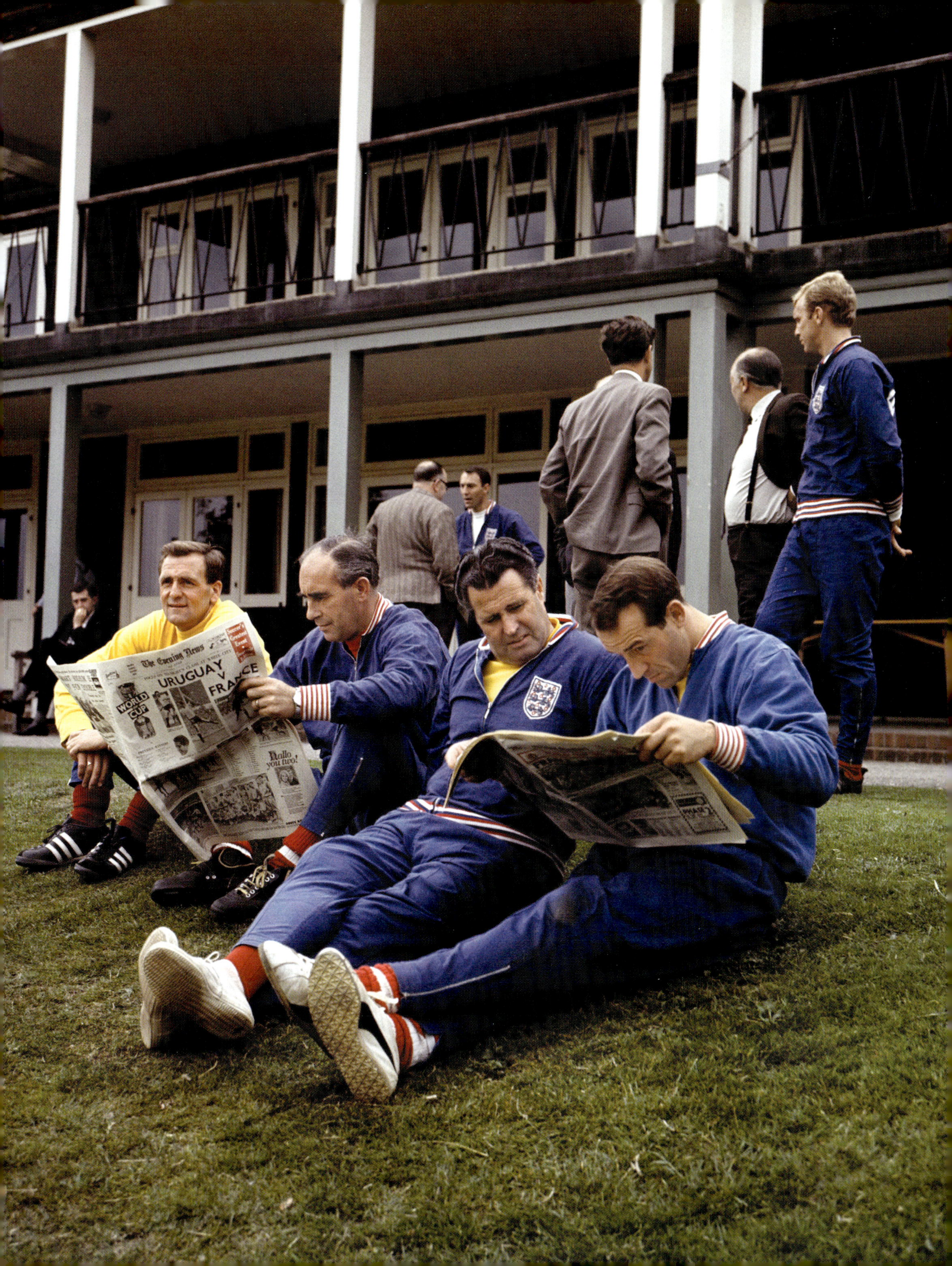
The Evening News
URUGUAY
V
FRANCE
WORLD CUP
Hallo you two!

> **It was not a classic England performance but three points from two matches looked OK from where I sat**

best balance, and Terry Paine was brought in to replace John Connelly. In the end, of course, he decided that the Peters–Ball combination was England's most effective option in the wide positions.

Having drawn with France, Mexico realised that another draw would give them an outside chance of qualifying. Subsequently, they too strung eight defenders across their penalty box, and they also had the benefit of a brave and agile goalkeeper in Ignacio Calderon.

Before the kick-off he knelt under the crossbar to pray and, initially at least, his prayers were answered. Roger Hunt had a perfectly good headed goal disallowed by the Italian referee Concetto Lo Bello after 35 minutes. The crowd of 92,570 whistled their disapproval and I think Lo Bello's decision angered the team and made them try even harder, but it was becoming clear that something special was required to break the Mexican stand-off.

Enter Bobby Charlton. Just before the interval he collected the ball in our half and began a powerful forward run. The Mexicans retreated before him until, about 30 yards from goal, he unleashed a thudding drive that flew beyond the dive of Calderon.

122 WORLD CHAMPIONS

That was the moment that set the 1966 World Cup alight and the sense of relief was overwhelming. At last we had given the crowd something to cheer. They were even happier when Bobby had a hand in England's second goal 15 minutes from the end. His through ball found Jimmy Greaves, whose cross shot was palmed out by Calderon. Roger Hunt, following up, scored from close range.

It was not a classic England performance but three points from two matches looked OK from where I sat. These were the days of two points for a win and one for a draw. The win lifted everyone and made us believe that we were going to have a real say in the outcome of the tournament.

Opposite: *England v Mexico. 1–0. Bobby opens England's account.*

Below: *Diana Rigg first joined Steed in* The Avengers *as Emma Peel in series four, which ran on ITV from October 1965 to March 1966.*

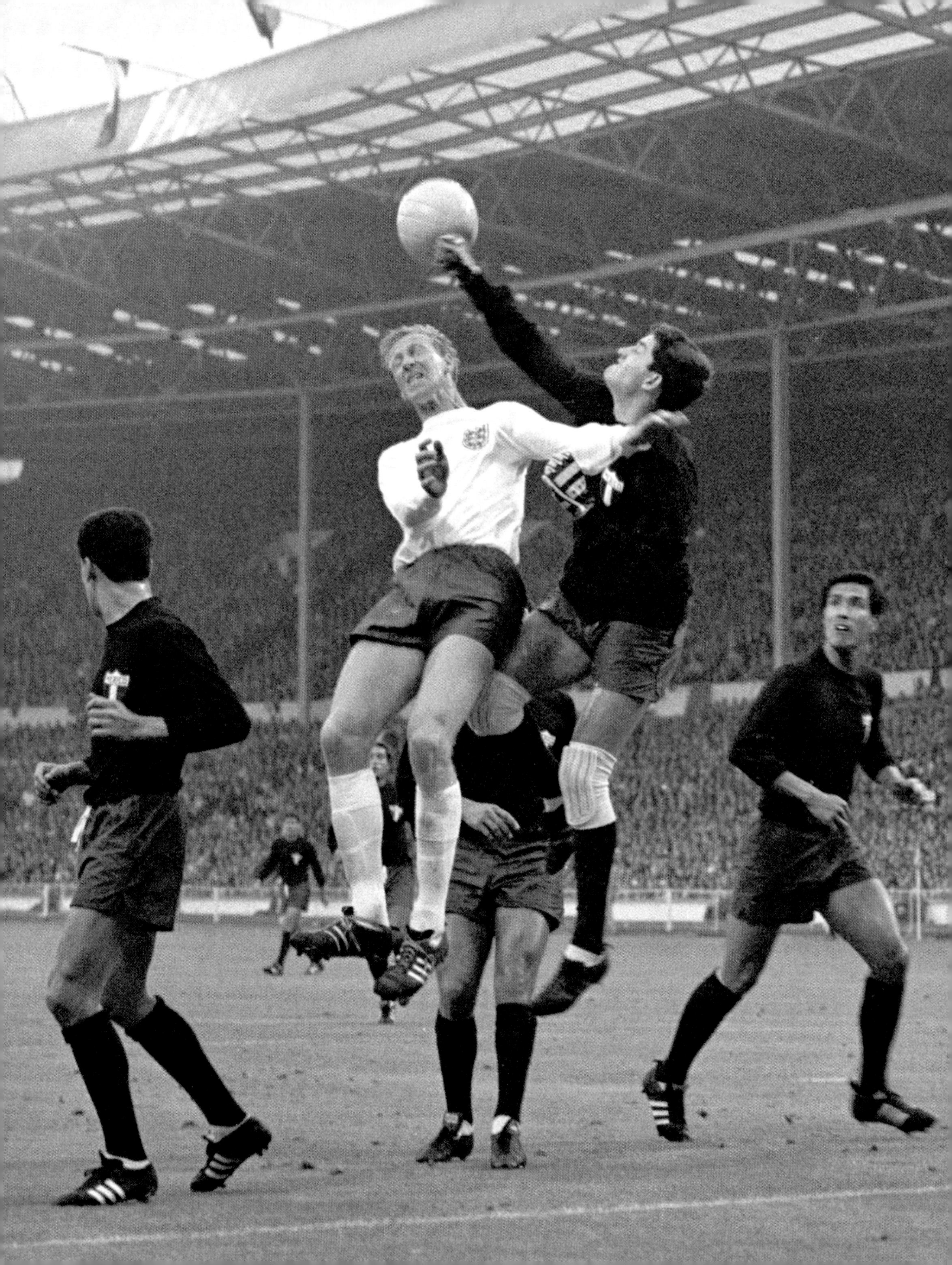

Opposite: *Calderon may have beaten Jack to the ball here, but his prayers before the game clearly weren't answered.*

Above: *2–0. And job done. Roger turns away to celebrate scoring England's second. Terry's already started the celebrations with arms raised.*

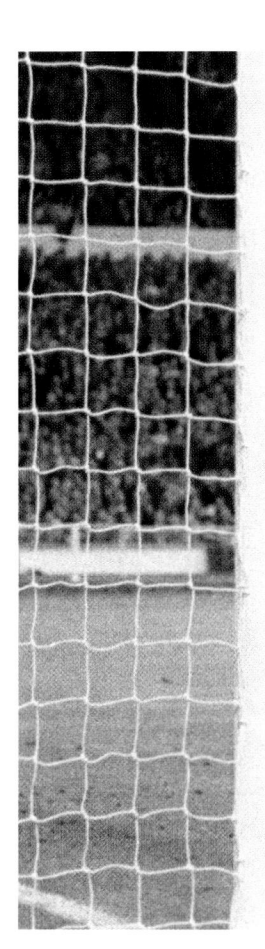

It was obvious that in Bobby Charlton we had a goalscorer for whom no defence could adequately legislate. He seemed to hit the ball with either foot with equal power and accuracy. No one knew for sure which was his stronger foot. I think he was best with his right but his brother Jack believed his left was his best. It didn't really matter. I bet Sven-Goran Eriksson wishes he had a player of his quality today.

The football played by Mexico and Uruguay had been disappointing but, quite naturally, the Fleet Street media pack devoted columns of newsprint to England's lack of attacking ideas. Hugh McIlvanney insisted in the *Observer*: 'Unless there is a dramatic injection of imagination in midfield and of vigorous initiative in attack, the dreams that have been cherished over three years of preparation are likely to dissolve miserably.'

England had four days to prepare for the final group game against France. The French had only one point, having lost to Uruguay and drawn with Mexico, and as the Uruguay–Mexico game had ended 0–0 the evening before, they knew they needed to beat England by two clear goals to qualify. That situation wouldn't occur now, of course. The last group games are all played at the same time.

The truth was that we were in pole position and could almost choose whom we met in the quarter-finals

In the build-up to 1966, BBC and ITV formed a consortium. They shared the coverage although both networks screened the final. The BBC was responsible for providing pictures to the rest of the world. Every game was covered – all in black and white, of course – which stretched both BBC and ITV to the limit.

TV was still in its infancy. There was, for instance, only one slow-motion machine in the country. The World Cup was the first sporting event to feature slo-mo in the coverage. Remember, too, in those days the BBC charter did not allow it to show advertising, so there were no perimeter adverts. The only advertising I remember at Wembley in 1966 was above the giant scoreboard. The *Radio Times* advert had been up there for years.

Although not all the games were broadcast live, the television companies were able to beam live coverage directly to our hotel. So we'd been able to watch the Uruguay–Mexico match in comfort. It was another dull game. Uruguay played like they knew a draw would be enough to qualify. The Mexicans couldn't break them down, so the following morning they were on the plane home.

At Alf's team-talk after training on the morning of the game, he insisted that we should not be swayed by the fact that only a convincing French victory could deny us a place in the last eight.

'We will not be complacent,' he said sternly.

The truth was that we were in pole position and could almost choose whom we met in the quarter-finals. If, for instance, we lost 1–0 to France we would qualify as runners-up in our group and face West Germany. If we beat or drew with France, we would finish as group leaders and meet Argentina.

In the dressing room before the match, Alf told us that qualifying was the priority. If that meant defending for 90 minutes we'd do it.

'Let them boo all they want,' he said. 'They'll be cheering if we qualify.'

Above: *Robert Shaw as King Henry VIII and Paul Scofield as Sir Thomas More, in* A Man For All Seasons *which won the 1966 Oscar for Best Picture. Scofield also won the Best Actor award.*

Opposite: *23 October 1966. Rescue workers continue to search for survivors after a coal slag heap slid into the South Wales mining village of Aberfan two days earlier, killing 144 people, of whom 116 were school children.*

Above: *England v France. 1–0. Roger taps the ball into the empty net.*

Opposite: *2–0. Roger with the head this time.*

He also said that he didn't want to see us pulling out of tackles. I think the 5–2 defeat against France in the Nations Cup at the very start of his England management still irritated him.

Alf introduced his third orthodox winger for this match, selecting Ian Callaghan at outside-right to replace Terry Paine in the only change to the team that beat Mexico.

A crowd of 98,270 squeezed into the stadium, confident that England would secure a place in the last eight. The French played with more adventure than either Uruguay or Mexico but their influential striker Robert Herbin twisted his knee after five minutes and had to limp through the rest of the match.

Roger Hunt scored both goals in England's 2–0 win. The first came in the 37th minute when he turned in a header from Jack Charlton that had cannoned off the bar. Roger looked suspiciously offside and the French were furious.

Jimmy Greaves and Bobby Charlton later had goals disallowed for offside but, with about 15 minutes remaining, Roger Hunt headed his second from Ian Callaghan's cross. For a moment, the French goalkeeper Marcel Arbour appeared to have saved it, but the ball was greasy because it had been raining. He fumbled and watched Roger's header roll behind him and into the net.

As Roger turned to celebrate his 15th goal in 16 internationals, I noticed that one of the French players, Jacques Simon, lay prostrate on the pitch, the victim of an ugly challenge by Nobby Stiles. Later Nobby admitted that it had been a bad tackle that he had simply mistimed.

Be that as it may, Simon was carried off the field while some among the Football Association hierarchy looked at each other and shook their heads. They didn't like the fact that Nobby had a reputation as a hard man and, in the days ahead, would put Alf in a very difficult situation by demanding that he drop Nobby from the team.

Jacques Simon lay prostrate on the pitch, the victim of an ugly challenge by Nobby Stiles

MOBIL WORLD CUP QUIZ

How much do you know about the history of the World Cup? Test your knowledge on the questions below.

1. When was the first World Cup competition held? *(Clue: The Mobil Oil Company was already 64 years old)* And where?

2. Who won the second and third World Cups? *(Clue: Mobil have a 30-million gallon per day refinery in that country)* And whom did they beat?

3. Where was the first post-war World Cup Final played? *(Clue: You could get there and back from London in a Mini on 4 gallons of Mobil Special—plus a 7,500-mile boat trip!)* And who won it?

4. In which year did Germany win the World Cup? *(Clue: It was the year before the first UK Mobil Economy Run)* And who was the runner up?

5. How many countries have entered for the World Cup this year: 16? more than 20? more than 30? more than 50? *(Clue: Mobil products are sold in more than twice as many countries)* And how many countries have won the World Cup more than once?

ANSWERS

1. 1930: Uruguay. 2. Italy: Czechoslovakia (1934), Hungary (1938), 3. Rio (Brazil): Uruguay. 4. 1954. Hungary. 5. Over 50: Uruguay (1930, 1950); Italy (1934, 1938), Brazil (1958, 1962).

THROUGHOUT THE WORLD—FOR MORE M.P.G. AND BETTER ENGINE PROTECTION

IT'S

Mobil

As I didn't play, I was not among those castigated by Alf when we returned to the Hendon Hall Hotel that night. He was not pleased. He didn't say anything to Nobby about his tackle but accused the lads of being complacent, excusing only the hard-working and goalscoring Roger Hunt. Ray Wilson was particularly hurt when Alf turned on him and said, 'There were one or two out there who thought they were good players – including you!'

There were other legacies of the French game. The match was significant for the last appearance of a winger in an England shirt in that tournament – and for the injury to Jimmy Greaves. When we got back to the hotel that night, I suspected that Jim would struggle to be fit for the quarter-finals.

In the opening three games, Alf had used three different line-ups. He'd tried three different wingers but none would feature when he named his side to face Argentina. It was in that match that, for the first time in the tournament, he played two midfield men in the wide positions – Alan Ball on the right and Martin Peters on the left. Wingers were about to be abandoned.

I think Alf felt that he had the best of both worlds with Martin and Alan. They were competitive, worked hard and defended diligently. In the case of Alan, Alf wanted him to block the forward runs of the Argentine left-back Silvio Marzolini.

He knew, too, that Martin could cross the ball as well as any winger. What's more he could cross the ball early, as he'd been taught at West Ham. This may have been in the back of his mind when he told me that I would be in the team against Argentina because Jimmy's leg wouldn't heal in time. It was desperately bad news for Jim but when I telephoned Judith to tell her that I would play in the quarter-finals, I couldn't conceal my delight.

I knew Argentina would be a real test. They were talented but provocative. To win, we would have to avoid getting embroiled in controversies, and play well. I'd watched the first three England games and knew that we had not played to our full potential in any of them. We'd finished on top of Group One without conceding a goal, but the level of performance had been unsatisfactory.

Traditionally, we played with a sense of adventure in English football, but Uruguay and Mexico were teams quite prepared to defend for 90 minutes. This attitude produces poor entertainment and we were getting blamed for it – unfair, I thought.

In fact, during the match against France, the comments of some of the spectators infuriated me so much that I had to tell one bloke exactly what I thought of him and his opinions. He'd really annoyed me with what he was saying about Jimmy and Roger, and I remember poor Judith tugging at my sleeve and telling me not to make a scene.

Opposite: *A quiz from the official World Cup programme. Those clues are a real help.*

He told me that I would be in the team against Argentina because Jimmy's leg wouldn't heal in time. It was desperately bad news for Jim but when I telephoned Judith to tell her that I would play in the quarter-finals, I couldn't conceal my delight

> *Nobby could niggle and irritate but his job was to win possession. He was tough and aggressive, but he wasn't vicious. I know because I played against him dozens of times*

We had just three days to prepare to meet Argentina. It was clear to us all that a storm was brewing because FIFA had released the fact that they had told the FA that if Nobby Stiles was 'reported to them again by a referee they would have to take serious action.' The day before the match, the Football Association sent emissaries to see Alf to suggest that he drop Nobby, at least for the next game because it was likely to be turbulent and fractious. They thought he would be a liability.

Alf refused even to consider such an action. He cited the fact that in three tough World Cup ties Nobby had collected just one caution. He said that Nobby was a pivotal figure in an England defence that had played, unchanged, for five consecutive matches without conceding a goal. Furthermore, he needed Stiles to man-mark the influential Ermindo Onega, and, finally, he said, 'If Stiles goes, I go.'

The FA backed down and Nobby remained in the team. It was another demonstration of Alf's devotion to his players. I think morale in the camp would have suffered had the FA forced Nobby out of the World Cup.

Alf had satisfied himself that Nobby's tackle on Simon had been a matter of poor timing. They'd had a brief chat.

'Did you mean it?' Alf asked.

'No Alf, I didn't,' Nobby replied.

Nobby could niggle and irritate but his job was to win possession. He was tough and aggressive, but he wasn't vicious. I know because I played against him dozens of times. Even so, I don't think he'd get away with some of those old-time tackles in the modern game. It was a more physical game in 1966.

What you also have to remember is that Nobby wore contact lenses because he was seriously short-sighted. He used to sit in the dressing room in his jock strap patiently trying to position his contact lenses.

I was ten years old at the time and leaving to go on our annual summer holiday with my parents and two sisters. Much to the frustration of my mother and sisters our departure was delayed by several hours to watch the match. My father and I thoroughly enjoyed the whole occasion - not so the females of the Botham family.

Ian Botham

They were not the small plastic ones you get today. He used to wear lenses the size of old pennies. They required lubricant to get them in and a suction pad on the end of a stick to pull them out again.

Even with them in, he couldn't see far. He used to tell Bobby Charlton, 'Stay within about fifteen yards of me because I can't see farther than that.'

On the morning of the match against Argentina Alf's two lieutenants, Les Cocker and Harold Shepherdson, pinned Nobby to the dressing-room wall at the end of training and said, 'Alf's stuck his neck out for you. Don't let him down.' He didn't.

Above: *Two days before the quarter-final clash with Argentina and Jimmy knows he won't be playing.*

GEOFF HURST

7

Argentina

When Bobby Moore led England out on to the pitch to face Argentina at Wembley, you could have cut the tension with a knife. The suspense had built remorselessly since Argentina's 2–0 win over Switzerland in Sheffield in Group Two four days earlier had made it likely that the two nations would meet in the quarter-finals.

I doubt if any England match, before or since, has generated the same level of hostility and suspicion during the build-up period. Alf Ramsey wasn't a manager who dwelt much on emotive issues before big matches but on this occasion his final words as we left the dressing room were, 'Gentlemen, you know what to expect today. Be ready for it.'

The strange thing is that England's football relationship with Argentina stretched back more than a century and had been very positive in its origins. Clubs such as Newell Old Boys and River Plate owed their existence to British tradesmen. In fact, the founder of the first league in Argentina in 1891 had been an English schoolteacher, Alexander Hutton. In the 1930s, when football in Argentina was threatened by illegal gambling, the FA in London agreed to supply a handful of referees to officiate until the scandalmongers were purged from the sport.

GEOFF HURST

WORLD CHAMPIONS

However, strong reasons existed for the mounting tension before this game. Although it was generally felt that Argentina lagged behind the Europeans in tactical terms, there was no doubt that their domestic football produced outstanding players. Not surprisingly, therefore, the Argentinians resented the loss of some of their top domestic players to European clubs, and indeed European nations. Three members of Italy's World Cup-winning team of 1934 – Luisito Monti, Raimondo Orsi and Enrico Guaita – had all been imported from Argentina. Monti had been centre-half in the Argentine team that lost 4–2 to Uruguay in the first final in 1930.

In all, more than 100 Argentine professionals left for Europe after the Second World War, including the great Alfredo di Stefano and Omar Sivori, who were capped by their new countries, Spain and Italy. Argentina complained bitterly that it would have been simpler to collect their team from around Europe for the 1958 tournament in Sweden.

Attitudes towards how the 'beautiful game' should be played also added to the heady mix of emotions that was brewing in the build-up. As was the case in most South American countries, the Argentines grew to believe they played a superior game. They argued that European football, and particularly that played in England, was overly physical and thrived merely because of sympathetic refereeing. Sir Stanley Rous's denial before the tournament began that he had instructed the World Cup referees to adopt a tolerant attitude to the tackling of the northern European teams seemed not to have prevented the South Americans thinking this was the case.

As for the English, they considered the South American game to be a hotbed of dirty tricks and sly underhand tactics. Only Brazil were beyond criticism. Argentina, on the other hand, were the worst exponents of the black arts and they reinforced this prejudice with a cynical, provocative performance against West Germany at Villa Park in Group Two. A bad-tempered match ended goalless, but not before Argentina's Jorge Albrecht had been sent off for an outrageous foul on Wolfgang Weber. His dismissal in the 65th minute was followed by that of the coach, Carlos Lorenzo, who had run on to the pitch to protest to the referee.

Argentina had some idea of what to expect from the crowd at Wembley because the Hillsborough fans jeered them whenever they touched the ball during their final Group Two match with Switzerland.

They recoiled with mock horror when they realised that their quarter-final opponents, England, intended to retain the 'questionable' services of Nobby Stiles, despite his indiscretion against the French and the consequent outrage at his behaviour.

Brazil, sadly, were already on their way home, complaining about the inadequacies of the referees, when we met Argentina. The fact that

Previous spread: *Pele looking accusingly at the Portuguese players who kicked him, and his team, out of the World Cup.*

Opposite: *A sad exit for the great man before half-time in the Brazil v Portugal game. Four years later it would be a very different story for Pele and the Brazilians.*

As was the case in most South American countries, the Argentines grew to believe they played a superior game. They argued that European football, and particularly that played in England, was overly physical and thrived merely because of sympathetic refereeing

> *Herr Kreitlein was in action straight from the kick-off... Argentina's plan was to stop us gathering any momentum. They embarked on a series of needless and quite provocative fouls that achieved the desired effect of breaking up our rhythm*

Pele had been kicked out of the match against Portugal before half-time – Joao Morais being the culprit – reinforced the belief that the South American teams were not getting a fair deal from the match officials. It all fuelled the growing tension as we prepared for the match on the afternoon of 23 July.

I remember standing in the tunnel, waiting to walk out on to the pitch, watching the Argentina captain winding up his team-mates. Antonio Rattin was a tall, imposing figure and you didn't need to speak Spanish to understand what he was saying about us. I didn't know it then but Señor Rattin was about to meet his match in the short, fussy, authoritative referee, Rudolf Kreitlein of West Germany.

Herr Kreitlein was in action straight from the kick-off. It was clear that Argentina's plan was to stop us gathering any momentum. They embarked on a series of needless and quite provocative fouls that achieved the desired effect of breaking up our rhythm.

The referee was constantly stopping the game and awarding fouls, but when Alan Ball was tripped on the edge of the penalty area he waved aside our appeals. This was all the crowd of 90,584 needed to start jeering the visitors.

Roberto Perfumo was the first booked, followed by Rattin, who stuck out a leg and tripped Bobby Charlton as he swept past him. Rattin complained bitterly to the referee and behaved as if the role of team captain gave him the right to run the match as well. This attitude inevitably brought him into conflict with the referee.

Undeterred by his booking, he treated Herr Kreitlein with obvious disdain, questioning any decision that went against his team. He just couldn't stop talking! The referee tried to impose some order and at one time, according to the distinguished football writer Brian Glanville, was: 'inscribing names in his notebook with the zeal of a schoolboy collecting engine numbers'.

```
I can tell you exactly where I was on July 30th
1966 - I was working as a packer at C&A in
Birmingham and I had a terrible crush on Bobby
Moore. I followed the World Cup avidly and knew
all the names of all the team members. Football
has never been the same for me since.
```

Julie Walters

WORLD CHAMPIONS

Above: *England v Argentina. Tension.*

    It wasn't an easy World Cup debut for me. I'd been detailed to harass Rattin, who was an outstanding player and at the heart of most of their best football, but he had an ugly side to his game. He lifted me into the air with one thuggish tackle out near the left touchline.

    There was never a moment's peace in that match. You felt that at any moment you might be fallen upon from behind. At least twice when the ball was nowhere near me I was kicked on the ankle.

A QUARTER-FINAL IS HELD UP FOR TEN MINUTES AS LATIN-AMERICAN TEMPERS FLARE OVER REFEREE'S DECISION

ANTONIO RATTIN (third from right), Argentine captain, arguing with the referee, Herr Rudolf Kreitlein, after being ordered off the field during the match against England at Wembley yesterday. With Rattin is Solari, and on the right is Bobby Moore, England captain.

ENGLAND WIN AFTER ARGENTINE WALK-OFF

By JACK CURNOW

ENGLAND, for the first time in five World Cup attempts, reached the last four of the competition when they beat Argentina 1-0 at Wembley yesterday after some of the worst happenings which have ever marred the game of Association Football.

The match was held up for ten minutes in the first half when Antonio Rattin, the Argentine captain, refused to leave the field after being sent off by the German referee, Herr Rudolf Kreitlein.

The whole Argentine team walked off the pitch and refused to play.

The game was marred, and several England players almost maimed, by a score of apparently vicious Argentine tackles, kicks and trips.

As he left the pitch after blowing the final whistle, Herr Kreitlein was jostled by a group of track-suited Argentines and one of them aimed a blow at his face.

A posse of policemen and uniformed Wembley officials sprinted forward, wrestled with the Argentines and Herr Kreitlein was hustled to his dressing-room. Half an hour later he left the stadium by a back entrance under police escort.

He refused to comment on the match. He has sent a report to F.I.F.A.'s disciplinary committee in an envelope marked "Private and Confidential."

'Wasted talent'

The England manager, Mr. Alf Ramsey, said afterwards he was delighted with the England's performance, and he added: "We have still to produce our best football.

"It will come against the right type of opposition, a team who come out to play football and not act as animals. It seems a pity that so much of Argentina's talent is wasted."

When Rattin was ordered off in the 35th minute, he refused to go. His offence seemed to be that of persistent arguing against the referee's decisions.

Right: Sunday Telegraph, *24 July 1966.*

The fateful moment for Rattin arrived about ten minutes before the interval. This time Luis Artime was cautioned for dissent and the towering Argentine captain, anxious once again to confirm his authority, impressed upon the referee the error of his ways. Once again, you needed no knowledge of Spanish to grasp the thread of his argument.

Rattin flourished his captain's armband in the referee's face. He gestured to the side of the pitch. He loomed over the tiny figure of Kreitlein. Suddenly, the referee pointed to the dressing room. He'd had enough of Rattin. He was off! The crowd, excited by the news that North Korea were beating Portugal 3–0 in Liverpool, suddenly realised what was happening.

'Off! Off! Off!' they chanted.

I was surprised that Herr Kreitlein sent off Rattin, not because he didn't deserve to go but because I just didn't think this small, balding referee had the courage to take such a decision. I've known many referees since then who would have lacked the nerve to take a decision like that in a match of such importance.

Rattin later protested that he'd only been asking for an interpreter. That was nonsense. I was right beside him and he changed immediately he realised he'd been sent off. Until that moment his attitude had been one of sneering contempt. I'd seen him spit on the pitch when Herr Kreitlein was close to him, but as soon as the referee pointed to the dressing room, Rattin was all amazement and hurt innocence. He started pleading softly and with humility. It was such a change of demeanour that I knew it was all an act.

Rattin had been sent off for 'violence of the tongue', the first player ever to be dismissed in a football match at Wembley. For eight minutes he and Argentina officials argued with Kreitlein and FIFA officials. Rattin refused to leave. At one point I thought Argentina were about to take their entire team off the pitch.

WORLD CHAMPIONS

It was an extraordinary scenario, beyond anyone's previous experience in English football. The referee, in my opinion, had little option, having seen his authority so brazenly violated, especially by a player wearing the captain's armband.

Ken Aston, the tall, mild-mannered former schoolmaster from Ilford who was head of the World Cup referees, finally restored some semblance of order. Rattin flounced off the field and the other ten Argentine players reluctantly strolled back and took up their positions. Herr Kreitlein blew his whistle and the match resumed.

Argentina were no easier to break down with ten men than they had been with 11. They erected a massed defensive wall and were clearly hoping to survive until the end of extra time when the semi-finalist would be decided by the toss of a coin.

In the dressing room at half-time, Alf stressed the need for patience and composure and made us very aware of the fact that they would try to even the score numerically by getting one of us sent off. Immediately after the restart I remember Roberto Ferreiro throwing himself over my trailing leg. He rolled about on the pitch as though he'd been hit by a runaway buffalo.

Then Jack Charlton collided with their goalkeeper, Antonio Roma. Both needed treatment. While Jack was lying on the ground he was kicked by one of the Argentine defenders. Bobby Charlton saw what had happened and raced to confront the man who had kicked his brother. He had to be restrained by Nobby Stiles and one or two others and when tempers had cooled, Herr Kreitlein booked both Charlton brothers for 'ungentlemanly conduct'.

I have to say that throughout the whole match, Nobby hardly put a foot wrong. The villain against the French, he did a thorough and very professional man-marking job on the Argentine midfield player Ermindo Onega and at the end left the field with an angelic smile on his face!

> **Rattin had been sent off for 'violence of the tongue', the first player ever to be dismissed at Wembley**

GEOFF HURST

141

Above and opposite: *1–0.*

I like to think that I played some role in his sense of satisfaction because, with less than a quarter of an hour remaining, I scored the only goal after Martin Peters had finally prised open the Argentine defence. It was enough to end Argentina's resistance and put England into the semi-finals of the World Cup. Martin, collecting a pass out on the left, turned towards the goal. He didn't know where I was on the pitch but he knew where I would be by the time he crossed the ball.

You could say that this was a goal that had been created on a training pitch in Essex long before the World Cup. Ron Greenwood

> *He crossed the ball early to the near post... I met the ball with a glancing header. It was a classic goal as far as I was concerned, straight out of the West Ham coaching manual*

had promoted the idea of an early cross to the near post, rather than the usual ball from the winger, which was traditionally delivered to the far post. Hours had been spent polishing this move and the goal at Wembley that day was due in no small part to the time Martin and I had practised it on the training ground.

He crossed the ball early to the near post, knowing there was a good chance that I would have got in front of my marker to meet it. That's exactly what happened and I met the ball with a glancing header. It was a classic goal as far as I was concerned, straight out of the West Ham coaching manual.

GEOFF HURST

143

Above: *Alf steps in ...*

Opposite: *Here They Come. The Monkees first appeared on BBC1 on 31 December 1966.*

Argentina's defenders were not expecting it. Each time I'd challenged for a ball at the back post I'd been bumped or knocked out of my stride before I'd even jumped.

The roar was deafening as the ball nestled in the Argentine net and I wondered how 'The Rat' felt. His absence meant that I'd been unchallenged when I attacked Martin's cross.

As I walked off the pitch at the end of that long afternoon, I felt that at last I'd done my bit for England in this World Cup. If I didn't do anything else, at least I'd scored the goal that secured our place in the semi-finals.

I was oblivious of the continuing drama as the players left the pitch. George Cohen was in the process of exchanging his shirt with Argentina's Alberto Gonzalez – a ritual observed all over the world – when Alf Ramsey suddenly halted the process. He would not let any of us swap shirts.

WORLD CHAMPIONS

GEOFF HURST

The butchers of Buenos Aires make football a farce

HURST HEADS ENGLAND INTO SEMI-FINAL

From DAVID MILLER: Wembley, Saturday

England 1, Argentina 0

ENGLAND ran out in the brilliant sunshine this afternoon in all-white — an unintentional symbol of purity which would not have been in character in some of their recent matches. Yet Argentina, in blue and white stripes, should instead have been in all black as the villains of what soon became an absurd spectacle, a farce of a match, not quite as bad as the Italy-Chile affair in 1962 in intensity, but worse in its duration.

That England finally emerged in the semi-final of the World Cup for the first time, to play Portugal here on Tuesday, following their third victory in this series and only their sixth ever in the finals, seemed almost an irrelevance after football had been degraded beyond endurance by an Argentine team with cultured feet and kindergarten minds.

Playing against 10 men for nearly an hour, England finally won with the only penetrating finish of the whole afternoon — a deep centre from the left by Peters with 13 minutes to go, headed home with perfect timing by his West Ham colleague Hurst, who was deputising for the injured Greaves.

This apart, there was little to cheer on an afternoon which is best forgotten (but which is likely to be considered by the FIFA disciplinary committee tomorrow afternoon). I am sorry that England's achievement was not gained with distinction, but then one has never thought them capable of it.

It was evident almost immediately that Argentina were technically the more accomplished players, and believing that the winners of this match would probably win the competition, I had an uneasy feeling that England had met their Waterloo. It was the Argentines themselves who determined otherwise.

Law of the jungle

The uneasiness soon became disgust as the butchers from Buenos Aires got to work, equally accomplished in every art of the chop, hack, trip and body check. Theirs is the law of the jungle.

There is a chronicle of their nonsense elsewhere. Sufficient here to say that with five players, Perfumo, Solari, Rattin, Artime and Mas, all booked, with their captain Rattin sent off for persistent arguing and obstruction of the course of the game following his own wicked foul on Bobby Charlton, with the trainers and manager Lorenzo holding up the game for ten minutes, and with several of their reserves attacking the referee at the end of the match, Argentina should be refused entry for the next World Cup.

If all they come for is to debase themselves and the game, they had better stay away. One shudders to think what might have happened with a referee of less perception and rigid, inflexible will than Rudolf Kreitlein, of West Germany.

His unquestionably was the performance of the afternoon, and had he abandoned the match when Rattin refused to leave the field, he would have been justified and Argentina must have forfeited it.

I am not vindictive, but for the first time ever I was delighted to see a player sent off. Rattin epitomised the rest of his side—a fine player totally without self control.

Still no attack

What is one left with on the credit side? Very little, for England, even against 10 men, struggled to find a way through. They have a defence, we know, but still no attack. Ball, Hurst and Hunt were lost for an answer for most of the game, and the system which allowed only three strikers is not one to win the crowds even if, as things are going, it still seems to win matches.

England have yet to give a really convincing display and Portugal will be a real test. Once already, earlier this year, Stiles has marked Eusebio out of a match, for Manchester United in the European Cup.

This afternoon Stiles was often chasing shadows as he battled to get to grips with the evasive Argentines, who moved backwards as often as forwards and looked content to play for a draw or even the chance of a lucky toss of a coin, until the middle of next week.

Against this sort of play England had no answer and there was one dreadful moment, seven minutes before England scored, when Mas had the chance to put Argentina in front. Jack Charlton was caught slow on the turn.

England's best patch was the first five minutes when Bobby Charlton hit a post from a corner kick with a low inswinger and Hurst went close from 25 yards. There was another highlight five minutes after half-time when Moore found Wilson in the left-wing position and his centre was hooked viciously by Hurst for the top right-hand corner of the net, only for Roma to make a superb save.

Alf Ramsey insists that England have yet to be given the chance to play their best football. To my mind they had it against France, and failed. The semi-final is rather late to start finding your form.

But at least it is something to be there, and Moore now playing magnificently, Jack Charlton and Wilson give one hope that Portugal will find goals harder to come by than they have so far.

As for Argentina, their appalling mentality is summed up by the player who said afterwards: "We were hoping to last out for a toss of the coin."

England.—Banks; Cohen, Stiles, Charlton (J.), Wilson; Moore, Charlton (R.), Hurst; Ball, Hunt, Peters.
Argentina.—Roma; Ferreiro, Perfumo, Albrecht, Marzolini; Rattin, Solari, Gonzalez; Artime, Onega, Mas.
Referee: R. Kreitlein (West Germany).

Quarter-final Results

England (Hurst)	(0) 1	Argentina	(0) 0 — at Wembley, 88,000
West Germany (Held, Beckenbauer, Seeler, Haller)	(1) 4	Uruguay	(0) 0 — at Hillsborough, 40,007
Portugal (Eusebio 4 (2 pen.), Augusto)	(2) 5	North Korea (Pak Seung Zin, Li Dong Woon, Yang Seung Kook)	(3) 3 — at Goodison Park, 40,248
Russia (Chislenko, Porkujan)	(1) 2	Hungary (Bene.)	(0) 1 — at Roker Park, 22,103

SEMI-FINALS

ENGLAND v PORTUGAL at Wembley, Tuesday, 7.30
WEST GERMANY v RUSSIA at Goodison Park, Liverpool, tomorrow, 7.30
Aggregate attendance so far 1,166,770; average 41,670.

World Cup football, 1966. Herr Rudolf Kreitlein, the referee, is escorted off the Wembley pitch at the end of the battle—and Mr. Ken Aston, the civilian behind him, who is the F.I.F.A. referees' liaison officer, is no doubt glad that he had not been in charge.

Jim Finney told 'You are right'

JIM FINNEY, the Hereford referee, was right to send off two Uruguayans at Sheffield. Who says so? Senor O. Barras, the Uruguayans coach.

"But it would have been fairer if one of the German players had gone off too," he added, but emphasised, "There is no hard feelings and we congratulate the Germans."

Other quotes from round the grounds included:

KIM EUNG SIR (North Korean F.A. Chairman): "I think the game was played very well. Both teams played fine football. I would like to express thanks to the people of Liverpool who gave us such good support."

OTTO GLORAI (Portugal's coach): "Eusebio received a leg injury in the final minutes but it is too early to say how bad it is."

Favourites . . . outsiders

One bookmaker yesterday promoted England to 5-2 joint favourites with Portugal to win the World Cup, with West Germany 11-4 and Russia 7-2. Another rates England 3-1 outsiders, with Portugal 2-1 and Russia and West Germany both 11-4.

Eusebio's four crush Korea

From TOM JACK: Goodison Park, Saturday

Portugal 5, North Korea 3

EUSEBIO must go down as the hero of this remarkable game—one that glistened with glorious talents, vibrated with tingling uncertainties, and raised the Goodison crowd to a peak of fervour never before aroused by aliens in Liverpool.

He hit home four goals with all the dark power that has made his the most glamorous name in the World Cup. It is his brooding menace that England must tame if they are to hold these all-conquering Portuguese in the semi-final.

But this is not to detract from the astonishing heroics of the Koreans, who seemed to have turned the soccer world upside down when they shot into a 3-0 lead early in the first half.

Rich reward

It seemed hardly credible that these little men, who had come out of the East as the subject of either humour or compassion, should have the Portuguese, fortune's and everyone's favourites now, in desperation.

They had seemed like callow schoolboys, all eagerness and innocence, against the solid grim professionals of the Portuguese. But their quick wits, fleet feet and sheer exuberance quickly brought them a rich reward.

Still, the Portuguese, whose all-round power made its presence felt in the end, must be classed among the greats in fighting back successfully from three down. Eusebio in particular, a ceaseless worker and schemer as well as a merciless striker, took his place among the unforgettables.

Little villainies

But it was the Koreans who were the crowd's darlings. The Liverpudlians, who had come overflowing with sympathy for these little underdogs of the competition, were full of sound and not a little fury from the start. They mixed their cheers for every darting move of the fit and lithe Koreans with boos for the little villainies of the Portuguese.

And they were in ecstacies within 30 seconds, savouring what seemed to be the biggest sensation of the Cup so far—a beauty of a goal by the Koreans.

A delicate pass from Han Bong Zin found Pak Seung Zin gliding forward on the edge of the area. He took the ball in his fast stride and it flew straight and true through a crowded defence to the corner of the net.

Then from the 22nd minute sensation piled upon sensation. Yang Seung Kook clipped another two home, both after delicate traceries of teamwork across the face of the goal.

It seemed hardly credible, but Eusebio quickly restored some of our faith in the natural order of things with the first of his golden goals—a swiftly fired rocket that sang its way home. And soon after he cracked home another from the spot.

One was always conscious in the second half of the strong dusky presence of Eusebio, backed by the glittering talents of Colunna, Simoes, Augusto, and the towering Torres. But as they settled to a quietly dangerous rhythm, the Koreans never stopped running and tackling.

However, their 'keeper had too often to be their saviour—and Eusebio was waiting in the wings to crush them. Another of his masterpieces of power and direction put the scores level; another of his penalties put Portugal in the lead, and from his corner an Augusto header settled the fate of the bold little Koreans.

All that was left to the Koreans now was a glorious, heartfelt farewell from their friends of Goodison.

Portugal: Pereira; Morais, Baptista, Vicente, Hilario; Graca, Coluna; Augusto, Eusebio, Torres, Simoes.
North Korea: Ri Chan Myung; Rim Yung Sun, Shin Yung Kyoo, Ha Jung Wong, O Yon Kyung; Pak Seung Zin, Jon Seung Hwi; Yang Seung Kook, Li Dong Woon, Pak Doo Ik, Han Bong Zin.
Referee: M. Ashkenazi (Israel).

RUSSIANS HANG ON GRIMLY

From MICHAEL WILLIAMS
SUNDERLAND, Saturday.

Russia 2, Hungary 1

HERE was a strange match; a World Cup quarter-final dominated by this drilled Russian team for the first hour only for a semi-final place to be all but knocked from their grasp by a brave Hungarian rally in those last desperate 30 minutes.

The game turned, or very nearly so, after 58 minutes when Bene, that astute little Hungarian winger who has scored four times in four games, cut in onto Meszoly's superb angled pass and thrashed the ball low past Yashin's right hand.

It was all Hungary needed. From a fumbling, terribly ordinary side who were two down and bore not the slightest resemblance to the team who so humbled Brazil at Goodison Park, suddenly everything began to click.

They surged forward, time and time again, as confidence took the place of uncertainty. Yashin was like some black panther on a hot tin roof as the ball bobbed hither and thither across his goal.

But though chance after chance came to Hungarian forwards and defenders alike, the ball simply would not go in the net again. Meszoly, flaxen-haired, all-purpose player, twice had his chance.

Meszoly delays

First Yashin got a somewhat fortunate right hand to a well placed low shot and next, as Farkas hooked the ball back from the bye line, Meszoly took so long over his shot that one felt he might try to unlace the ball first. Anyway it was blocked, and Meszoly wrung his hands in despair.

But this was a bad miss. It was nothing to the one perpetrated by Rakosi 10 minutes from time. Now it was Nagy who chipped the ball across, everyone missed it and there was the little winger ready to thunder it into the empty net on the bounce.

Alas, his foot never so much as connected. It was almost as if Nicklaus had played an air shot in the Open Championship. It was Hungary's last opportunity, Russia never gave them another.

In the end one could reflect that it was only justice. Russia have been coming along very nicely these past two weeks and though I would not readily back them to win the Cup, they are nevertheless going to be difficult to unseat.

Chislenko pounces

Hungary were a goal down after only five minutes. Malofeev forced a corner on the left, Banishevskiy tapped it quickly to Porkujan and when Gelei failed to hold a stinging low shot, Chislenko pounced to score a simple goal.

It failed to upset Hungary but with Khusainov and Sabo taking hold in mid-field, a second Russian goal always looked more likely than a Hungarian equaliser. One Malofeev headed against the bar and then, two minutes after half time, came the second goal.

Khusainov took a free-kick, the stretching Meszoly tragically touched his header just out of Gelei's reach and Porkujan swept the ball home. And that, so we thought, was that. And so it was. Just.

Russia: Yashin; Ponomarev, Shesternev, Voronin, Danilov; Sabo, Khusainov; Chislenko, Banishevskiy, Malofeev, Porkujan.
Hungary: Gelei; Kaposzta, Szepesi, Meszoly, Matrai; Sipos, Nagy; Bene, Albert, Farkas, Rakosi.
Referee: Juan Gardeazabal (Spain).

GERMANS THRASH URUGUAY'S NINE

GOLF COURSES

FRIEND

is no

FOR all the scores of people who take up golf each year, it is unlikely that more than a handful come to show any great interest in the game's history, but even those with only a sparing knowledge of days long ago will probably be aware of the remarkable number of famous players who have emerged from the Channel Islands.

Harry Vardon, son of a gardener, and Ted Ray, the only English professionals to have won the United States Open championship, were born not far from the links of Royal Jersey; Vardon actually in a cottage that stood on the edge of the course at Grouville. The Boomers, the Chevaliers, the Renoufs, and the Gaudins all learned their golf either there or at La Moye, the other 18-hole course on the island. Guernsey, for their part, can claim Herbert Jolly and Henry Cotton's mother, who almost certainly gave the great man his first sight of golf from his pram at the home of the Royal Guernsey club.

Regrettably my travels have not yet allowed the chance of a round at Guernsey, an omission I hope may be rectified in the autumn, but happily I am familiar with both

FOR T

How Toria g her speed

By JOHN CHAMIER

DOES Toria's conquest of those 1,940 miles Round Britain mean a new look at the place of multi-hulls in yachting? The answer is no—and yes.

Multi-hulling will anyhow remain an acquired taste. The race, however, showed that trimarans and catamarans can take what the occasion offered—and the occasion was fresh as often as not. True there was windward work, but the greater part of the circuit was covered with a free wind.

So it happened that the 300-mile Harwich-Plymouth hitch, which should have been the longest turn to weather of the lot, was planed by Toria in front of fresh northerlies and easterlies. Beating to windward is a multihull's weakest point of sailing. In tough weather it's her greatest test of structural soundness as well, and escaping these conditions Toria completed the 2,079 miles of the race in a sea time of 11 days 17½ hours.

This race having proved itself, will the sequel be run widdershins or counter-clockwise? That beat from Shetland to St. Kilda against a beefy sou'wester—oh, brother!

Bright ideas from armchairs apart, cats and tris have proved that design and construction have advanced no end. Toria's average of 10 knots over the 520 miles Lerwick-Harwich highlights this—that's real travelling.

Kissing the water

Toria is a great example of design thought. She is a big boat. At 42ft. overall, the only longer boats in the race were Hasler's Summer and the old 1930 8-metre Severn. But the combined beams of these two hardly equalled half of Toria's 22 feet. Toria's subsidiary hulls are empty and her main hull, in which her entire accommodation is contained has a beam of only 4ft.

But for the purposes of racing her designer-skipper, Derek Kelsall, has

FOR T

Trickles a

By JAMIESON BENNETT

UNLESS there is an early break in the weather, prospects of trout fishing on the Tweed and its numerous tributaries during the August holiday month will be pretty grim.

Some of the tributaries are mere trickles and the hill burns in the foothills of the Cheviots and the Lammermoors, so beloved by the worm fishers, are hardly worth a visit. But the prospects, though poor, are not entirely hopeless.

A long rod, a bag of worms (well scoured in moss before use) and a light nylon cast with a Stewart tackle, is the right combination to beat the conditions. You will have to set the alarm clock for a 6 a.m. start, however, if you want to catch the trout in the thin streams that are barely heavy enough to cover the back fins.

Fly is not out of it entirely. A

Jiggery-topery by

By DEREK FLETCHER

> I was sat in a cricket dressing room watching England beat Germany after being bowled out for a 'duck' on the Saturday morning. England winning made up for it. I never thought that four years later I would become a first-class county cricket umpire and after 18 months a Test umpire. If someone had asked me in 1966 if I would become a cricket umpire I would have said 'you are joking'.
>
> *Dickie Bird*
> Dickie Bird MBE

Herr Kreitlein, his shirt torn at the shoulder, needed to be escorted from the field by Ken Aston and a squadron of police officers. The Argentine manager Carlos Lorenzo stood in front of England's team doctor Alan Bass rubbing his forefinger and thumb together in a gesture that was, I guess, supposed to symbolise an exchange of money.

Even the England dressing room was no sanctuary. I couldn't stop smiling until one of the attendants shouted above the bedlam, 'The Argentines are hammering on the door. They want to fight!'

Suddenly, a chair came flying through the door.

'Send them in!' shouted Jack Charlton. 'Send them in! I'll fight them all!'

'Yes, send them in,' repeated Nobby Stiles, tucked away safely behind big Jack.

Thankfully, at this point the police arrived and cleared the corridor outside our dressing room, but it wasn't over. In a TV interview a jubilant Alf Ramsey said that we had still to produce our best football.

'It will come,' he said, 'against a team that wants to play football and not act as animals.'

Animals! That remark was to haunt Alf for years. His comments were broadcast around the world and the diplomatic turbulence caused still generates ripples of unease whenever England play Argentina.

It was sad that a sporting event should provoke such a furious row between the European and South American nations. At one point, the South Americans, shocked and offended by Alf's outburst, threatened to pull out of FIFA because of what they claimed was a European conspiracy. On the day we beat Argentina, Uruguay were beaten 4–0 by West Germany and had two players, Horacio Troche and Hector Silva, sent off by an English referee, Jim Finney.

Animals! That remark was to haunt Alf for years. His comments were broadcast around the world and the diplomatic turbulence caused still generates ripples of unease whenever England play Argentina

Opposite: Sunday Telegraph, *24 July 1966.*

WORLD CHAMPIONS

In the aftermath, the FIFA disciplinary committee asked the FA to censure Alf for his 'unfortunate remarks'. Denis Follows, the secretary of the FA, had a quiet word with Alf who then issued a short statement making it clear that no insult had been intended.

Argentina, though, were fined the maximum 1,000 Swiss francs. Rattin was suspended for four matches, Onega and Ferreiro for three matches each. The two Uruguayans were also banned for three games and their team-mate, Julio Cortes, who had kicked referee Finney after the final whistle, was handed a six-match suspension.

Argentina returned home complaining bitterly of discrimination against them and the other Latin countries. They cited the appointment of a German referee for their match at Wembley and said in a statement that he was 'absolutely biased in favour of England'.

They also reiterated that Rattin was merely requesting an interpreter when he was sent off, but I was told that Kreitlein could speak English and Spanish, as well as his native German.

Opposite: *The shocking scenes in the West Germany v Uruguay quarter-final, where English referee James Finney sent off Horacio Troche ...*

Above: *... and Hector Silva, resulting in both players receiving three-game bans.*

Below: *All smiles and high hopes. Prior to the tournament, Uruguay's Julio Cortes was besieged by autograph hunters. But it all ended on a sour note with his six-match ban for kicking referee Finney after his team crashed 4–0 to the Germans.*

Opposite: *31 March 1966 – General Election day. The three main party leaders were: Prime Minister Harold Wilson, Labour; Jo Grimond, Liberal; and Ted Heath, Conservative. Labour were returned to power with a landslide majority of 96.*

Argentina's sense of injustice lingered for decades. It was avidly recalled by them in 1986 when Diego Maradona's 'Hand of God' goal knocked England out of the World Cup in Mexico and again in 1998 when David Beckham was sent off as England lost a penalty shoot-out in France. The ill-feeling was still there in 2002 when a Beckham penalty gave England a 1–0 win in Sapporo, but I was delighted that England's 3–2 win in Geneva in a warm-up match for the 2006 World Cup passed without any serious incidents, on or off the pitch.

On that July evening in 1966, we were far too busy celebrating our victory to realise how the events of the afternoon would reverberate for years, polarising European and South American football. That night, the only thing that mattered was England's progress to a semi-final group that consisted entirely of European teams. The much-fancied Hungarian team had lost 2–1 to the USSR. Portugal and Eusebio had overhauled a 3–0 deficit to beat North Korea 5–3 and the Germans had beaten Uruguay 4–0.

The Illustrated London News

MARCH 26, 1966 2s 6d

THE ILLUSTRATED LONDON NEWS

THE GENERAL ELECTION

Wilson: "You know Labour Government works"

Heath: "Action not words"

Grimond: "For you for ALL the people"

8

Portugal

In the hours that followed the win over Argentina, the players came to the conclusion that the nation was getting behind us – at last!

The newspapers, so often carping and critical in the past, now viewed Alf's 'wingless wonders' and his 4-4-2 formation as a tactical breakthrough of profound significance.

The national team was just three days and 90 minutes away from the World Cup final and suddenly all the pundits and correspondents, all the prophets of gloom, were predicting that England could win the tournament.

Portugal had a team capable of brilliance. Many considered them favourites for the title following their 3–1 win over Brazil in the first round. They were the highest scoring team in the tournament. They'd hit nine in their three games in Group Three and five more in that extraordinary win over North Korea in the quarter-final, and, in Eusebio Ferreira, they had one of the world's truly great players. They'd needed Eusebio to salvage the game against the North Koreans but their entire cast list was impressive. Mario Coluna, Antonio Simoes, Jose Torres and Jose Augusto were ranked among the top players in Europe.

GEOFF HURST

Opposite: *The 1966 20th Royal Film Performance – Born Free – attracted some of the leading lights of the 1960s. Catherine Deneuve arrived in London, with her husband David Bailey, to attend ….*

Above: *… also there were Woody Allen and Ursula Andress.*

Previous spread: *The stitches in Jimmy's shin were healing. But not quite fast enough for him to be back in the line-up for the semi-final.*

Alf stressed that we would need to be at our best to beat them. There was no room, he said again, for complacency. His attitude was typically diligent. He even studied some newsreel film of Eusebio taking penalties and then sat and watched it over and over again with Gordon Banks. Eusebio almost always hit his shot to the goalkeeper's right, so they came to the conclusion that if Gordon dived that way, there was a good chance that he could make a save, if it became necessary.

The win over Argentina had reinforced the belief in the dressing room that World Cup glory was within our grasp. We'd always trained well, but now there was an extra edge to it. I remember Bobby Moore saying that he viewed playing Portugal like, he suspected, many top First Division sides viewed playing West Ham. In other words, Portugal were a fine technical team and would give us a good game, but there was little about them to worry us.

I trained hard for two days knowing that Jimmy Greaves would expect his place back in the team, assuming he was fit. The stitches in his shin injury were healing and I thought he would probably be recalled. He was the great goalscorer in English football and it was unthinkable that he would be left on the sidelines if fit.

I wasn't sure that I was doing my chances of selection much good when I asked Alf whether I could train in my tracksuit. He'd insisted throughout the preparation for the tournament and in all training matches that players wore numbered bibs – usually red or white.

He told us that he didn't want us to wear tracksuits but that was how I had always trained at West Ham. I weighed about 12st 10lb and was one of the heavier members of the squad. I liked to sweat in midweek. Whether it did me any good physically I don't know, but I believed it did and that was what mattered.

GEOFF HURST

> *Jimmy, we were told, still wasn't quite right so Alf kept faith with the 11 men who played against Argentina. It was the first time he'd fielded an unchanged team in nearly three years*

Anyway, the morning after the Argentine game I told him that I thought it would benefit me if I trained in my tracksuit. I knew it would disturb the symmetry of the numbered bibs but I thought that I could probably pull one on over the tracksuit top. He looked at me for an age and then said, 'All right, Geoffrey. If it matters to you that much, go ahead.'

From then on, I kept my tracksuit on – and felt better for it. Then I wished I had asked him earlier. Instead of speaking my mind I had conformed but, until recently, I had been a very junior member of the squad. I should have trusted Alf to know the difference between someone being awkward and someone genuinely worried about breaking an old habit.

My request did my selection chances no harm at all. Jimmy, we were told, still wasn't quite right so Alf kept faith with the 11 men who played against Argentina. It was the first time he'd fielded an unchanged team in nearly three years. From the quarter-final onwards he picked the same 11 players for six consecutive matches, which is still an England record.

So, Alf's 'wingless wonders' began to take root. Jimmy's injury, plus the fact that he'd gone five games without scoring, meant that I had a place alongside Roger Hunt. The failure of the three wingers to find any consistent form meant that Alan Ball and Martin Peters were given responsibility for the wide areas.

Bobby Charlton, of course, had the free creative role in midfield, supported by his faithful Manchester United team-mate Nobby Stiles, who provided security in front of the back four.

The back line was already an institution – Cohen, Moore, Charlton J. and Wilson, with Gordon Banks in goal just in case anything went wrong. That defence played together for 11 consecutive games between July 1966 and April 1967.

The night before we faced Portugal at Wembley, we watched the other semi-final between West Germany and the USSR on TV. This match attracted a crowd of 38,273 to Goodison Park.

Unfortunately, an FA publication released before the tournament began gave the impression that, should England win their group, they would play their quarter-final at Wembley and the semi-final at Goodison Park. My understanding is that no such decision was ever taken but the fact that it had even been thought about seemed to fuel suspicions.

It was the duty of the World Cup committee to choose the venues, but this merely promoted the conspiracy theory favoured by the South Americans. They claimed that Sir Stanley Rous had favoured his home country by ensuring they played all their matches at Wembley.

In fact, the decision to stage England's semi-final at Wembley was

> I can't recall where I was when Kennedy was assassinated, or exactly where when my kids were born, or even when Joe Bugner won his last fight, but the '66 World Cup. Who doesn't?
>
> I had been reporting with the 'London Evening News', which actually sold more copies than the majority of national papers today.
>
> In Blackpool for a big fight, so big I can't recall it, and the best hotel had reduced prices for children. So they came along with 'Her Indoors' dying to don Kiss-Me-Quick hats.
>
> Work done, I explained that breakfast must be early because the big match must not be missed. With traffic jams, all stops were barred, including pleas for pees, not to mention Cokes and chocolate bars.
>
> By the time Barnet was looming the dying strains of 'Abide With Me' were heard on the radio and I was testy and impatient, blaming the lengthy journey time on the lateness of Her Indoors packing bags etc. We reached our abode as the first whistle blew. Phew.
>
> The only embarrassment of that great day was auctioning for charity the 'original' shirt of Moore. I bought it myself because it was England white. I could not face an irate buyer who might have rumbled the phoney.
>
> *Reg Gutteridge*

based on finance. England against Portugal at Wembley guaranteed a sell-out crowd. West Germany against the USSR didn't. Nonetheless, I believe Sir Stanley Rous wanted England to play in Liverpool and was outvoted.

I don't think the England players would have worried in the least bit about playing at Goodison Park. As Bobby Moore pointed out after training one day, most of us had played far more club games at Everton's ground than we had at Wembley.

> **From the quarter-final onwards he picked the same 11 players for six consecutive matches, which is still an England record**

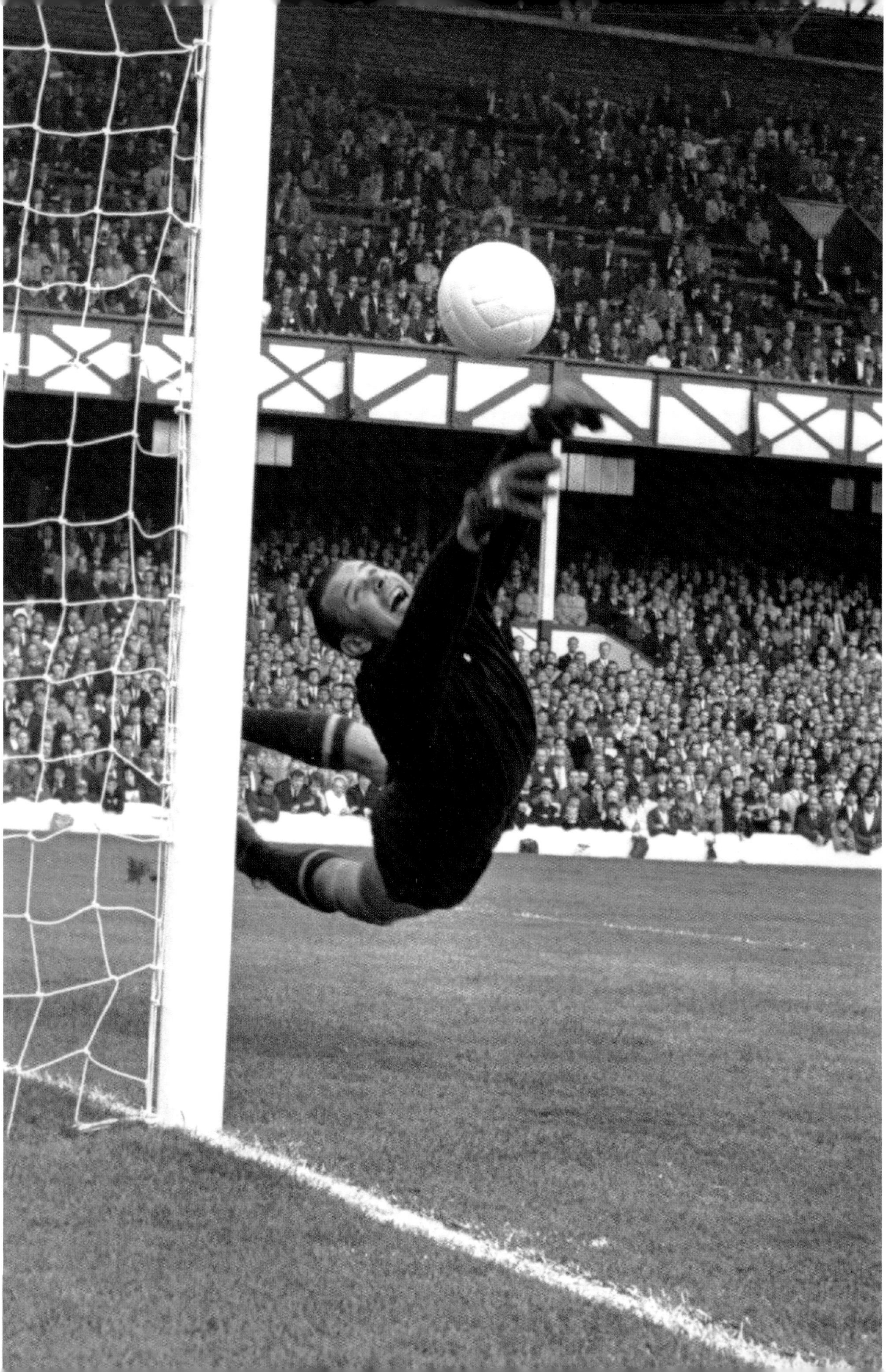

The Germans and the Soviets produced an ill-tempered match, illuminated briefly by the majestic goalkeeping of legendary Russian Lev Yashin. He was 40 at the time, approaching the end of a 78-cap international career. Yashin spent 25 years with Moscow Dynamo and remains the only goalkeeper in history to win the European Footballer of the Year award, which he did in 1963. In a measure of his reputation and popularity, Pele, Eusebio, Bobby Charlton and Franz Beckenbauer all turned out for his farewell match in Moscow in 1971. He was such a hero in the USSR that he was awarded the Order of Lenin, the highest honour available to him.

Ironically, after the game, team coach Igor Morozow blamed him for contributing to the USSR's defeat by the Germans. Remember that this match was played just 20 years after the end of the Second World War when both nations had lost millions of men in the fighting on the Eastern Front. Needless to say, there was no love lost between them. It was a wretched match littered with fouls. After just 15 minutes the Russians lost the services of Iosif Sabo, who launched himself recklessly at Franz Beckenbauer and was injured in the process. Sabo stayed on the pitch but spent the remaining 75 minutes hobbling about, making no useful contribution. With no replacements allowed, having a player injured so early in the game was seriously bad news.

Then, just before the interval, a strong tackle by Karl-Heinz Schnellinger hurt Igor Chislenko and gave the Germans possession. Schnellinger, with the ball at his feet, swept along the left flank and crossed to Helmut Haller who ran on and scored.

Although limping, Chislenko tried to play on, but it was no surprise when he lost the ball to Siegfried Held and, in his anger and pain, kicked out at the German. The Italian referee Concetto Lo Bello had no option but to send him off.

So, for the rest of the game the Russians played with just nine fit men on the field and the Germans, quite understandably, were happy to retain possession and let the clock run down, although Franz Beckenbauer did score a second goal.

From our point of view, watching the match wasn't the most rewarding or useful of exercises. As Alf pointed out to us, with the Soviets depleted for half the game, we had to remember to judge the strength of the Germans in that context.

We did notice that, with just a few minutes remaining, their goalkeeper Hans Tilkowski dropped a left-wing cross that he should have held. Valeriy Porkujan swiftly capitalised on the mistake, scoring from close range.

I remember making a mental note of Tilkowski's error. The Germans had won 2–1 and looked solid and resourceful but, if we qualified for the final, I thought that we'd have a good chance of winning.

Opposite: *Lev Yashin. In majestic form in the semi-final against West Germany, even though the Russians were defeated.*

Yashin spent 25 years with Moscow Dynamo and remains the only goalkeeper in history to win the European Footballer of the Year award

> *Nobby knew how to handle Eusebio but would have to be at his sharpest. Eusebio had scored a total of seven goals so far in the tournament, against Bulgaria, Brazil and North Korea*

First, though, we had to beat the Portuguese. Just as the FIFA hierarchy had predicted, a huge crowd of 94,493 squeezed into the old stadium for the greatest sporting event at Wembley since the 1948 Olympic Games.

Alf had prepared us thoroughly and it was clear from his team-talk that he believed Nobby Stiles could be one of the most influential figures in the match. Nobby had been given the task of marking danger man Eusebio, the European Footballer of the Year. It was a task he had fulfilled successfully already that season.

Five months earlier, United had faced Eusebio's club Benfica twice in the European Cup quarter-finals. Nobby had marked the great Portugal striker, denying him a goal on both occasions. United won the first leg 3–2 at Old Trafford and the second 5–1 in Lisbon, where a teenaged sensation called George Best scored twice.

Nobby knew how to handle Eusebio but would have to be at his sharpest. Eusebio had scored a total of seven goals so far in the tournament, against Bulgaria, Brazil and North Korea. A big, charismatic, muscular striker from Mozambique, he had succeeded the injured Pele as the tournament's most exotic star.

The 'Black Panther', as Eusebio was called, played for Benfica for 13 years, scoring 316 goals in 294 matches. He won the Portuguese title seven times and appeared in four European Cup finals, one of them against Manchester United at Wembley in 1968, when he was again marked by Nobby.

Unlike some of his team-mates, Eusebio was a real gentleman from the old school and I have always remembered the way he congratulated the United goalkeeper Alex Stepney when he saved the shot that would have won Benfica the European title.

When he retired, after scoring 41 goals in 64 international appearances, Benfica erected a statue to the great Eusebio Ferreira de Silva outside their Stadium of Light in Lisbon.

According to my dear wife – who is my memory – I was living in Dublin and working as the lead singer with a showband called the Chessmen. You see, the groups had taken over from the solo artists in 1964, so for two years, up until 1966, I was an actor on television in series like 'Maigret', 'No Hiding Place' and 'Desperate People'.

Ricky Valance

Above: *England v Portugal. 1–0. Bobby turns to celebrate with the rest of us after he side-footed us into the lead.*

However, all that interested us as we walked on to the Wembley pitch that Tuesday evening in July 1966 was how we could prevent Portugal from capitalising on this great asset in their ranks. Alf had entrusted the job to Nobby but we all knew it would take enormous diligence and discipline. As we lined up before the kick-off, Nobby was smiling from ear to ear. Almost to a man, the crowd were chanting his name.

Portugal were a talented, attacking team, but a darker side had emerged when Joao Morais perpetrated one of the most cynical acts of the tournament with an outrageous foul that sent Pele limping out of the World Cup. There was no doubt, either, that Portugal had some problems defensively. To concede three goals in 20 minutes to the international novices of North Korea must have been a cause for concern.

Alf had picked over their team, their strengths and weaknesses, and told us what to expect, and as we kicked off we were confident that we were good enough to beat them. It was a cool evening and it had been raining earlier in the day. That meant the pitch was fast and slick, and this suited us. Unusually, there were few questionable tackles. In fact, there were few tackles of any sort. It was a match that simply blossomed into a celebration of good open football played in a

GEOFF HURST

If you can't beat a bull

join him!

Get the best of a bull with Bovril

wholesome spirit – a real contrast to the war of attrition with Argentina. It provided spectacular entertainment and, for many, was the best match of the tournament.

It's a fact that 23 minutes passed before the French referee, Pierre Schwinte, whistled for a foul – Martin Peters obstructing Eusebio. Indeed, Portugal didn't commit a single foul throughout the first hour. What are the chances of such restraint in the modern game?

The match was decided by the excellence of two players – Nobby Stiles and Bobby Charlton. In a great exhibition of man marking, Nobby tracked Eusebio tenaciously, rarely allowing him time to fashion any real threat to the England goal.

Bobby? Well, this was perhaps the match that established his credentials as a world star. It was his best game of the tournament – some say the best he ever played for England. He scored both our goals and it was his brilliance on the night, rather than Eusebio's, that separated the teams.

The first goal came after 30 minutes. Portugal had no outside-right that night, so Ray Wilson had plenty of time and space to exploit on his left flank. He hit a forward pass that found Roger Hunt, who immediately scuttled towards goal with the ball at his feet. Jose Pereira, the Portugal goalkeeper, raced from his six-yard box and threw himself at Roger's shot to block it, but he couldn't hold the ball. Bobby, running in to support, met the loose ball at the edge of the penalty area, side-footing it past the grounded Pereira into the net.

That goal instantly lifted much of the tension that was coursing through the England team. Eusebio was wilting from Nobby's persistent challenges and on the one occasion he did break free to hit a rare shot, Gordon Banks' save turned the ball away from the foot of a post.

In the dressing room at half-time, Alf stressed that Portugal were bound to raise the tempo in the second period. No one, he said, likes to dip out at the semi-final stage. I remembered how disappointed I'd been just three months earlier when West Ham had lost to Borussia Dortmund in the semi-final of the European Cup Winners' Cup. I also remembered my jubilation the year before when we'd beaten Real Zaragoza in the semi-final of the same tournament.

Nothing is quite as shattering as defeat in the semi-final. Even losing in the final is better than failing to take part because you tripped at the last hurdle. These were the thoughts going through my mind as we started the second half, just 45 minutes away from the World Cup final.

As the second half unfolded, I also remember thinking how much I was enjoying myself. For all the importance of the occasion, it was still possible to enjoy a soft Wembley evening and take pleasure from what you were doing.

Opposite: *Bovril, the traditional warming half-time drink, advertised in the official World Cup programme … for a summer tournament.*

> *Bobby? Well, this was perhaps the match that established his credentials as a world star. It was his best game of the tournament – some say the best he ever played for England*

Above and opposite: *2–0.*
And one of Bobby's best ever.

The ball and the players were never still as the pattern and flow of the game twisted and turned on the skill of a Charlton pass or a Eusebio dribble. I think it was the first time that I felt I actually belonged in the team. I had a level of confidence in my own ability that I'd not enjoyed before when playing for England. It was as though a little voice was whispering to me, 'Relax, Geoff! You have every right to be out here with these great players.'

So I was still full of running when, with 12 minutes left, I stole the ball from Jose Carlos as we chased a pass from George Cohen. I swung past Carlos and looked up at the options. Once again I could see Bobby Charlton cruising forward in support.

I waited a full second before rolling the ball into his path. On that turf, with the ball running so straight and true, it was as easy as a shot in training for a marksman such as Bobby Charlton. Probably a match earlier, I wouldn't have had the nerve to wait for him to come forward.

Without breaking the pattern of his stride Bobby met my pass on the edge of the Portuguese penalty area. His thudding shot had hit the

WORLD CHAMPIONS

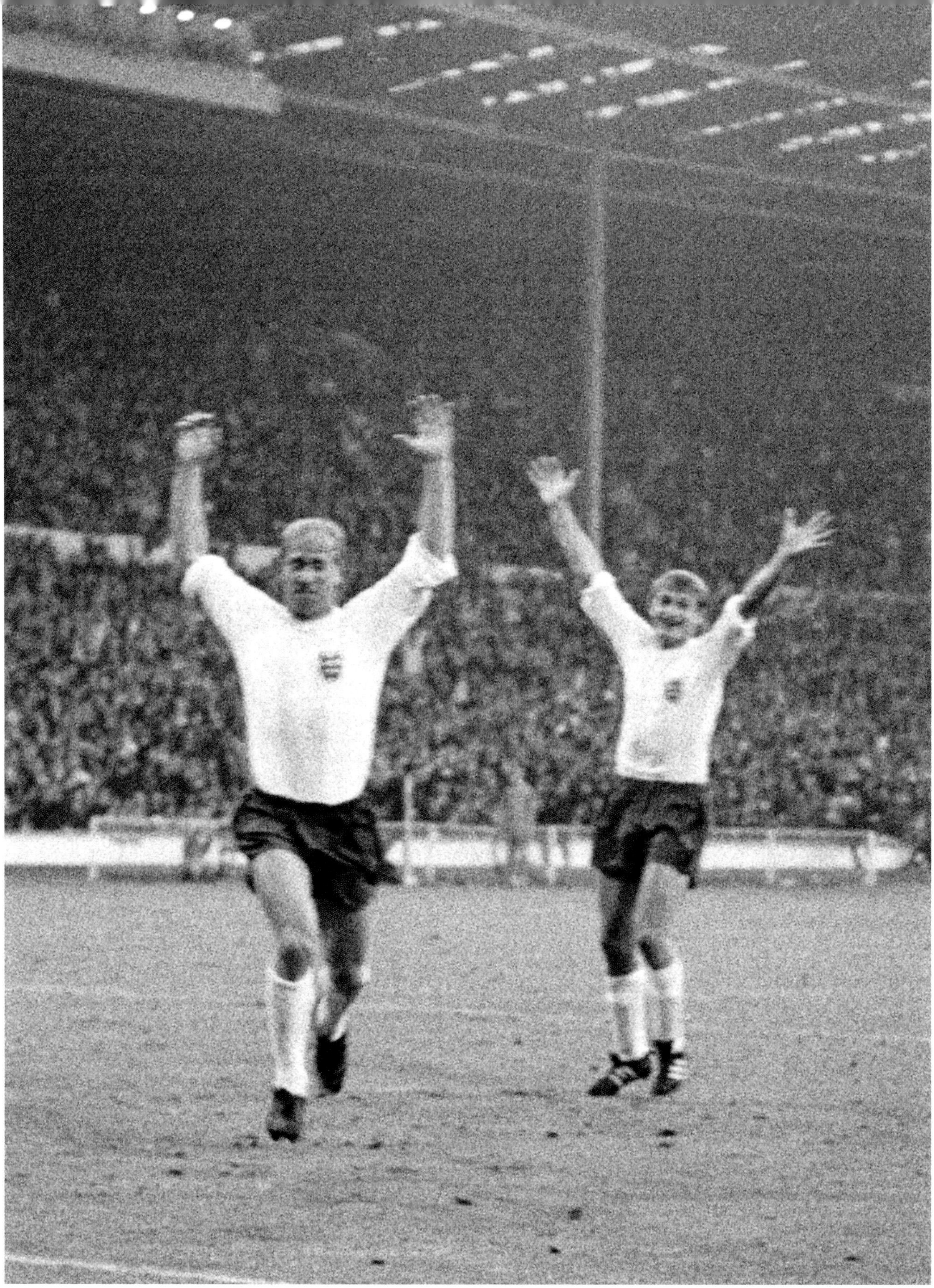

back of the net before most people fully realised what had happened. Bobby was not just a great goalscorer, but a scorer of great goals. That was one of his very best.

As the crowd erupted, their cheers echoing around the great bowl of the stadium, he raised his arm, turned and began to walk back to the centre circle. We all embraced him and even some of the Portuguese shook his hand.

It wasn't over, though. Three minutes later Antonio Simoes crossed from the right and the giant Jose Torres met the ball at the back post and headed over Gordon Banks. Jack Charlton, who'd had a real battle with Torres – both men are well over six feet tall – put out a fist and punched the ball away before it crossed the line.

Jack didn't argue. It was plain for all to see that the referee had no option but to award a penalty to Portugal. If Jack conceded a penalty in

Below: *2–1. It should have been all over. But Eusebio's penalty gave Portugal hope.*

Opposite: *It wasn't to be for the Portuguese. Eusebio had done all he could but England were through to the World Cup final.*

166　　　　　　　　　　　　　　　　　　　　　　　WORLD CHAMPIONS

the same circumstances today, he would be sent off and miss the next match – in this case the World Cup final. Forty years ago he wasn't even booked.

Instead, he covered his face with his hands and watched as Eusebio faced Gordon Banks. Would 'Banksie' remember to dive the right way? He had intended to but, at the last moment, changed his mind. He was moving to his left as Eusebio struck the ball, waist high, to his right. Usual spot! Eusebio gave 'Banksie' a consolation pat on the cheek as he picked the ball out of the net.

Still it wasn't over. Mario Coluna, a formidable figure in midfield, shot just wide with five minutes remaining and then Simoes, with only Gordon Banks to beat, had a fabulous chance to equalise. A goal looked certain until Nobby appeared from nowhere with a superb covering tackle to deflect the shot wide of a post. Nobby was outraged by England's slack defending – and let them know it!

Then, finally, the referee blew his whistle. It had been a wonderful match played in the right spirit. As I walked off I looked up at the giant scoreboard above the Wembley terraces showing the scoreline – England 2 Portugal 1.

I felt quite pleased with myself. Having struggled to get into the side initially, I'd scored the winning goal against Argentina and set up the winner for Bobby Charlton against Portugal. It was a relief to leave the field feeling satisfied with my contribution. Life couldn't get much better for a professional footballer.

I remember trying to console a tearful Eusebio. He had energised the final minutes as the Portuguese, driven on by the inspiring Coluna, had poured

GEOFF HURST

167

Opposite: *One more hurdle to overcome.*

forward in desperate search of an equaliser, but we'd clung on and thoroughly deserved our victory.

It was an emotional moment. One or two of our lads shed a tear in the dressing room, but Alf was uncharacteristically buoyant and frivolous as he dodged between players offering his congratulations. It was, he said, England's best game since he'd been manager.

'Gentlemen! Gentlemen!' he shouted. 'I don't often talk about individuals but I think that you would all agree that Nobby has today turned in a very great professional performance.'

We all cheered Nobby who was wrestling with his contact lenses. He'd subdued one of the world's great players without once laying a boot on him. He'd relied entirely on the speed of his interceptions and his positioning.

Above the din in the dressing room I heard a cry from Jack Charlton.

'Alf! Alf! We can have a drink tonight can't we?'

'No Jack,' Alf said, 'we can't!'

However, Alf had allowed the players' wives to visit the Hendon Hall Hotel that night. By the time we got back at about 11p.m. they were already there and he bought a round of drinks for us all – just the one drink each, he said. After about an hour the wives were ushered out of the hotel and we all drifted off to bed.

The manager was close to fulfilling his prophecy and he would allow nothing and no one to get in his way.

WEST GERMANY

22 Selected Players

1 Hans Tilkowski
2 Horst Höttges
3 Karl-Heinz Schnellinger
4 Franz Beckenbauer
5 Willi Schulz
6 Wolfgang Weber
7 Albert Brülls
8 Helmut Haller
9 Uwe Seeler
10 Siegfried Held
11 Lothar Emmerich

12 Wolfgang Overath
13 Heinz Hornig
14 Friedel Lutz
15 Bernd Patzke
16 Max Lorenz
17 Wolfgang Paul
18 Klaus-Dieter Sieloff
19 Werner Krämer
20 Jürgen Grabowski
21 Günter Bernard
22 Josef Maier

The names and numbers of the players taking part in each match will be announced over the public address system prior to the kick-off. This information should be inserted in the space provided on the relevant page for each game, covered between pages 44 and 55.

Les noms et les numéros des joueurs selectionnés seront annoncés par moyen du haut-parleur avant le coup d'envoi de chaque match. Ces renseignements sont à ajouter à la page qui convient, c'est-à-dire entre la page 44 et la page 55.

Die Namen und Nummern der Spieler welche an jedem Spiel teilnehmen, werden per Lautsprecher vor dem Anstoss bekannt gegeben. Diese Angaben können an der hierfür für jedes Spiel vorgesehenen Stelle—Sieten 44 bis 55—eingetragen werden.

Los nombres y números de los jugadores que toman parte en cada partido serán anunciados por los altavoces antes del comienzo del partido. Esta información debe ser incluída en la casilla correspondiente en la página relativa a cada partido, incluida entre las páginas 44 y 55.

9

Match number 32 – the final tie

Saturday, 30 July 1966 is the most famous day in the history of English football – the day England won the World Cup, a source of enduring pride for a nation and its people.

For Alf Ramsey it was the spectacular culmination of three years of hard work and dedicated planning. For Bobby Charlton, Ray Wilson and Bobby Moore it was a fitting reward for years of loyal service on the international stage. For Martin Peters and me, it was the unbelievable climax to a meteoric six-month rise to international recognition. For Jimmy Greaves it was an unforgettable day for an entirely different reason.

GEOFF HURST

Previous spread: *One more game to go. I was on a high but nerves were raw. Neither Martin nor myself knew whether or not we'd be playing. Distractions such as strolling down to Hendon and signing autographs were very welcome.*

Above: *The Day Before. Lunchtime. Jimmy, sitting next to me, was fit and neither of us knew at that stage which one of us would get the nod from Alf. My glance up to the camera speaks volumes about my anxious state.*

Opposite: *From the* Sports Argus, *30 July 1966. Even the cartoonists of the day, such as Norman Edwards, were hedging their bets.*

Martin and I, sharing our hotel room in the leafy north London suburb, spent the four days between the semi-final victory over Portugal and Match 32 – the World Cup final – in a state of suspense and anxiety. Those days were full of questions and whispered speculation. All 22 players in the squad wanted to know the same thing – who would be playing against West Germany in the final at Wembley?

Some, of course, didn't need to be told. Four of our five world-class players knew they would be in the team – Gordon Banks, Bobby Moore, Ray Wilson and Bobby Charlton. The fifth, Jimmy Greaves, thought he was fit enough to play. The nation wanted him to play. He was, after all, the greatest goalscorer of his generation, but no one was sure that Alf would recall him. If he did, the man most likely to make way for him was me. At least, that's what I thought. Roger Hunt may have been vulnerable, too, but he was far more experienced than I was.

The back four had been unchanged in the previous seven matches so there was no reason to suppose that Jack Charlton and George Cohen would not line up alongside Bobby and Ray in defence. They were all fit and free of injury problems.

Mentally and physically, I was at my peak. I think most of us were. The mood in the camp was upbeat. The dissenting voices, carping on about the lack of wingers, had disappeared before the game against Portugal and that performance was the first to receive universal acclaim. We had played as a coherent unit and emerged triumphant. Suddenly, after weeks of doubt, everyone believed England were unbeatable. Harold Wilson, the Prime Minister, made hurried plans to return from Washington to attend the final. Tickets for the game were changing hands at 20 times their face value and even the nation's housewives, who had complained about too much World Cup football on TV, were hooked.

None of us knew it at the time but Alf said later that he'd decided within minutes of the Portugal victory to keep an unchanged team against the Germans. The fact that he kept his innermost thoughts to himself was typical and ensured that there was a bit of an edge in training. Certainly in my case, I believed that I needed to look strong and focused because, deep down, I suspected that Alf would recall Jimmy Greaves once he knew he was fit.

> **Mentally and physically, I was at my peak. I think most of us were. The mood in the camp was upbeat**

GEOFF HURST

Above: Radio Times *announced that Doctor Who was back on 5 November 1966 in a six-part adventure entitled 'The Power of the Daleks' ...*

Opposite: *... and for the very first time the Doctor regenerated, from William Hartnell to Patrick Troughton.*

Nobody will ever know for sure whether Alf did indeed decide to commit himself to an unchanged team so soon after the Portugal victory. It would not have been typical of Alf to decide to leave out a player of Jimmy's stature before he knew whether he'd be fit – but it seems that one other was also facing the possible axe.

Bobby Moore was England's greatest captain, much admired by Alf, but it now seems that at one point the manager contemplated dropping him from the team for the World Cup final.

I wasn't aware of this until many years later when a group of the 1966 team met for a reunion some time after Bobby had died. We were talking about old times and how Alf preferred to keep his cards close to his chest in matters of team selection. George Cohen recalled overhearing, purely by chance, parts of a conversation between Alf and the only two men he confided in – Les Cocker and Harold Shepherdson.

They were discussing Bobby Moore and, specifically, his contribution in the matches against Argentina and Portugal. George quite clearly remembers Alf saying that he wasn't sure whether to play Bobby against the Germans.

'How d'you think Norman would do?' he asked Les Cocker. Les knew as much about Norman Hunter as anyone because he was Don Revie's coach at Leeds, where Norman played.

The rest of the lads were as astonished as I was by George's recollection of Alf's conversation. No one doubted the authenticity of George's claim but we all agreed that to have left 'Mooro' out would have been unthinkable. During the rest of the evening, the conversation kept returning to the same subject. This was hardly surprising as it was the first time we'd given such a scenario any thought.

WORLD CHAMPIONS

GEOFF HURST

Although West Germany had been surprise winners of the World Cup in 1954 – the Hungarians had been favourites – they had never beaten England

We felt that it was significant, for instance, that when we played the Germans at Wembley in February 1966 – my debut game – Norman had played, and played well, although not at centre-back. Previously considered untouchable in the heart of the England defence, Bobby went into the World Cup knowing that he had a rival who, pertinently, was Jack Charlton's defensive partner at Leeds. Norman was a good player and if Bobby hadn't been around would have won far more than 28 England caps.

Back in July 1966, though, in the days before the final, the newspaper back pages were dominated by feverish speculation about Jimmy Greaves and his state of fitness. The Germans also had a problem that, for a time, threatened to rob them of young Franz Beckenbauer. He was just 20 but it was already clear that he would become a major world star.

He'd scored four goals – two against Switzerland and one each against Uruguay and the USSR – but he'd picked up two cautions, the second in the fractious semi-final win over the USSR. As is the case today, this meant a minimum one-match suspension but, 40 years ago, FIFA allowed some room for manoeuvre. According to the rules at the time, each caution had to be 'confirmed' by the FIFA disciplinary committee. An 'unconfirmed' caution required no further action, i.e. no suspension.

Two days after Germany's semi-final win, the FIFA disciplinary committee met and decided not to confirm Concetto Lo Bello's second booking of Beckenbauer. He was therefore free to face England in the final.

This was great news for the Germans, and I remember Alf reassuring us, insisting that it would make no difference. They'd be more worried about Bobby Charlton, he said, than we would be about young Franz.

Although West Germany had been surprise winners of the World Cup in 1954 – the Hungarians had been favourites – they had never beaten England. In fact, they'd embraced full-time professionalism only two years earlier when they introduced a national league. Until 1964, the game at the highest level in West Germany had been played in four regional divisions.

As a pre-war, unified Germany, they had drawn 3–3 with England in Berlin in 1934, lost 3–0 at Tottenham the following year and lost again, spectacularly, 6–3 in Berlin in 1938 when the England players were photographed giving Hermann Goering the infamous Nazi salute.

East Germany lost 2–1 in Leipzig in 1963 and West Germany lost 3–1 at Wembley in 1954, 3–1 in Berlin in 1956, 1–0 in Nuremberg in 1965 and 1–0 at Wembley in 1966. The division of Germany was a consequence of the Second World War and, although it may be hard for some to imagine now, many people throughout Europe still nursed memories of the conflict.

Opposite: *The final instalment of Sergio Leone's 'The Man With No Name' trilogy was released in the UK in 1966.*

For Three Men
The Civil War
Wasn't Hell.
It Was
Practice!
CLINT EASTWOOD
"THE GOOD,
THE BAD AND
THE UGLY"
co-starring
LEE VAN CLEEF
ALDO GIUFFRE
and with
MARIO BREGA
also starring
ELI WALLACH
in the role of Tuco
Screenplay by AGE-SCARPELLI, LUCIANO VINCENZONI and SERGIO LEONE
Directed by SERGIO LEONE
Music by ENNIO MORRICONE
Produced by ALBERTO GRIMALDI FOR P.E.A. — Produzioni Europee Associate, Rome
TECHNISCOPE® TECHNICOLOR®
Re-released thru
United Artists
A Transamerica Company

Above: Batman – The Movie, *starring Adam West as Bruce Wayne/Batman and Burt Ward as Dick Grayson/Robin, pitted the Dynamic Duo against their four classic adversaries: the Penguin, the Riddler, the Joker and Catwoman. 1966 also saw the TV series hit ITV on 21 May, with the same actors in the lead roles. Holy Global Football Tournament, Batman!*

In my opinion, a residue of lingering bitterness towards the Germans helped create the atmosphere in which the final was played. My wife Judith's father had been a paratrooper in the war and at the end of the match that July afternoon he was in tears. Most of the players had relations who had fought between 1939 and 1945. Having won the war, to an entire generation of Englishmen it was inconceivable that the nation's footballers would lose a match against the Germans. Across much of the rest of the world, though, England were unpopular finalists.

The French were still resentful following their defeat, the Scots were envious, all of South America believed that the tournament had been loaded in favour of the host nation and everyone else thought that our football was boring and cautious. As far as we were concerned, this was great news. It reinforced our self-belief, generated defiance in the dressing room and bound us closer together as a unit.

Our final training session at Roehampton was on Friday morning. Jimmy had pronounced himself fit but Alf had told the press that he would be having a fitness test that morning. Jim went through the routine and was, to all intents and purposes, fit to play in the World Cup final 24 hours later.

Ever since the semi-final I'd been going over the various permutations in my mind and each time I came to the same conclusion – Jim *must* play. He was the finest marksman in English football. At that stage in his career he had 54 caps and 43 goals. No one had scored more goals for England. How could anyone leave him out of the final if he was fit?

What made matters more difficult for me was the fact that he and I were pals. I'd always held him in high esteem as a player and I got to know him as a person when he trained with West Ham just before his big move to AC Milan in 1961.

His icy professionalism in front of goal had always impressed me and sometimes seemed at odds with his irreverent attitude to football off the field. He enjoyed a laugh and a joke and I suspect that sometimes Alf found his relaxed attitude irritating.

It would have been much easier for me in the days before the final had Jim been a complete stranger. It couldn't have been a picnic for him, either. Since the age of ten he'd never really had to look at a teamsheet. He knew his name would always be there. As a youngster in east London, and with Chelsea, AC Milan and Spurs, it was as certain as night follows day that when the team was announced it would consist of Jim and ten others.

```
I did some gardening in the morning then went off
to watch the match. I must have been one of only
a few Scots who actually wanted England to win it.
I thought it was a fantastic game. Just brilliant.
   When the game was over, I went back home and
into the garden to finish off, when I see my next
door neighbour coming down the street carrying a
can of stout. He shouted, 'Alex, have you heard
the result? We've won the World Cup! And I'm off
to celebrate.' I called back to him, 'Great, but
don't invite me, with just one can of stout.'
Some party that would be.

       Alex Ferguson
Sir Alex Ferguson
```

> *Ever since the semi-final I'd been going over the various permutations in my mind and each time I came to the same conclusion – Jim must play. He was the finest marksman in English football*

Opposite: *Not every magazine in the summer of 1966 was caught up in World Cup fever.*

> *Now, perhaps for the first time, he was wondering whether he'd play. I'm sure that, like me, he never wanted to play in any one game as much as he did in the World Cup final*

Now, perhaps for the first time, he was wondering whether he'd play. I'm sure that, like me, he never wanted to play in any one game as much as he did in the World Cup final. To be honest, I wasn't going round at the time saying 'poor old Jimmy'. I was thinking to myself, 'At least I've got a chance.'

I asked Judith to bring my transistor radio from home so that I had some distraction during the days of waiting. Martin and I would stroll down the hill into Hendon to look at the shops and spent hours convincing each other that we'd both be picked. I think I did a better job convincing him than he did convincing me that I would get selected ahead of Jim.

I used to watch Alf during training for any hint of encouragement, any sign that might reassure me. There wasn't one. If Les Cocker grinned at me, I'd think, 'Perhaps he knows something but he can't tell me!'

Alf realised that many of his players, especially the younger ones – Martin and Alan Ball as well as me – were desperate to know whether we'd play. Finally, after training that Friday, he began a process that he'd been thinking about for a couple of days. He had already told the media that he would not announce his team publicly until noon on the day of the match, but he'd made up his mind to tell his players individually the day before.

On Saturday July 30th I was working the Domino Club in Manchester and doing working men's clubs early. The Beatles had come along at that time and people like me, Marty Wilde, Billy Fury etc were considered old hat. It took some time for us to come back into fashion.

I was playing in goal at the time for the Showbiz XI. In the team at that time were Sean Connery, Tommy Steele, Tony Newley, Mike and Bernie Winters, Ronnie Corbett, Bernard Bresslaw etc. On the Sunday afterwards we played out of our skins - the news had made us feel like giants. I remember we got drunk and ended up at the Stork Club in the West End.

Jess Conrad

BEAUTY
WHAT
NOW?
WHAT
NEXT?

GEOFF HURST

WORLD CHAMPIONS

As we drifted away from the training pitch, Alf quickened his pace until he was beside me. No one else was in earshot.

'I want you to know that you'll be playing tomorrow,' he said. 'I'm telling you now because I want you to relax and sleep properly tonight, but keep it to yourself. I won't be telling the others.'

It was hard to contain my elation but I was determined to observe Alf's wishes and keep my secret. I was also naive enough to think that I was the only one who knew. Later in the day, I discreetly telephoned Judith with my news. I was so immersed in my own sense of satisfaction, so bursting with excitement and anticipation that I failed to notice one or two other players walking around smiling ridiculously. I must have looked exactly the same to them.

Early that evening Alf took us all to the cinema. We gathered in the hotel lobby after dinner and followed Alf and Les Cocker down the hill to the cinema in Hendon high street. We strolled out in a long file, chattering away like children on a school outing.

We had no accompanying policeman. In fact, we had no security at all. I only ever remember a single uniformed constable at our hotel when we were staying there, and the police motorcycle escort that helped us negotiate the traffic on match days. Today when the England squad meets, the security cordon is very evident – a sign of the times, I guess.

On that July evening in 1966 we attracted a few curious glances from passers-by. Some of the passengers in cars waved and the drivers blew their horns but otherwise we were left alone.

I had still not told anyone, apart from Judith, that I'd been selected but I watched Alf moving quietly among the players. Was he telling them? I didn't realise it at the time but later Martin Peters told me that in the cinema foyer Alf took him to one side and said, 'You'll be playing tomorrow. Don't tell anyone else. I haven't told the others.'

We watched *Those Magnificent Men in Their Flying Machines*. It was a relaxing way to spend the evening before the World Cup final. Alf loved it and later said that it was the best film he'd ever seen.

Later, when Martin and I were back in our hotel room, I just couldn't keep my good news bottled up any longer.

'Don't whisper it to a soul, Martin, but the boss has told me I'm playing tomorrow,' I said.

'Great!' smiled Martin. 'So am I.'

By the following morning it was fairly clear who knew and who didn't. Ten of the 11 had been told the previous day they were playing. The one man who hadn't been told was Alan Ball.

It was late morning on Saturday, 30 July when Alf told Alan that he would face the Germans that afternoon. Why did he leave it so late before telling him? We have discussed it among ourselves over the years.

Opposite: *What do you do the night before playing in the World Cup final? Wandering out to see a film was perfect for us. Magnificent even. Eric Sykes, Terry-Thomas and Stuart Whitman prepare to take to the skies in their flying machines. Dastardly deeds undoubtedly ensue. Alf loved it.*

'I want you to know that you'll be playing tomorrow,' he said. 'I'm telling you now because I want you to relax and sleep properly tonight, but keep it to yourself. I won't be telling the others'

> *Like me, most of my team-mates believed that I was the player likely to be left out if Alf decided to play Jimmy Greaves*

Like me, most of my team-mates believed that I was the player likely to be left out if Alf decided to play Jimmy Greaves, but Alan has a different theory. He believes that he would have been left out had Alf decided to play Jim. Alan thinks that Alf would have reverted to a 4-3-3 formation to confuse the Germans. Had this been true, Alan would have been sacrificed, England's midfield strength would have dropped to three but the striking strength would have increased to three – Roger Hunt, Jimmy and me.

Personally, I'm not sure Alf would have considered that to be a realistic option. As it turned out, Alan, the baby of the team, played the game of his life. He blossomed as others wilted. At the end Alf said to him, 'Young man, you'll never play a better game.'

On Saturday morning I was told that Jimmy Greaves, who was sharing with Bobby Moore, was already packing his bags and getting ready to leave. That evening, as soon as the match was over, he slipped out of Wembley and went on holiday with his wife.

I felt for Jimmy but we were both professionals. I had a great opportunity ahead of me and had to focus on the challenge. I couldn't afford to think about anything else that day. Jimmy would have understood that. We didn't talk. It wasn't a matter of avoiding the issue. The chance simply never came along.

Afterwards, I felt the subject was best left alone. It was not something I wanted to raise with him. We're friends and we were business associates at one time in the late seventies. We still see each other socially but what happened in 1966 is something we have just never spoken about. I don't suppose we ever will.

For Martin and me, though, the great life-changing adventure was just beginning. We had breakfast in our room in a mood of mounting

---

On the day England won the World Cup I had been invited to appear on 'Juke Box Jury', which in those days was transmitted live. David Jacobs and the rest of the panel were put 'on hold' because of the World Cup running over on its TV time. Tom Jones had a new release on the show as well as Ringo Starr's 'Yellow Submarine', which I have to admit I voted would never be a hit!

Sir Jackie Stewart

anticipation. Martin rang his wife Kathy, who had just moved into their new house in Barkingside. She had moved house on her own while Martin was away preparing for the World Cup.

I shaved, read the papers, did all the usual things. I ordered another pot of tea from room service. I remember a brief sense of frustration as I looked out over the hotel grounds. It was a bright day but it had been raining. That at least settled one issue in my mind. When I played I always preferred to wear boots with moulded rubber studs. Jimmy

Above: *The Beatles' classic album* Revolver *entered the UK charts on 13 August 1966 and remained at No. 1 for seven weeks.*

Above: *Jack and Bobby's mum, Cissie, arriving at King's Cross on her way to see her boys before the game.*

Greaves used to say that he felt rubber studs gave him 'an extra half a yard' and I agreed. I felt I was a bit quicker in moulded rubbers, but I couldn't wear those boots on a wet pitch because I'd be sliding all over the place.

When I saw the rain that morning I knew I'd have to wear boots with nylon screw-in studs, which were longer and gave a better grip on wet or soft surfaces. Choosing which studs to use was one thing but the make of boots was already decided. We'd all agreed to wear adidas boots – except Gordon Banks who had been persuaded by Puma to wear their brand.

There were no big boot sponsorships in those days. The business of endorsing products was still in its infancy, but adidas had approached us because the TV coverage meant that their boots would be seen around the world. As I recall, they paid us about £300 each to wear their boots, which, by the standards of 1966, was not to be sneezed at.

WORLD CHAMPIONS

Later that morning I went for a walk and met Nobby Stiles as I left the hotel. He was on his way to church, a bit later than usual, to say a few prayers. He probably felt that we might need some divine help that afternoon. I remember thinking to myself that he was lucky to find a Catholic church in Golders Green.

Looking back, it's remarkable to think that he and I and other members of the squad could stroll about quite freely on the morning of the World Cup final. In similar circumstances today, the appearance of Wayne Rooney would bring Golders Green to a standstill.

Just as surprisingly, we were allowed visitors. Jack Charlton, whose wife Pat was back at home in Leeds expecting a baby, and Bobby were summoned to the lobby where their parents had suddenly turned up. Their dad was a coal miner and their mum was Jackie Milburn's sister. They probably knew as much about football as Jack and Bobby. I guess any last-minute advice would have been welcomed.

At midday we had lunch. I had my usual pre-match meal – beans on toast and a pot of tea. Then we filed in to a private room for the team-talk where Alf spoke to us for about 30 minutes. We'd already watched a recording of the Germans in action and Alf simply reminded us of a few key points.

He'd clearly given a lot of thought to the threat posed by Beckenbauer. We assumed that the young German would attack us from deep midfield positions. Alf reminded Nobby that, if such a scenario developed, Beckenbauer would be his responsibility. It didn't turn out that way, though. Helmut Schoen sacrificed Beckenbauer's attacking potential and asked him to police Bobby Charlton, a task that occupied him fully for 120 minutes.

Within a few minutes of the team-talk we were climbing on to the bus for the short trip to Wembley. A handful of fans cheered us on our way. You could sense the tension in the bus but the mood among the players was very positive. The Germans had never beaten England. Why should it be any different today?

Wembley Way was seething with a flag-waving mass of excited fans. They thumped on the flanks of the coach and the chant of 'England! England!' seemed to grow as we approached the grey bastion of the Empire Stadium.

As I stepped off the coach and walked down the high concrete tunnel to the dressing room, I had no idea what was awaiting me out on the pitch. At that moment, I was just concentrating on getting in. The England dressing room was as manic as the concourse outside the stadium. The place was heaving with TV crews, photographers, members of various Football Association committees, members of the Wembley staff. Even the man who made the half-time tea was wandering around with his autograph book.

GEOFF HURST

Looking back, it's remarkable to think that he and I and other members of the squad could stroll about quite freely on the morning of the World Cup final

The scene was very un-Ramsey like. I was sitting next to Bobby Moore, who liked a bit of peace and quiet as he prepared for a match.

'Have you counted the people in here?' he said. He wasn't happy.

Slowly the place began to empty of all the outsiders and finally Alf was alone with the players. He went to those he considered critical to his game plan to stress individual points. He shook hands and said 'Good luck' to every player. We could hear the noise from the crowd intensifying. The atmosphere was electric.

The crowd was marvellous that day. Players like to tell you that they don't hear the crowd but that is only true in the sense that you learn to ignore the abuse. You can sense whether the stadium is with you or not. At no stage during that long afternoon did they falter. It was not just that they wanted us to win. The feeling we had as players is that the crowd – 96,924 – was *certain* we would win. They had no room for doubts. With that kind of belief pouring down from the terraces, we could hardly fail to have confidence in our ability to lift the Cup.

The band of the Royal Marines was still entertaining the spectators when Alf told us it was time to go. I was amused as I watched 'Mooro' and Martin go through their usual pre-match ritual. Martin waited until Bobby had put his shorts on and then pulled on his own. He was trying hard not to look triumphant but Bobby had seen all this. He discreetly took his off and waited until we were walking up the tunnel to the pitch before putting them back on!

Martin also liked to be at the end of the line as the team walked out on to the pitch but so did Jack Charlton. There was no argument. Jack was the senior man, Martin the newcomer. Jack walked out last.

Bobby Moore, shorts finally in place, led us along the cavernous tunnel that leads to the running track around the pitch. We stood patiently in line at the top of the tunnel waiting for the Germans to emerge from their dressing room.

The Swiss referee Gottfried Dienst, a German speaker, was already at the top of the tunnel. The tall silver-haired linesman standing alongside him was, I later learned, Tofik Bakhramov, a veteran of the Second World War. Although actually born in Azerbaijan, he is most commonly remembered as 'the Russian linesman'. He was to have an important role in the drama about to unfold.

Below: *I didn't see him, but this is the ticket that got Hunter Davies in to see the game.*

Opposite: *Wembley Way on the day of the final.*

ALL SPORT SUN
Daily Mirror
THE WORLD CUP PAPER
Daily Mirror
PRIVATE

WORLD CHAMPIONS

Above: *At last. Uwe Seeler and Bobby watch Gottfried Dienst toss the coin before kick-off. The 'Russian linesman' is looking at his watch.*

After a couple of minutes we heard the 'clack, clack' of boots on concrete and the Germans joined us at the top of the tunnel – Haller, Schnellinger, Beckenbauer, Overath, all the top names. As we suspected, it was the team that had beaten the USSR in the semi-final.

As we walked out into the stadium the noise from the crowd took my breath away. It crossed my mind that the entire country would be watching and it sounded as though most of them were there in person. I noticed a big banner in the crowd that read: 'Nobby Stiles for Prime Minister!'

Odd thoughts ran through my mind. Judith's dad had predicted before the match that I'd score a hat-trick. Ridiculous, I thought. I'd scored twice in my previous seven England games. A single goal would be an achievement but, essentially, I wanted to get through the 90 minutes without embarrassing myself or betraying the faith that Alf had shown in me.

It was the team that had beaten the USSR in the semi-final

GEOFF HURST

> **All truly good teams rally when they go a goal behind. This was now going to be a real test of our powers of recovery**

Siegfried Held kicked off and initially the Germans looked comfortable and completely unmoved by the fervour of the Wembley crowd. I felt a need to make an impression and got my chance after just six minutes.

A right-wing cross from Nobby was headed out by Horst Hottges, but only as far as Bobby Charlton. He returned the ball high into the penalty area and I jumped to meet it with the German goalkeeper Hans Tilkowski. Neither of us was prepared to yield an inch and Tilkowski came off worse in the collision of the heavyweights. He lay still on the pitch and needed treatment before climbing back to his feet.

I felt we were just beginning to find our rhythm when, after 13 minutes, Held hit a long speculative ball from the left to the far side of the England penalty area. It looked harmless until Ray Wilson, completely unchallenged, headed the ball straight to the feet of Helmut Haller. It was an uncharacteristic error by Ray. Haller quickly controlled the ball and, spotting his opportunity, drove a low shot beyond Gordon Banks into the far left-hand corner of the net.

It was not a hard shot and Jack Charlton, arriving late on the scene, might have blocked it had he stuck out a leg. He felt sure, though, that Gordon would save it. What he didn't know was that Gordon was unsighted and couldn't see Haller striking the ball. So his reaction to the shot was inevitably late.

WORLD CHAMPIONS

Conceding a goal had a galvanising effect on us. It was the first conceded in open play and the first time that we had been a goal down. All truly good teams rally when they go a goal behind. This was now going to be a real test of our powers of recovery. In our favour was the fact that we had a lot of time to put it right.

We didn't have to wait long. Six minutes later, the creator of our equaliser was Bobby Moore. Tripped by Wolfgang Overath, Bobby quickly picked up the ball and placed it as the referee blew for the foul.

He was going to take the free kick immediately but waited just for a second because he'd seen me, 40 yards ahead, moving across the German penalty area. 'Mooro' struck the ball with perfect precision. He knew exactly where I was going because it was the sort of thing we'd worked on dozens of times on the West Ham training pitch.

I ran in from the right, met the ball with my head and steered it low past Tilkowski who, I guess, was a little uncertain about challenging me after our earlier clash.

It took me a second or two to realise that I'd scored a goal in the World Cup final but, as the crowd roared, I knew that if I achieved nothing else in life, I would have a place in the history books for that single moment.

Opposite: *One down.*

Above: *1–1.*

WORLD CHAMPIONS

Opposite and above: *2–1.*

Before the match, I suspected that I might get that kind of chance. I knew I'd cause the Germans problems in the air. They played with a sweeper, Willi Schulz, and three markers – Wolfgang Weber, Karl-Heinz Schnellinger and Horst Hottges. Weber was the only orthodox central defender and Hottges, a full-back, was given the job of marking me. When he picked me up from the kick-off, I immediately thought that I might get a chance to show that I was better than he was in the air.

I'd given this some thought before the game and reckoned that, with only one genuine central defender, they'd have trouble marking both Roger Hunt and me. So, from the start, it was my intention to take up positions that were unfamiliar to Hottges. As a full-back, he was used to marking wingers and I suspected that he would be at a serious disadvantage trying to shadow me in the centre of the field. The Germans didn't make many tactical errors, but this was one – and a costly one for them.

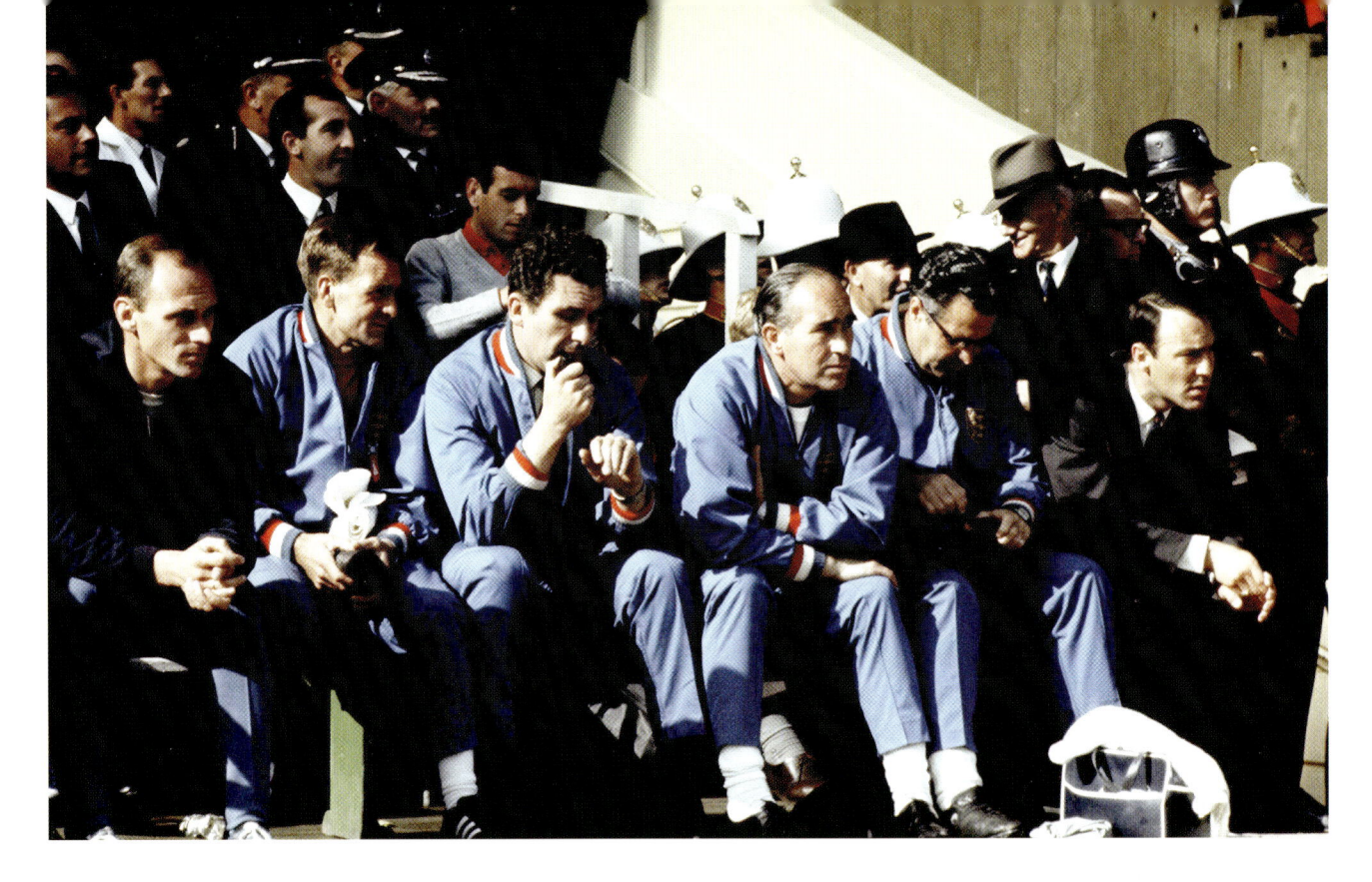

WORLD CHAMPIONS

Just before half-time, Ray Wilson made yet another surge down the left. I was able to outjump Hottges to meet his cross and steer the ball into the path of Roger Hunt. It was a good chance but Roger miscued the ball and Tilkowski, raising his arms like a man in prayer, blocked the shot. Would Jimmy Greaves have done better in the same situation?

Sadly, we hadn't played particularly well in the first half but in the dressing room at half-time there was no hint of criticism from Alf.

'Keep doing the simple things well,' he said. 'You're doing fine – but you can do better.'

Two things had become obvious during the opening 45 minutes. The first was that the German youngster Beckenbauer was so engrossed in the task of shadowing Bobby Charlton that he posed no real threat to our goal.

The second was that England's youngster Alan Ball, bristling with energy and endeavour, had the legs to outpace Schnellinger. As the game unfolded, Alan's contribution grew more and more significant. He was dragging Schnellinger all over the place and, just 13 minutes from time, his persistence broke the deadlock.

He won a corner and took it himself. The Germans failed to clear it and the ball fell loose at my feet on the edge of the penalty area. I hit a shot that ballooned off Weber and arced into the air. As the ball fell, both Martin Peters and Jack Charlton, in the penalty area for the corner, were within range. Jack hesitated – 'I was thinking "Blimey! This is coming to me!"' he now tells everyone. Martin didn't hesitate. The more natural finisher, he seized the opportunity, stepped forward and while Jack was still thinking about it, drove the ball into the net.

It was at this point in the match, with the minutes ticking away, that the German reputation for durability took root in the Wembley soil. The match was as good as over. We thought so. Most of those in the crowd thought so, too – but the 11 German players didn't think that at all. With just minutes to go, 'Mooro' was his usual picture of calm. Bobby Charlton implored us to focus, to remain diligent. Suddenly, he had the opportunity to put the match beyond the Germans.

Roger Hunt, collecting a pass from Martin Peters, turned and raced towards the goal, finally laying the ball into the path of Bobby. A goal then would have sealed it, but Bobby stumbled and miskicked the ball wide.

A disappointment, but even so the match was over – surely it was over. In the last minute, Jack Charlton jumped for a high ball with Held. I thought Held had backed into Jack but Herr Dienst, the referee, thought otherwise. He awarded the Germans a free kick on the left, just outside the penalty area.

Opposite: *Jimmy was there giving his support from the bench throughout the whole game, as Alf looked on impassively...*

... even when others found the drama almost unbearable.

As the game unfolded, Alan's contribution grew more and more significant. He was dragging Schnellinger all over the place and, just 13 minutes from time, his persistence broke the deadlock

Above: *2–2.*

Opposite: *'Go and win it again.'*

Lothar Emmerich hit a strong, left-footed shot that ricocheted around the penalty area, hitting both Held and Schnellinger before arriving at the far post from where it was driven home past the lunging Ray Wilson by Wolfgang Weber.

Wembley was silent, apart from the clutch of disbelieving German fans. I was exhausted – we all were – as we trudged back for the restart. Bobby Charlton kicked off and the referee immediately blew the whistle to signal the end of 90 minutes.

We'd been *that* close! Suddenly, we were faced with extra time and, in the circumstances that afternoon, I have to say that the prospect of a further 30 minutes appeared daunting.

Forty years later, barely a person in England does not have at least some idea of what happened next. First, Alf gathered the players around him. He knew we were tired but he told us not to lie on the pitch. That's what the Germans were doing.

'Look at them,' he said. 'They're finished. They're flat out on their backs.'

> When Weber equalised for Germany I leapt up in amazement and broke a light shade. The goal was so unexpected, coming as late as it did.
>
> John Motson

WORLD CHAMPIONS

They were, too. He told us that we'd been the better team over 90 minutes.

'You've won it once,' he said. 'Now go and win it again.'

He was brief and to the point. He never wasted words but those he used were inspirational. He lifted our spirits once more. What mattered now was our state of fitness. Would all those grinding training sessions under Les Cocker pay off?

All over the country, those who could bear it were crouched around TV sets or radios. I learned later that many people simply couldn't stand the tension and had to go out into the street or garden. In the stadium the crowd roared once again as extra time began.

In those 30 minutes, little Alan Ball was a whirlwind of perpetual motion. He didn't stop. Even today I don't know where he found the energy. Overall, I thought we were the fitter team. We kept our shape and our discipline. Bobby Moore made sure of that. There was an unobtrusive authority about his performance that day. He had an air of superiority and, even in those final draining minutes, played with the kind of self-assurance that suggested he was out for an afternoon stroll.

The Germans, on the other hand, were clearly struggling. Within minutes of the restart 'Bally' robbed the flagging Uwe Seeler, swept forward and hit a shot that Tilkowski turned over the bar. Moments after that, Bobby Charlton released a 20-yard shot that hit Tilkowski's left-hand post.

We'd played ten minutes of extra time when Nobby Stiles drove a pass from the centre circle out to the right for Alan Ball to chase. With

> 'Look at them,' he said. 'They're finished. They're flat out on their backs'

GEOFF HURST

199

WORLD CHAMPIONS

his socks down round his ankles, 'Bally' set off in pursuit, outpaced Schnellinger and hit a low early cross to the edge of the penalty area.

I ran to meet the ball. If anything, I made my run a little too early. This meant that instead of moving on to the ball, it was falling slightly behind me as I reached the edge of the area. I needed to adjust my stance and take a couple of touches to get the ball into a shooting position.

Then, to get the power required to strike it properly, I had to fall back. I connected beautifully but, in doing so, toppled over, so I probably had the worst view in the ground as the ball struck the underside of the bar and bounced down on to the line.

My next clear memory is of Roger Hunt, to my left, halting his run forward and wheeling away, raising an arm in the air. Had there been any doubt about the validity of the goal in Roger's mind, he would have continued his run and supplied the finishing touch.

My own feeling is that it would have been the easiest thing for Roger to do. The natural instinct for any striker in those circumstances is to put the ball in the net if he feels it's necessary. Roger didn't think his intervention was required.

Opposite top: *On its way...*
Opposite bottom: *... and in ...*
Above: *... or is it?*

Above: *Yes. 3–2.*

At that moment I had no doubt that it was a goal but within seconds the Germans were appealing to the referee. Dienst had blown his whistle because the ball was out of play. When it bounced out from under the crossbar Weber headed it away and some argue that, in a race for the ball, Weber might have beaten Roger.

I looked across to the linesman. Tofik Bakhramov had raised his flag and now 22 pairs of eyes, and those of the referee, were closing in on him. Besieged by protesting German players, the Swiss referee and the tall, silver-haired linesman conferred. Dienst asked him whether the ball had crossed the line. Bakhramov said that it had. The referee pointed to the centre spot. The goal stood. We were in front again. I couldn't believe it. I'd now scored twice in the World Cup final.

I didn't know it at the time of course but that goal was to become one of the most controversial incidents in the history of football. Did the ball cross the line? I don't know the answer and I never will.

I can no more claim with certainty that the ball crossed the line than the Germans can claim that it didn't. Having listened to all the arguments and watched the replay hundreds of times on TV, I have to admit that it looks as though the whole of the ball did not cross the line. At the time, though, I desperately wanted to believe that it was a goal.

I can understand the anger and frustration of the German players that day. Their fury has diminished but they've never forgiven us. In 1975 when West Germany played England at Wembley in a friendly match, Franz Beckenbauer was still in their team.

They trained at Wembley the night before the match and when they walked on to the pitch they noticed that the goalposts hadn't been erected and the pitch had not been marked out. Beckenbauer turned to his team-mate Berti Vogts and said, 'See, Berti, they've removed the evidence!'

Thankfully, my third goal meant that the World Cup final of 1966 was not decided by the opinion of a Swiss referee and a Russian linesman. With hindsight, it would have been sensible not to have a Soviet official involved. The other linesman was Karol Galba from Czechoslovakia.

As I pointed out earlier, many people throughout Europe still nursed memories of the Second World War and FIFA would have been better advised to select all the match officials from countries that had played no part in it.

For decades afterwards, the Germans claimed that the Russian linesman's war experiences had influenced his judgement. I don't know whether that was the case, but I do know that I was delighted to meet his son in 2004 when I was asked to unveil a statue in Tofik's honour in his home town of Baku in Azerbaijan. Tofik, who became a national hero through his service to football, had died in 1993, a month after Bobby Moore.

Happily, there was no doubt about the validity of England's fourth goal. The Germans had been knocking a stream of high balls into our penalty area in a desperate search for the equaliser. Seeler had the best chance to level the score again but he failed to connect with Held's headed pass.

Then, as the crowd whistled for the end, the Germans launched yet another attack. This time Bobby Moore intercepted a cross from Schulz, catching the ball on his chest. He looked upfield to see who was free to accept a pass. Bobby was in our penalty area, a dangerous place to be with the ball at his feet.

Only seconds remained. Jack Charlton was having kittens. The Germans were beginning to close down on Bobby.

UK No. 1 album throughout the World Cup tournament: *Sound of Music* soundtrack. No. 1 for 70 weeks in total from 1965 to 1968. The second highest number of weeks at No. 1 for any album. *South Pacific* soundtrack holds the record

Above: *4–2.*

'Kick the ****ing thing out of the ground,' Jack screamed. He said later that had a Leeds United defender taken such a risk in the penalty area in the final seconds of a critical match, he would probably have been suspended for a month by the manager – but this was Bobby Moore. Instead of kicking the ball out of the ground, he turned back into the penalty area with the ball at his feet. The Germans were frantic to regain possession but Bob was a picture of composure. He looked up and then hit the killer pass to me.

> When the fourth goal went in I remember helping out in defence enabling you to stand up-field waiting for the ball!
>
> *Roger Hunt*
> Roger Hunt

WORLD CHAMPIONS

It was the perfect ball. My first thought was not to give it away. We had to keep possession. I sensed that Overath was chasing me as I raced towards the German goal. Then I was aware of Schnellinger, having abandoned 'Bally', heading towards me from the side.

By this time I was about ten yards from their penalty area. I still don't know where I got the strength from to make that run. I'd been flattered a few minutes earlier when, after a similar long run, Hottges had gestured to me to slow down. He was in a worse state than I was.

Seconds remained. Kenneth Wolstenholme was telling a nation glued to their TV sets, 'Some people are on the pitch ... they think it's all over.'

I heard 'Bally' calling me as he burst forward in support. I decided to hit the ball with every last ounce of strength I had. Even if I missed the target the ball would bury itself in the crowd behind the goal and retrieving it would waste a few seconds.

Strangely, just as I shaped to hit the ball, it struck a divot in the pitch, bouncing up fractionally higher than I anticipated. Because of this, I caught the ball with the hard part of my instep and it literally flew like a bullet – past Tilkowski and straight into the net.

> The Germans were frantic to regain possession but Bob was a picture of composure. He looked up and then hit the killer pass to me

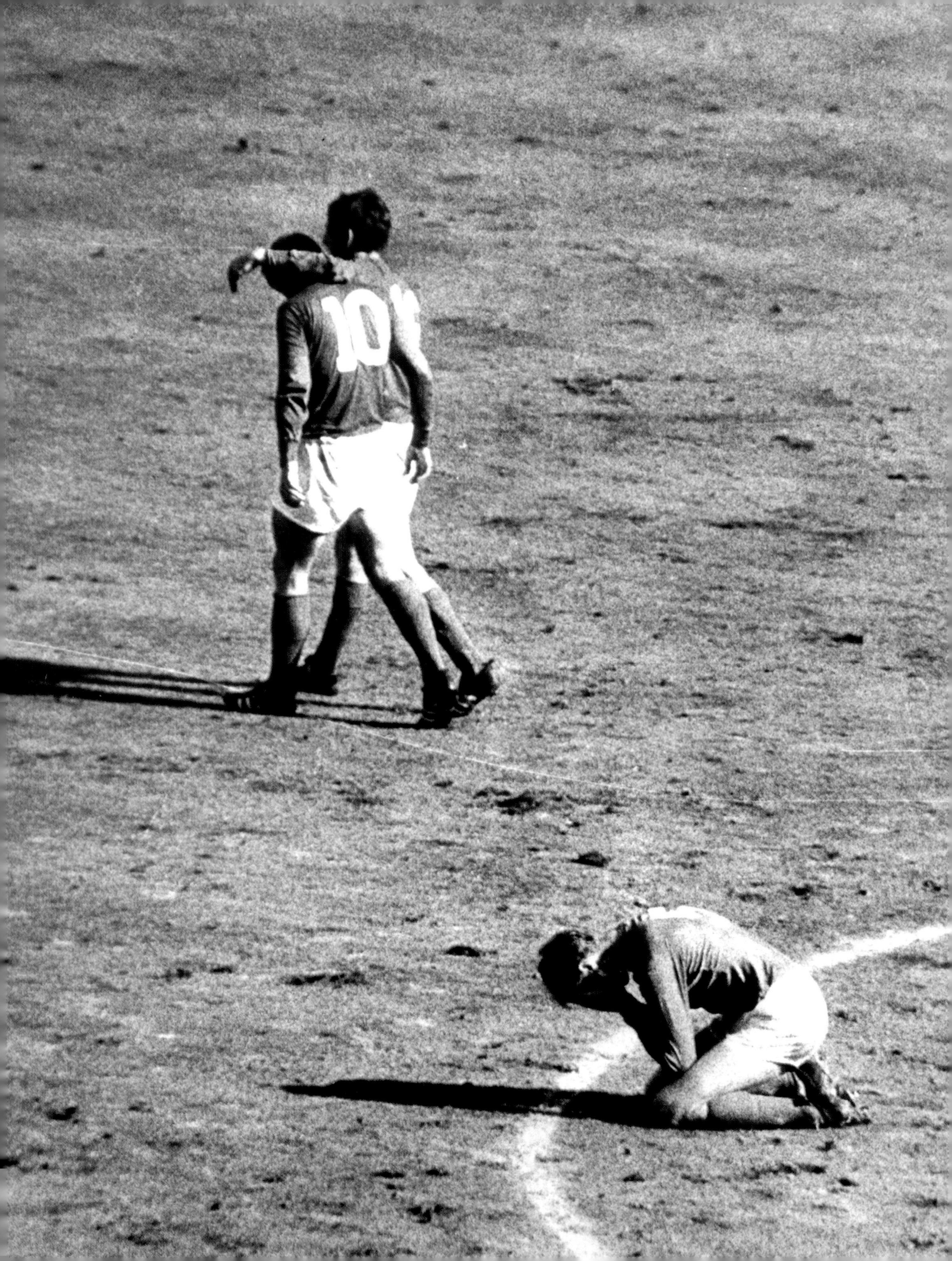
10

It was at this point that Wolstenholme concluded his famous piece of commentary with the words, '... it is now!'

It certainly was over. We'd won the World Cup and I'd scored three. Alan Ball was the first to jump on me. I just stood there, happy, exhausted, disbelieving. Judith's dad had been right. He said I'd score three!

Youngsters were running on to the pitch. Jack Charlton slumped with his head in his hands. My legs were trembling. Alf sat on the trainer's bench, practically expressionless, as Wembley exploded with noise and emotion.

The Germans didn't touch the ball again. Well, most of them didn't. Somehow the match ball was ghosted out of the stadium by Helmut Haller. Many years later, the *Daily Mirror* and Richard Branson agreed to pay £80,000 to retrieve the ball from Helmut's son's cellar.

I'd given the match ball no thought at the end of the game. Gottfried Dienst had blown the full-time whistle immediately I struck the fourth goal. Play never resumed. Amid the frenzy and jubilation, a thought nagged at the back of my mind. Did my third goal count? I wasn't worried about the second but had he blown the whistle before my third went in?

Everyone was congratulating me on my hat-trick but I wasn't convinced. I remember, once we had returned to the dressing room, walking back out to the pitch just to check the scoreboard. Sure enough it said England 4 West Germany 2.

> *It certainly was over. We'd won the World Cup and I'd scored three. Alan Ball was the first to jump on me. I just stood there, happy, exhausted, disbelieving*

I remember the World Cup of 1966 with very fond memories. Just prior I was invited to spend a holiday with Bill Tucker, the orthopaedic surgeon, at his home in Bermuda and whilst there he asked me if I would like ten tickets to see the games. I said yes and bought them. On my return home I gave the tickets to family and friends and we enjoyed the games up to and including the final when, of course, England won. Thanks Geoff!

Sir Henry Cooper OBE KSG

Opposite: *The final whistle.*

10
The party

The Football Association's official report into the World Cup final of 1966 said: 'No more gripping finale could have been offered as a product of the scriptwriter's art. If it had been fiction instead of fact, it would have been regarded incredulously.'

Not many would disagree with that summing up of a remarkable sporting occasion. Apart from the crowd at Wembley, a global TV audience of around 600 million had watched a dramatic and compelling match. Just consider this – an equaliser in the last minute of normal time, a goal still being disputed 40 years later and an England victory finally sealed with the last kick of a 32-match tournament.

As for my disputed goal, the FA report claimed that the official film confirmed the authenticity of the goal: 'The motion picture cameras established unquestionably the validity of the goal.'

For me, it was a life-changing 120 minutes. Almost everything that has happened to me since can be traced back, in some way or other, to that afternoon at Wembley.

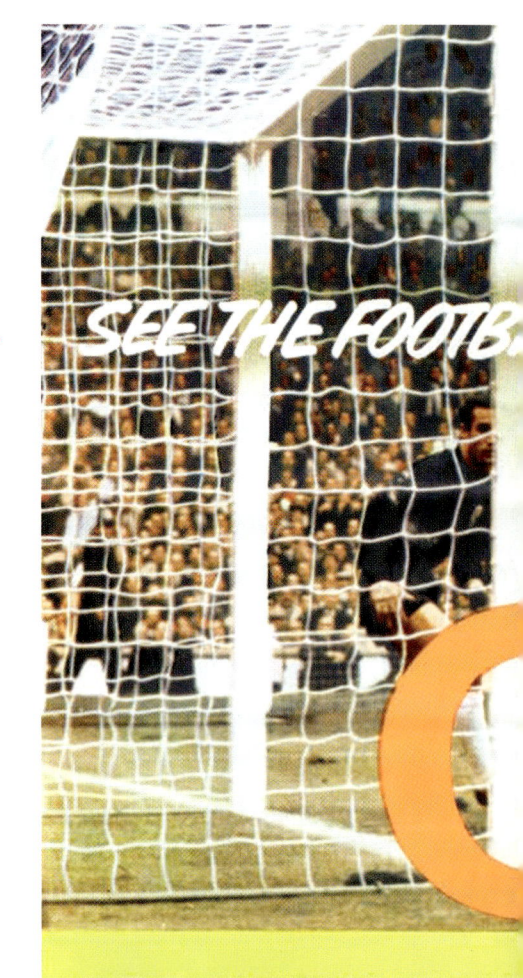

L STARS OF 16 NATIONS IN
GOAL!
THE COMPLETE FILM OF THE
WORLD CUP 1966
ON THE GIANT SCREEN IN
TECHNICOLOR & TECHNISCOPE
LLS
OF
OUR!
COMMENTARY WRITTEN BY BRIAN GLANVILLE · NARRATION BY NIGEL PATRICK · MUSIC COMPOSED BY JOHN HAWKESWORTH
DIRECTED BY ABIDINE DINO & ROSS DEVENISH · PRODUCED BY OCTAVIO SENORET · A COLUMBIA PICTURE
A BLC RELEASE

WORLD CHAMPIONS

Fame and celebrity hit us all with the speed of an express train. Exhausted and jubilant as I climbed the 39 steps at Wembley to shake hands with the Queen, I had no idea what life had in store for me. As captain, Bobby Moore was first up the steps to the royal box and, typical of the man, dried his hands on the velvet frontage before accepting the golden Jules Rimet Trophy from the Queen.

We jogged a lap of honour, with the crowd cheering both us and the Germans. Then we persuaded a bashful Alf to have his photo taken with the trophy and after a tumultuous hour in the dressing room we all tumbled aboard the team bus for the journey into the West End.

The streets were thronged with flag-waving fans as we made our way to the Royal Garden Hotel in Kensington High Street for the official reception. The police had closed the area to traffic to allow the crowds to congregate outside the hotel.

Limousines delivered the great and the good, including the Prime Minister, members of his cabinet, all the FIFA bigwigs and practically every FA official and functionary. The players and officials of the four semi-final nations were there, too.

Fame and celebrity hit us all with the speed of an express train

> **To be honest, most of the players couldn't wait to get away. We sat there politely in our official suits**

The key absentees were the players' wives, who had to eat separately in another part of the hotel, and sadly Jimmy Greaves. We all thought of him that evening but, quite obviously, he wanted to be alone.

It was a sumptuous, but stuffy, banquet and at some point we went with Alf to the balcony where we waved to the crowd below. The newspapers the next morning said that London had not seen such celebrations since VE Day, 21 years earlier.

To be honest, most of the players couldn't wait to get away. We sat there politely in our official suits, listening to the speeches and picking at the roast beef. Most of us wanted to join our wives and families and go somewhere less formal to celebrate. I remember nodding at a few of the German players but they seemed as anxious to get away as we did.

I'd made plans to go out with Judith and friends after the official dinner, just as we often did after a Saturday match. I asked Martin Peters, Alan Ball, Nobby Stiles and John Connelly and their wives to join

GEOFF HURST

Sunday Mirror

6d. July 31, 1966. No. 173

WORLD BANKERS PLEASE NOTE:

Britain's reserves went up yesterday by one valuable gold cup

GOLDEN BOYS!

Triumphant balcony line-up by the England team. Manager Alf Ramsey is waving fourth from left. Holding the World Cup—skipper Bobby Moore.

The players' coach arrives... and thousands cheer their idols.

LIKE Royalty, they stand on the balcony to hear the cheers of the great crowd.

This was the England team last night after their great 4—2 World Cup win against West Germany.

The conquering heroes had driven in a coach from Wembley to the Royal Garden Hotel in Kensington.

There they were cheered by thousands of fans blocking the road.

It was the West End's wildest night since VE night—in May, 1945. Hooting cars jammed the streets. In Trafalgar-square young people leaped into the fountains.

In Kensington, many of the excited fans broke through the police barriers to shake hands with their Soccer idols.

Every commissionaire in the normally sedate hotel helped the police to get the team inside for a champagne reception given by the Government.

At the reception, Premier Harold Wilson met Mr. and Mrs. Robert Charlton, the proud parents of England stars Jack and Bobby.

"I wish you'd had more children," quipped the Prime Minister.

Mrs. Charlton replied: "So do I. I could have done with eleven."

World Cup Special—Pages 6, 15, 16, 17 and 32

us at Danny La Rue's club in Hanover Square. It was one of London's hotspots at the time.

The wives waited for ages, tut-tutting as wives do, but at about midnight we set off in a fleet of taxis. In the end, Martin and Kathy Peters decided not to come. She had just completed a house move on her own and I think after such a long time apart they just wanted to be together.

At Danny La Rue's they made a fuss of us. Danny was on stage when we arrived and he stopped the show to announce that the World Cup winners had just turned up. Everyone stood up and applauded and the band played 'When the Saints Come Marching In'. We danced and drank and had a laugh. They presented us with a cake and I think, by this time, the drama of the day was beginning to take its toll. Even at this point, with the other revellers applauding this little knot of World Cup heroes, it didn't strike me that we had done anything special. It was a bit unreal. We were back in the hotel by three.

The wives waited for ages, tut-tutting as wives do, but at about midnight we set off in a fleet of taxis

GEOFF HURST

215

Above: *Bobby, myself and Martin proudly wearing our suits and enamel badges, just about to head in for the official dinner.*

Opposite: *'Can I have my ball back?' Helmut Haller sportingly congratulates me at the reception....*

So were most of the other lads. There were exceptions. Jack Charlton, the worse for wear, spent the night on the sofa of a complete stranger in east London. Next morning, as he sat on the patio trying to recover, a woman looked over the garden fence and said, 'Hello, Jackie.' She was a neighbour of his, visiting friends in London. They lived a few doors apart in the coal-mining village of Ashington in Northumberland.

The following morning most of us were back together again, reading the newspapers over breakfast and discussing where we'd been the night before. Judith and I went for a walk in Hyde Park. As we left the hotel a newspaper photographer stopped us and asked if he could take a picture. It was something I would have to get used to.

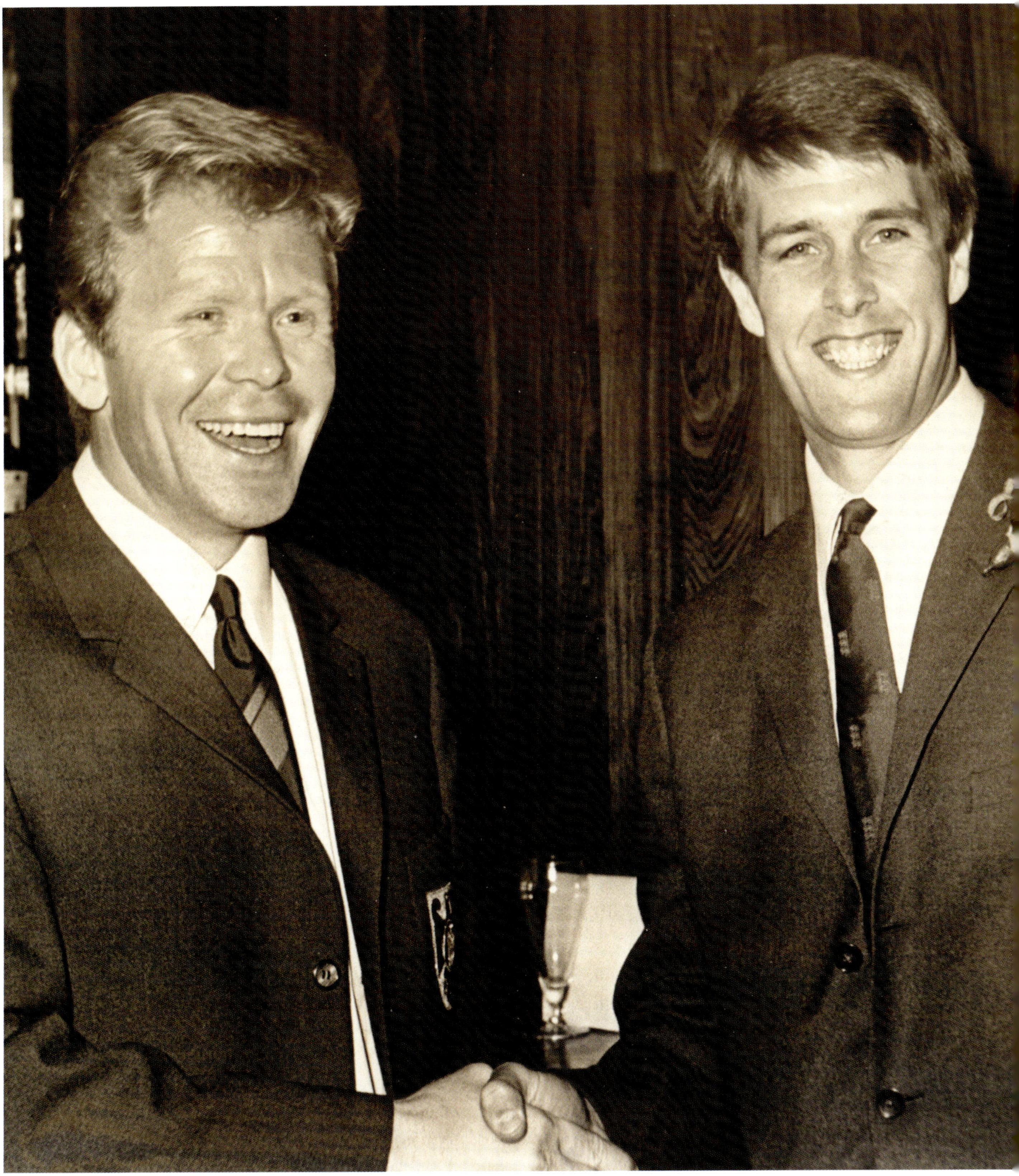

Above: ... and then off to dinner ...

Opposite: ... but not with the wives ...

About midday we were driven to the ATV studios for a lunch hosted by Eamonn Andrews. During a quiet moment, Alf explained to us the bonus arrangements proposed by the FA. For winning the World Cup we were to share £22,000 – not a fortune but still a considerable sum in those days. The FA proposed that the money be divided between the 22 of us according to how many games each had played in the tournament.

This meant that those who had played in all six games, such as Gordon Banks, Bobby Moore and Bobby Charlton, would receive

218　　　　　　　　　　　　　　　　　　　　　　　　　　　WORLD CHAMPIONS

significantly more than someone like me, who had played in three, or John Connelly or Terry Paine, who each played in only one match.

It says something for the team spirit in the squad that the senior players immediately put their heads together and persuaded Alf to change the arrangements. They felt the money should be shared equally between the players, regardless of the number of games played. So we each received £1,000.

It was the right decision. Years later, when I went into coaching and management, I realised that those who didn't play were often as

Above: ... at least until some of us made it to Danny La Rue's later that night.

Opposite: *A proud moment. Receiving the* News of the World's Man of the Match *award from Tom Finney.*

important as those who did. The players left on the sidelines are often the ones who determine the mood within a squad of players, especially when you are away from home for a long time.

Then, suddenly, it was all over. Handshakes, farewells, see you next time – 'Perhaps Geoffrey, perhaps,' said Alf ominously – and then, quietly, we all went back to our lives. We'd spent eight weeks together, won the World Cup and now it was over.

I assumed everything would return to normal but life was never quite the same after that for any of us. We were heroes and it took all of us time to come to terms with our new status.

Judith and I were driven back to our £5,000 semi-detached chalet bungalow in Hornchurch, Essex. It was our first marital home. Martin and Kathy Peters were taken to their new house in Barkingside. Halfway home a car ran into the back of them. No one was hurt but the accident happened outside a block of flats. People were peering down from their balconies.

I saw the final alone in a darkened room in
Bellingham, near Catford, south London, where
I was still living with my parents. They went
shopping! Can you believe it? I bet they were on
their own in Bromley.
   At 2-1 I nipped into the room next door for a
glass of Scotch - I felt I needed to celebrate
the event in some way. When I got back the
Germans had equalised and there were no action
replays to tell me what had happened. I sank the
Scotch in one to get over the shock.
   But I had tears in my eyes when Mooro collected
the Cup, as I did when my, by then, friend, died
in 1993.

Bob

Bob 'The Cat' Bevan

Then, suddenly, it was all over. Handshakes, farewells, see you next time

GEOFF HURST

221

Above: *The morning after the final before. Very happy to read the papers while waiting for breakfast.*

Opposite: *Sunday Express, front and back.*

When they finally arrived home, the telephone was ringing. The newspapers already knew that they'd been in a crash and the headlines the next morning read: 'World Cup hero in car smash!'

We were all used to signing autographs at our clubs but nothing had prepared us for the level of adulation that followed the World Cup. Strangers stopped us in the street, in shops, in the bank, on the train, in restaurants. We were asked to open shops, attend prize-givings and judge beauty contests.

It was all very flattering but I never took it too seriously. One cinema in Ilford asked me to go on stage to present a mini car to a competition winner. As I stood in the wings, the MC gave me a huge build-up and finally announced, 'A big hand please ladies and gentlemen for our very own World Cup hero – George Hurst! Come out here George and show yourself!'

On that Sunday afternoon, though, when I finally returned home to Hornchurch, I really had no idea what lay in store. We drove round to Judith's mum's house to pick up baby Claire, went home and I cut the

WORLD CHAMPIONS

SUNDAY EXPRESS

JULY 31 1966 — Founded by LORD BEAVERBROOK — PRICE 6d

WORLD CUP SOUVENIR

England team mobbed—biggest cheer of all is for Alf Ramsey

Goal-getting smiles... by Peters, Hurst and Hunt

IT'S JUBILATION NIGHT

Sunday Express Reporter

IT WAS LIKE a Coronation night when England's victorious World Cup footballers drove from their Hendon headquarters to a banquet and reception in Kensington last night to celebrate their 4—2 triumph over West Germany in the final at Wembley.

Banners and Union Jacks were strung everywhere along the route. Thousands stood on the pavements. Thousands more cheered from windows, from balconies, even from roofs as the team's bus drove by.

Long before the team arrived at the Royal Garden Hotel the whole area around the hotel was jammed full. The Automobile Association reported that traffic all over the West End was at a complete standstill.

Outside the hotel every car with a Union Jack started a new chant of "*England, England.*" There were cheers for a largely unsmiling Russian team which drove in a few minutes before eight — and more cheers (and a few boos) for Mr. Harold Wilson, who arrived with his wife.

But all the cheers of the deliriously happy crowd were dwarfed by the tumultuous roar that greeted the arrival of the Conquering Heroes.

As the bus pulled on to the hotel forecourt the cheering...

Callaghan

Big Yard swoop: 12 held

Sunday Express Reporter

ELEVEN MEN and a woman were arrested yesterday in a 12-hour operation by special briefed squads of Scotland Yard detectives was one of the biggest mass arrest operations ever known in London.

The arrested people were taken to West Central police station in the early hours of the morning. They had been picked up in a closely co-ordinated military style operation in the Greater London...

Eleven of the 11 arrested were charged last night and will appear at Bow Street court tomorrow on various charges...

Harry Trum... is taken ... hospital

ENGLAND—CHAMPIONS OF THE WORLD

England (1) 4   West Germany (1) 2

Hurst 3,   Haller,
Peters   Weber

(After extra time; score at 90 mins., 2-2)

At Wembley — attendance 93,000

AROUND 5.15 p.m. YESTERDAY the most triumphant and tumultuous din I have ever heard rose from the stands and terraces of Wembley Stadium. From every side of what has been described as "this historic cathedral of football" a blaze of Union Jacks waved as people, unashamedly gripped by emotion and patriotism, danced, wept, and hugged each other.

For as the whistle of Swiss referee Gottfried Dienst sounded the end of the truly manly and magnificent battle it meant that at last West Germany had conceded defeat.

England had WON.

England who gave honour to the rest of the earth, were FOOTBALL CHAMPIONS OF THE WORLD.

ALAN HOBY reports from Wembley

SWOOPED

● Martin Peters (16) and Roger Hunt (21) turn in triumph after Peters had cracked England's second goal

DANNY BLANCHFLOWER comments

Now I must pay tribut...

Right: Guardian, *1 August 1966. Totally relaxed and natural.*

Opposite: The Times, *1 August 1966. Not all the papers made a big splash about Martin's accident.*

We were all used to signing autographs at our clubs but nothing had prepared us for the level of adulation that followed the World Cup. Strangers stopped us in the street, in shops, in the bank, on the train, in restaurants

Football bliss—Geoff Hurst, scorer of three goals for England, with his wife in Kensington Gardens yesterday

lawn. Then I washed the car. It was pretty much like any other Sunday afternoon.

There was the inevitable sense of anti-climax, but it wasn't long before the new season started and Bobby, Martin and I were being cheered on to the pitch at Upton Park. Yes, on Saturday, 20 August, just three weeks after the World Cup final, West Ham faced Chelsea and lost 2–1. Can you imagine today's managers and players accepting that situation? I can't.

For me, World Cup success brought international recognition and a new six-year contract worth £140 per week. At the start of the year I'd been earning £45 per week. I also had an approach from the well-known American sports agent Mark McCormack who wanted to represent me. I was intrigued, but turned him down when I realised his company wanted 20 per cent of everything – including my salary from West Ham.

224   WORLD CHAMPIONS

In the wider world, England's success in 1966 laid the foundations for sweeping changes in the way the game was played. Alf's 'wingless wonders' had been a tactical triumph. Other coaches around the world took note. Some vilified England for a lack of flair and a reliance on work rate but eventually everyone was experimenting with 4-4-2.

Alf had demonstrated the value of efficiency, discipline, team work and defensive organisation. These qualities had made England difficult to beat. The downside of this was that there was no longer room for individual talent or unpredictable genius. Under Alf, every player had to fit into his basic strategy.

On the home front, football's boom years followed the 1966 World Cup. Many predicted a bleak future for the game but in England the crowds couldn't get enough. These were the days before wall-to-wall TV. If you wanted to see top-class football, you had to get out of your armchair and go to the stadium. In 1965–66, 27 million fans watched football in the four divisions of the Football League. By 1967–68 that figure was more than 30 million.

The rest of the world may have damned us with faint praise but no one can take away the fact we were the champions – and deservedly so in my opinion.

Above: *After our stroll in the park it was off to the ATV studios for a nicely understated lunch. You can see how much fun we are having.*

Opposite: *And then reality bites. Back in training with four days to go before the start of the new season.*

It has been said that England's victory in 1966 was the worst thing to happen to football. I agree with that in this respect only. Our victory set a benchmark against which all future England teams would be measured. None has got any closer to that standard than Bobby Robson's 1990 semi-finalists. Perhaps our successors have simply found it too big a challenge.

The truth is that anything short of winning the World Cup must be regarded as failure – as we all discovered in Mexico four years later.

GEOFF HURST

11 Whatever happened to?

So, what was the legacy of 1966? Was England's triumph in the World Cup final good for the game or was it, as Denis Law, claimed, 'The start of ten years of bad football'?

Denis had made a point of playing golf on the afternoon of the final, considering it disloyal for a patriotic Scotsman to watch England in such circumstances.

He was one of my idols and I understood how he must have felt when he finally heard that England had won the World Cup. It was, he said, a shock that he would never get over! I've always considered his after-match comments to be mischievous rather than malicious.

He said that he thought Alf's decision to play without wingers was the worst thing that had happened to the game because, according to him, it killed the art of scoring goals. He predicted that the game would become boring and predictable if Alf's system were copied. Others – Pele for instance – agreed with him.

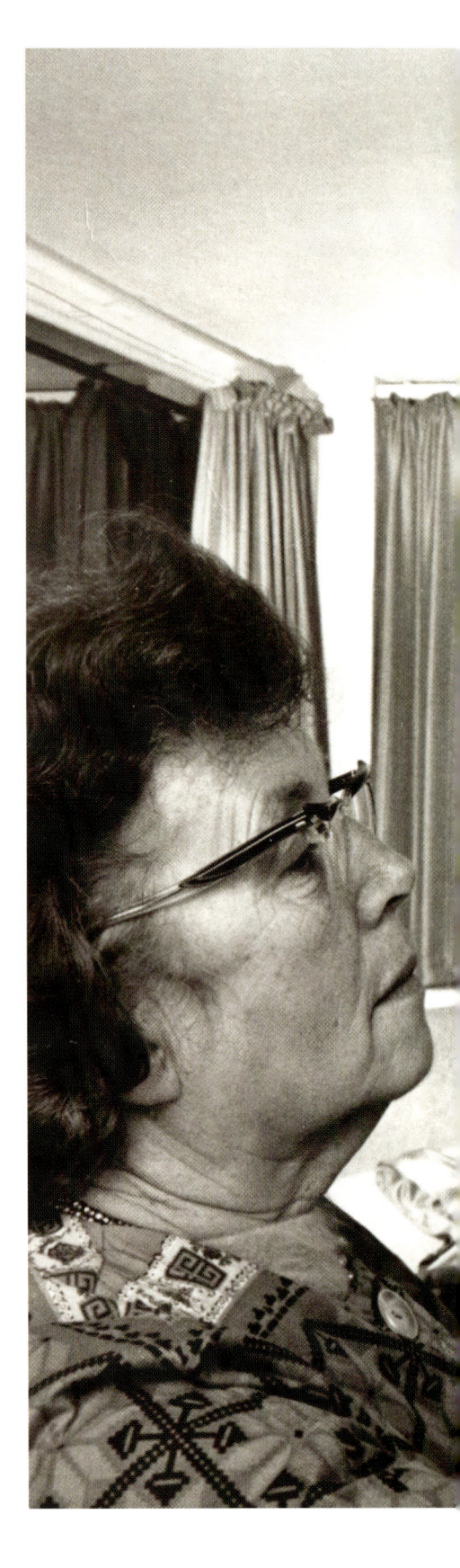

GEOFF HURST

Previous spread: *Winning the World Cup changed all our lives forever. Now I was of interest to sculptors ...*

Above: *... Bobby and I attended the Men of the Year lunch in November, alongside Atlantic rowers Sgt. Chay Blyth and Capt. John Ridgway ...*

Opposite: *... Jimmy, Bobby, Johnny Hollins and I met Miss World 1966 (Reita Faria from India) ...*

Nevertheless, many coaches decided to emulate Alf's tactics. In this sense, Alf's influence was indeed immeasurable. Some felt that his team exceeded the sum of its parts but there was no doubt that the team was successful, and for that reason it was copied.

So, without really intending to, Alf took football into a new age. The days when flying wingers such as Tom Finney and Stanley Matthews rampaged along the flanks were over. Alf organised defensive systems that restricted time and space and forced coaches to rethink their tactics.

Managers in the old First Division were the first to see the benefits of the Ramsey strategies. Just like Alf, they wanted teams that were hard to beat. While entertainment levels may have suffered, match attendances after the World Cup spiralled upwards.

Then, in 1968, Manchester United became the first English victors in the European Cup, providing an early hint of the approaching dominance of the First Division clubs on the continental stage. So it wasn't all bad news.

GEOFF HURST

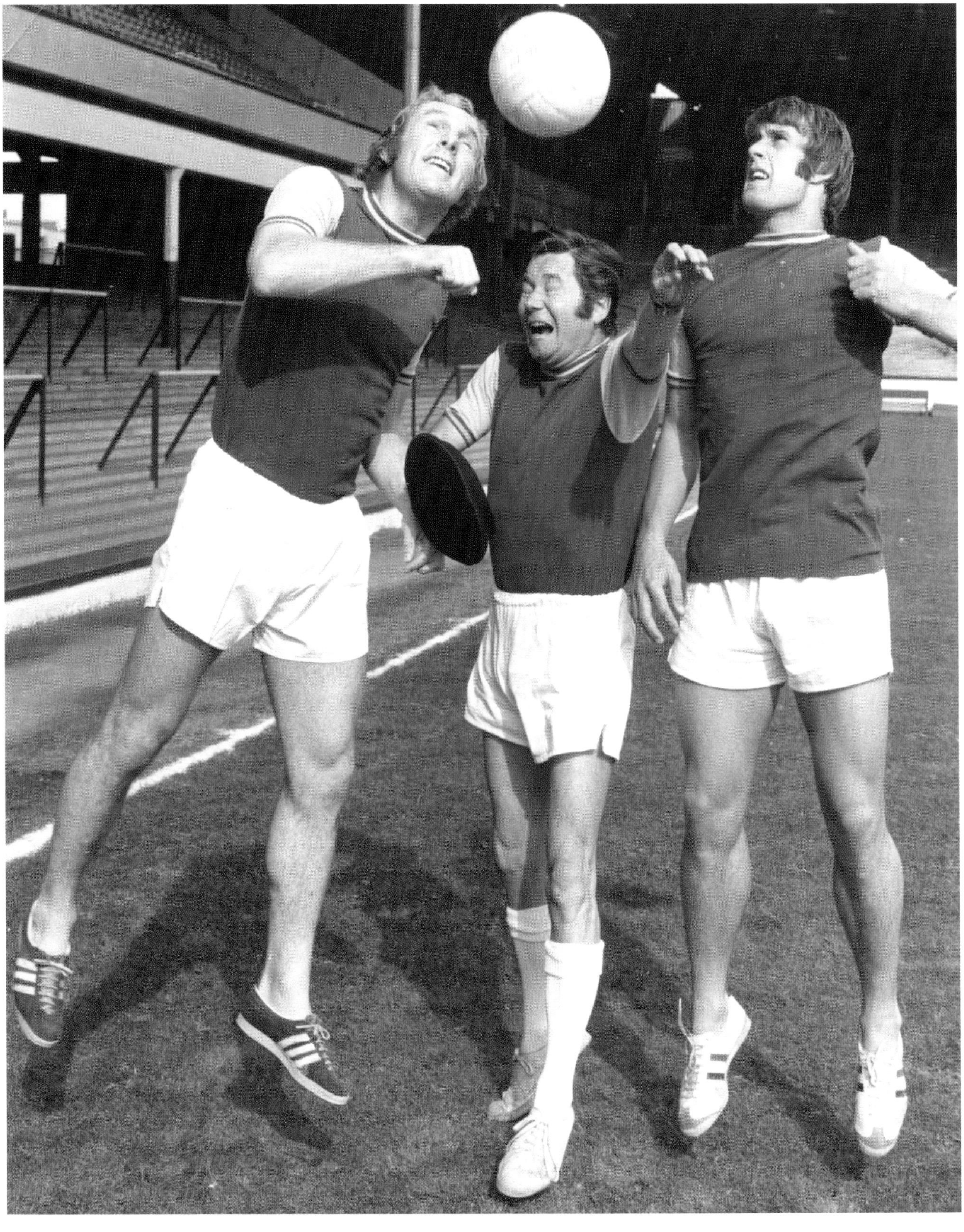

I would argue that Alf was simply the first to recognise the way the game was evolving. He produced a system that got the best out of the talent he had available. We had some tremendous individual players in 1966 but the one thing we all had in common was – Alf Ramsey. He brought us together and convinced a good bunch of lads that they could become world-beaters.

For the mother nation of football, winning the World Cup was the yardstick by which all that followed would be judged. It has since been argued that the victory in 1966 set an impossibly high benchmark. I don't see it like that at all. I see it as a realistic challenge that all those who have followed have failed to meet. It hasn't been a problem in Brazil – they've won the world title five times. The Germans and Italians have similarly risen to the challenge. They've both won it three times.

For the moment, Alf remains a unique figure, the only manager to steer England to victory in the World Cup. Since his departure, Don Revie, Ron Greenwood, Sir Bobby Robson, Graham Taylor, Terry Venables, Glenn Hoddle, Kevin Keegan and Sven-Goran Eriksson have

Opposite: ... we hung around with big-time celebrities ... and Reg Varney from On the Buses ...

Above: ... and years later we met Princess Diana at the 40th anniversary of the Queen's coronation.

Above: *'The Shrimp'. Jean Shrimpton, supermodel and an icon of Swinging Sixties London.*

all been entrusted with the job of leading England. Three more coaches have had the job on a caretaker basis – Joe Mercer, Howard Wilkinson and Peter Taylor. No one has matched Alf's achievement.

I know Alf bitterly regretted his failure to retain the trophy in Mexico in 1970. If anything, his team was better than in 1966 and the quarter-final defeat by the Germans in the heat of Leon, where we had led 2–0 with 40 minutes remaining, was a narrow thing.

Only five of the 1966 team remained to face the Germans that day – Bobby Charlton, Alan Ball, Bobby Moore, Martin Peters and me.

The World Cup-winning team played together just three times after that wonderful Wembley afternoon in July 1966. First against Northern Ireland in Belfast in the October and then the following month we played twice at Wembley – against Czechoslovakia and Wales. We beat the Irish 2–0, drew 0–0 with the Czechs and beat Wales 5–1 to take our unbeaten run of matches to 19.

The sequence had to come to an end some time. It was just unfortunate that it had to be at the hands of our friends from Scotland. Their team included a gloating Denis Law! In April 1967 England met Scotland in a European Championship qualifying tie at Wembley. These

Above: The Frost Report, *David Frost's satirical current affairs follow-up to his satirical current affairs sketch show* That Was The Week That Was, *made its debut on 10 March 1966. It brought the two Ronnies (Barker and Corbett) together for the first time and also launched John Cleese's TV career.*

were always special occasions. The Scots poured down to London and a crowd of 99,063 squeezed into Wembley.

Of the six games I played against Scotland this was the solitary defeat, but it was the one that mattered, particularly to the Scots. Denis, a wonderful player, scored the opening goal and, with 12 minutes remaining, it looked as though that would be enough to win the match. Incredibly, four goals arrived in those last minutes.

Bobby Lennox drove home a second for Scotland and, with five minutes left, Jack Charlton scored for England. Jimmy McCalliog made it 3–1 and, in the dying seconds, I scored with a header. It wasn't enough. The Scots had won and while we were bitterly disappointed they were naturally jubilant.

Denis insisted that the Scots should now be declared world champions. He even claimed that Alf's decision to replace Roger Hunt with Jimmy Greaves, the first team change he'd made in seven games, strengthened England and therefore enhanced the value of the Scottish victory!

I always thought it was something of a hollow win for them. This was still in the days before substitutes in international games and we

Opposite: *Remembering '66 didn't help us repeat the achievement in '70.*

Above: *19 games unbeaten until Denis Law opened the scoring at Wembley in 1967, steering the Scots to a 3–2 victory. Anyone but Denis ...*

were forced to carry three injured players for much of the match. Jack broke a toe in the 15th minute and spent the rest of the game hobbling round at centre-forward. Ray Wilson and Jimmy Greaves were later injured and Bobby Charlton finished the match playing at left-back.

In a sense, that defeat was the beginning of the end of the team of '66. In the following months Alf brought in Peter Bonetti, Keith Newton, Alan Mullery, Brian Labone and Norman Hunter, and began to rely less and less on George Cohen, Roger Hunt, Jack Charlton, Jimmy Greaves and Nobby Stiles.

Alf's team spanned three decades in the evolution of English football – the fifties, sixties and seventies. Bobby Charlton made his England debut in 1958 and the last of us to pull on the white shirt was the baby of the team, Alan Ball, who played his final game for England in 1975.

Alf was unceremoniously sacked by the Football Association following the failure to qualify for the 1974 World Cup, and by then 'Bally' and Martin Peters were the only members of the 1966 team still playing. The first members of the team to retire from international football were George Cohen and Roger Hunt. They played their last match together in the 2–0 win over Northern Ireland in November 1967.

WORLD CHAMPIONS

GEOFF HURST

'Big' Jack was a straight up-and-down centre-half without frills

Roger's England career spanned six years. He spent 11 great years at Liverpool, finished his club career with Bolton and then devoted all his energies to building up a successful haulage company with his brother. I sometimes see 'Hunt' trucks on the motorways.

He and Rowan now live in Warrington, Lancashire, and Roger spends a lot of time on the golf course and always attends the 1966 reunions. He's good fun and has a dry sense of humour that he demonstrated to perfection when I once asked him for his memories of that afternoon in 1966.

He wrote back to me: 'What I remember most about the fourth goal is helping out in defence, enabling you to stand upfield waiting for the ball!'

George Cohen's international career was relatively short, spanning just three years, but in that time he won 37 caps and finished on the losing side three times only. He spent his entire career with Fulham and when he finally hung up his boots at the age of 28 because of a knee problem, he had a successful second career in the property business.

He and his wife Daphne live near Tunbridge Wells and act as hosts at one of the hospitality suites at Craven Cottage on match days. He's still good to listen to because he talks such sense about football, especially when the conversation gets round to defending.

I'm sure he'll admit that he wasn't the most talented footballer in the team but I think he was physically the strongest and this must have helped him in his successful fight against cancer. He is the uncle of the World Cup-winning rugby player, Ben Cohen.

Ray Wilson had a 63-match international career and when he retired he concentrated on his undertaker's business in Yorkshire. Whenever he met one of us he'd always flourish a business card and say, 'You're not looking too good, you know, you better take one of these.' His sense of humour remains as wicked as ever. If you ask 'How's business?' he usually replies, 'Very good. Lot of flu about in our area!'

He lives with his wife Pat in Halifax and spends much of his spare time walking. I've promised I'll join him one day for a long trek over the Yorkshire Dales.

There's nothing pretentious about Ray, and you could say the same about Jack Charlton. 'Big' Jack was a straight up-and-down centre-half without frills. He made very little attempt to embrace the fashions of the day in the 'swinging sixties', which explains why Alan Ball's jokes about Jack's dress sense often had the dressing room in stitches.

Apart from his playing success with England and Leeds, he enjoyed a wonderful management career with Middlesbrough, Sheffield Wednesday, Newcastle and, most notably, the Republic of Ireland. In management terms, Jack was the most successful of the boys of '66. In seven years under Jack, Eire qualified for the finals of the 1988 European Championship and the finals of the World Cup in 1990 and 1994.

Soon after they'd qualified for the first time, we were at a function together. He was the after-dinner speaker, something he did well and often. We met in the bar and he said to me, 'What am I going to do, Geoff? Qualifying for the World Cup has wrecked my summer. I had it all planned – shooting, fishing, a few speaking engagements and a holiday.'

Below: *24 January 1966. George Harrison marries Patti Boyd at Epsom Registry Office.*

> **Nobby remains a much-loved figure in professional football**

When Kevin Keegan suddenly quit as England manager in 2000, Jack was with the rest of the 1966 team on a reunion cruise. We all tried to persuade him to apply for the job but he wouldn't consider it.

'I have too much to do with my shooting and fishing,' he said.

'Quite right, Jack,' said Ray Wilson who, incidentally, was voted 'best mingler' by the rest of us on that cruise because of the ease with which he mixed with other passengers.

These days, Jack lives with his wife Pat near Newcastle. As well as the shooting and fishing, he is still an outstanding after-dinner speaker. He makes me laugh as soon as he stands up to speak. He can be mercilessly funny when talking about his team-mates from 1966. Nobby Stiles is a long-suffering target of Jack's humour but takes it all in his stride. I remember Jack pointing him out in the audience at a dinner some years ago.

'How could people all over the world be so frightened of him,' he joked. 'Look at him now – a pathetic little man!'

Nobby remains a much-loved figure in professional football and when we are all together in public nowadays, he's often the one who

240   WORLD CHAMPIONS

gets most requests for photographs and autographs. His toothless jig of delight around Wembley, with socks around his ankles and the Jules Rimet Trophy in his hands, remains one of the nation's abiding memories of that afternoon.

Nobby, too, is a popular after-dinner speaker but he's cut back on his workload since he had a heart scare. He finished his playing career with Middlesbrough and Preston and after four years as manager of Preston from 1977 to 1981, he went back to Old Trafford to work on the coaching staff.

He and his wife Kay, the sister of Johnny Giles, are the most unaffected couple and still live in the same house in Stretford, Manchester, where they have spent most of their married life.

Twice a League Championship winner with Manchester United and, like Bobby Charlton, a European Cup winner, Nobby played the last of his 28 games for England against Scotland in April 1970. Alf took him to Mexico for the 1970 World Cup, but he didn't play. It was good just to have his enthusiasm in the dressing room.

For most of his England career, Nobby roomed with Alan Ball and they became very good pals, which they still are. In 1966, 'Bally' was full of boyish enthusiasm with an abundance of the self-belief that took root five years earlier when Bolton Wanderers told him that he would never be big enough to be a professional footballer. 'Bally' became one of the best midfield players of his generation, winning 72 caps. His distinguished playing career finally ended in 1982–83 with Bristol Rovers at the age of 38.

He shares with Jack the distinction of a successful management career, with Blackpool, Portsmouth (twice), Stoke City, Exeter City, Manchester City and Southampton, where he now lives. I think, though, he sometimes found the attitude of the modern-day player difficult to understand.

Still as lively and passionate as he was when playing, he now works in the media and is in demand as an after-dinner speaker. Sadly, his

Opposite: *One of our treasured get-togethers. Banksie's golf day in 1990, with Sir Alf. Big Jack must be in the bar...*

Above: *... or he might have been at the World Cup in Italy, managing Ireland.*

Martin's place in the history of the game is secure. After all, only two English players have scored goals in the World Cup final and he's one of them

> There was an expectant air around the East End of London the day our three heroes in claret and blue took on West Germany with the help of eight other players whose names I can't remember. I worked at Brown's supermarket in East Ham at the time, but dear Mr Brown gave us all the afternoon off as he didn't feel trade would be very brisk with the big game on the telly. When Kenneth Wolstenholme said, 'They think it's all over...', well it wasn't for me. I had to catch a 101 bus back to East Ham. It took an eternity. Cars hooted and claret and blue scarves hung from all the windows, as strangers linked arms to sing 'I'm Forever Blowing Bubbles'.
>
> When I arrived home my dad, a staunch West Ham supporter himself, and constant inhabitant of the wooden steps of Upton Park's Chicken Run (a part of the ground Geoff Hurst will remember well as many of his penalty kicks ended up there), had to ask me the score as he'd been under his Ford Prefect all afternoon, trying to sort out a knackered clutch. Yes, my dad worried me at times. I told him Geoff Hurst had scored a hat-trick. He scrubbed his hands with Swarfega and told me it was a shame he hadn't done it against Chelsea at the end of the season. In the evening I went to the Hammers pub in East Ham High Street and endlessly toasted my three West Ham heroes. So although I remember the 30th July well, I'm not too clear about the day after.
>
> Richard Digance

wife Lesley died last year after a long illness. She is missed by all the other wives. They met regularly at 1966 reunions and all became close friends. Judith and I always enjoyed Alan and Lesley's company, particularly when they joined us for a winter holiday in Australia.

Judith still speaks to most of the wives regularly, but none more often than Kathy Peters. Their friendship dates back more than 40 years to when Martin and I were youngsters at West Ham – and explains the size of the telephone bills we both face each month!

Martin and Kathy live in a leafy cul-de-sac in Shenfield, Essex, but Martin's roots are in the East End. His dad was a lighterman on the Thames and Martin would have gone on the river, too, but for the fact that he was such a talented sportsman. He was good at everything, but outstanding at football. He was the most versatile player of the 1966 team and when his long career with West Ham, Spurs and Norwich finished, he briefly tried management with Sheffield United.

After that, he and I teamed up again and worked for the same company in the motor insurance business for a long time. He's semi-retired now but still hosts a lounge at Tottenham on match days and works the after-dinner circuit. He remains as slim as a pencil. You'd think he was still playing football, but golf is his game these days.

Some may feel that the World Cup spotlight since 1966 has focused on Bobby Moore and me, but Martin's place in the history of the game is secure. After all, only two English players have scored goals in the World Cup final and he's one of them.

His after-dinner speaking routine contains an inescapable truth: 'Geoff is revered for his three goals in the final but if I hadn't scored the second, we'd have lost 2–1.' You can't argue with that!

Gordon Banks was the world's best goalkeeper in 1966 and was still ranked number one four years later when he pulled off that epic save

1966 Christmas No. 1 single: 'Green, Green Grass of Home' by Tom Jones. No. 1 for seven weeks

Below: *Save of the Century.*

Above: *Two years later Gordon lost his eye in this car accident.*

Opposite: *Bobby's last game: 28 April 1973, against Chelsea. Was he looking for a new career as a referee? Johnny Hollins certainly seems to think so.*

from Pele in Guadalajara. At one time, in 1965, I thought I might play with him at club level because he almost joined West Ham, but he went to Stoke City instead. I've never forgotten that his save from my penalty in the 1972 League Cup cost West Ham a place in the final. Shortly after that, West Ham sold me to Stoke and I was delighted at the prospect of finally playing alongside 'Banksie' in the First Division.

I'd played just eight games for Stoke when, in October 1972, just after he'd helped Stoke beat Chelsea in the League Cup final, Gordon was injured in a car crash and lost an eye. He was voted Footballer of the Year in 1971–72 but the accident ended his career, although he did play briefly in North America. Like most of the rest of us, he also tried his hand at management – with non-league Telford.

He and his German wife Ursula still live in Stoke-on-Trent. Gordon is also a favourite on the after-dinner circuit where he always receives a great reception with lines such as, 'I've got one eye, broken ankles, broken fingers, broken arms and hip replacements, but some wag will always ask, "You still playing Gordon?"'

WORLD CHAMPIONS

GEOFF HURST

The biggest challenge they've had to face since West Germany equalized. Keeping their cholesterol down.

It might have been the German forwards the England team had to watch in '66. But nowadays it's their cholesterol, as our football heroes recently discovered. To help they've gone for a substitution, switching their usual spread for Flora pro.activ. Thanks to natural substances called plant sterols, Flora pro.activ has been clinically proven to reduce LDL cholesterol by an average of 10-15%, when you move to a healthy diet. Maybe Flora pro.activ can help you towards the goal of lower cholesterol too. If you'd like more information, call 0800 027 1322 or visit www.floraproactiv.co.uk

Dramatically cuts cholesterol.

Bobby Moore played until 1978. He moved to Fulham in 1974 after 16 seasons in West Ham's first team, finally retiring after more than 1,000 senior matches. His last big Wembley occasion came in the 1975 FA Cup final when he played against his old club West Ham, who beat Fulham 2–0.

He flirted unsuccessfully with management at Oxford City, Eastern Athletic in Hong Kong and Southend United, and wrote a letter of application to the Football Association when the England manager Don Revie suddenly quit in 1977. The FA gave the job to Ron Greenwood. In 1990 he became a commentator for the Capital Gold radio station.

A year later, a few months after undergoing an operation for suspected colon cancer, he married his second wife Stephanie. He and Tina had divorced in 1986. His health slowly deteriorated though he still worked regularly for Capital. He died in February 1993, a week after watching England play San Marino at Wembley. He was 51. A few days before he died he called me at home. It was a strange phone call from Bobby, but Judith recognised the significance of it. I didn't realise it at the time but it was his way of saying goodbye.

A few days later, while driving in the north of England, I heard a news flash on the radio telling me that Bobby Moore had died. I knew he was ill but it was still a brutal shock. He had been part of my life and was only eight months older than me. Judith and I drove to West Ham to pay our last respects, along with thousands of others. The gates at Upton Park were festooned with flowers, scarves and messages from the fans. They'd built a shrine to Bobby. It was a moving, tearful occasion for both of us.

Above: *17 March 1966. Arkle and Pat Taafe on their way to their third consecutive Cheltenham Gold Cup.*

Above: *Roger, George, Alan, Ray and Nobby. A wrong righted at last.*

Each of Alf's World Cup-winning 11 has a niche in history but perhaps the reputation that will survive longest belongs to Sir Bobby Charlton

On hearing the news, Pele described him as 'the best defender I ever played against' but it was Alf Ramsey who best summed up Bobby's contribution to English football. 'I believe it would have been impossible to win the World Cup without Bobby as captain,' he said.

Each of Alf's World Cup-winning 11 has a deserved niche in history but perhaps the reputation that will survive longest belongs to Sir Bobby Charlton who is one of the greatest players in the history of the game. Despite the appalling experience he suffered in Munich in 1958, Bobby made a full recovery and emerged as the greatest English footballer of the last century. His achievements are unrivalled – the World Cup, the European Cup, three League Championships and three FA Cups with Manchester United. He was also voted Footballer of the Year in 1966. What he didn't win wasn't really worth winning. He was a prolific goalscorer but I believe he was at his best as a midfield organiser. For me, he was the pivotal figure in Alf's strategy.

He finally retired as a player in 1973 after 17 years in United's first team. He was briefly the manager of Preston but in 1980 returned to Old Trafford where he became a director. He remains an influential figure on the board and a confidant of Sir Alex Ferguson.

Bobby Charlton graced the game in an era that was different from today and, like Bobby Moore, his sportsmanship and sense of fair play provided parents and teachers with an example to set before children. His standards were high, his values deep and he was loved throughout the football world. He remains a wonderful ambassador for the nation, a man full of gentle dignity. We worked closely together during the Football Association's attempts to secure the right to host the 2006

World Cup, and it was plain to see the esteem in which he is still held around the world.

Bobby was knighted in 1994, a belated recognition of his huge contribution to football. Alf had been knighted in 1967, and quite right, too. Bobby Moore was awarded the OBE at the same time and, in later years, Gordon Banks, Jack Charlton, Martin Peters and I were awarded the same honour.

It wasn't until the New Year's Honours list of 2000 that the 'forgotten five', as they were described by the tabloid newspapers – George Cohen, Nobby Stiles, Ray Wilson, Roger Hunt and Alan Ball – were finally given the MBE. A wrong was righted when the Queen handed out those medals. I believe that by recognising some, and not others, you promote the idea that some contributed more. That wasn't the case. Ours was a team victory and if one man deserved greater praise than any other in 1966 it was not one of us but Sir Alf Ramsey.

Below: *What memories. What men.*

Statistics

Europe

Group 1
Bulgaria, Belgium, Israel

Belgium v Israel 1 – 0; Bulgaria v Israel 4 – 0; Bulgaria v Belgium 3 – 0; Belgium v Bulgaria 5 – 0; Israel v Belgium 0 – 5; Israel v Bulgaria 1 – 2

	P	W	D	L	F	A	Pts
Belgium	4	3	0	1	11	3	6
Bulgaria	4	3	0	1	9	6	6
Israel	4	0	0	4	1	12	0

Play-off (in Florence): Bulgaria v Belgium 2 – 1

Bulgaria qualified

Group 2
West Germany, Sweden, Cyprus

West Germany v Sweden 1 – 1; West Germany v Cyprus 5 – 0; Sweden v Cyprus 3 – 0; Sweden v West Germany 1 – 2; Cyprus v Sweden 0 – 5; Cyprus v West Germany 0 – 6

	P	W	D	L	F	A	Pts
West Germany	4	3	1	0	14	2	7
Sweden	4	2	1	1	10	3	5
Cyprus	4	0	0	4	0	19	0

West Germany qualified

Group 3
France, Norway, Yugoslavia, Luxembourg

Yugoslavia v Luxembourg 3 – 1; Luxembourg v France 0 – 2; Luxembourg v Norway 0 – 2; France v Norway 1 – 0; Yugoslavia v France 1 – 0; Norway v Luxembourg 4 – 2; Norway v Yugoslavia 3 – 0; Norway v France 0 – 1; Luxembourg v Yugoslavia 2 – 5; France v Yugoslavia 1 – 0; France v Luxembourg 4 – 1; Yugoslavia v Norway 1 – 1

	P	W	D	L	F	A	Pts
France	6	5	0	1	9	2	10
Norway	6	3	1	2	10	5	7
Yugoslavia	6	3	1	2	10	8	7
Luxembourg	6	0	0	6	6	20	0

France qualified

Group 4
Portugal, Czechoslovakia, Romania, Turkey

Portugal v Turkey 5 – 1; Turkey v Portugal 0 – 1; Czechoslovakia v Portugal 0 – 1; Romania v Turkey 3 – 0; Romania v Czechoslovakia 1 – 0; Portugal v Romania 2 – 1; Czechoslovakia v Romania 3 – 1; Turkey v Czechoslovakia 0 – 6; Turkey v Romania 2 – 1; Portugal v Czechoslovakia 0 – 0; Czechoslovakia v Turkey 3 – 1; Romania v Portugal 2 – 0

	P	W	D	L	F	A	Pts
Portugal	6	4	1	1	9	4	9
Czechoslovakia	6	3	1	2	12	4	7
Romania	6	3	0	3	9	7	6
Turkey	6	1	0	5	4	19	2

Portugal qualified

Group 5
Switzerland, Northern Ireland, Holland, Albania

Holland v Albania 2 – 0; Northern Ireland v Switzerland 1 – 0; Albania v Holland 0 – 2; Switzerland v Northern Ireland 2 – 1; Northern Ireland v Holland 2 – 1; Holland v Northern Ireland 0 – 0; Albania v Switzerland 0 – 2; Switzerland v Albania 1 – 0; Northern Ireland v Albania 4 – 1; Holland v Switzerland 0 – 0; Switzerland v Holland 2 – 1; Albania v Northern Ireland 1 – 1

	P	W	D	L	F	A	Pts
Switzerland	6	4	1	1	7	3	9
Northern Ireland	6	3	2	1	9	5	8
Holland	6	2	2	2	6	4	6
Albania	6	0	1	5	2	12	1

Switzerland qualified

Group 6
Hungary, East Germany, Austria

Austria v East Germany 1 – 1; East Germany v Hungary 1 – 1; Austria v Hungary 0 – 1; Hungary v Austria 3 – 0; Hungary v East Germany 3 – 2; East Germany v Austria 1 – 0

	P	W	D	L	F	A	Pts
Hungary	4	3	1	0	8	3	7
East Germany	4	1	2	1	5	5	4
Austria	4	0	1	3	1	6	1

Hungary qualified

Group 7
USSR, Wales, Greece, Denmark

Denmark v Wales 1 – 0; Greece v Denmark 4 – 2; Greece v Wales 2 – 0; Wales v Greece 4 – 1; USSR v Greece 3 – 1; USSR v Wales 2 – 1; USSR v Denmark 6 – 0; Greece v USSR 1 – 4; Denmark v USSR 1 – 3; Denmark v Greece 1 – 1; Wales v USSR 2 – 1; Wales v Denmark 4 – 2

	P	W	D	L	F	A	Pts
USSR	6	5	0	1	19	6	10
Wales	6	3	0	3	11	9	6
Greece	6	2	1	3	10	14	5
Denmark	6	1	1	4	7	18	3

USSR qualified

Group 8
Italy, Scotland, Poland, Finland

Scotland v Finland 3 – 1; Italy v Finland 6 – 1; Poland v Italy 0 – 0; Poland v Scotland 1 – 1; Finland v Scotland 1 – 2; Finland v Italy 0 – 2; Finland v Poland 2 – 0; Scotland v Poland 1 – 2; Poland v Finland 7 – 0; Italy v Poland 6 – 1; Scotland v Italy 1 – 0; Italy v Scotland 3 – 0

	P	W	D	L	F	A	Pts
Italy	6	4	1	1	17	3	9
Scotland	6	3	1	2	8	8	7
Poland	6	2	2	2	11	10	6
Finland	6	1	0	5	5	20	2

Italy qualified

Group 9
Spain, Rep of Ireland, Syria (withdrew)

Rep of Ireland v Spain 1 – 0; Spain v Rep of Ireland 4 – 1
Play-off (in Paris): Spain v Rep of Ireland 1 – 0

Spain qualified

Group 10
England

England qualified

South America
Group 11
Uruguay, Peru, Venezuela

Peru v Venezuela 1 – 0; Uruguay v Venezuela 5 – 0; Venezuela v Uruguay 1 – 3; Venezuela v Peru 3 – 6; Peru v Uruguay 0 – 1; Uruguay v Peru 2 – 1

	P	W	D	L	F	A	Pts
Uruguay	4	4	0	0	11	2	8
Peru	4	2	0	2	8	6	4
Venezuela	4	0	0	4	4	15	0

Uruguay qualified

Group 12
Chile, Ecuador, Colombia

Colombia v Ecuador 0 – 1; Ecuador v Colombia 2 – 0; Chile v Colombia 7 – 2; Colombia v Chile 2 – 0; Ecuador v Chile 2 – 2; Chile v Ecuador 3 – 1

	P	W	D	L	F	A	Pts
Chile	4	2	1	1	12	7	5
Ecuador	4	2	1	1	6	5	5
Colombia	4	1	0	3	4	10	2

Play-off (in Lima): Chile v Ecuador 2 – 1

Chile qualified

Group 13
Argentina, Paraguay, Bolivia

Paraguay v Bolivia 2 – 0; Argentina v Paraguay 3 – 0; Paraguay v Argentina 0 – 0; Argentina v Bolivia 4 – 1; Bolivia v Paraguay 2 – 1; Bolivia v Argentina 1 – 2

	P	W	D	L	F	A	Pts
Argentina	4	3	1	0	9	2	7
Paraguay	4	1	1	2	3	5	3
Bolivia	4	1	0	3	4	9	2

Argentina qualified

Group 14
Brazil

Brazil qualified

North and Central America

Group 15

Sub-Group 1: Jamaica, Netherlands Antilles, Cuba

Jamaica v Cuba 2 – 0; Cuba v Netherlands Antilles 1 – 1; Jamaica v Netherlands Antilles 2 – 0; Netherlands Antilles v Cuba 1 – 0; Netherlands Antilles v Jamaica 0 – 0; Cuba v Jamaica 2 – 1

	P	W	D	L	F	A	Pts
Jamaica	4	2	1	1	5	2	5
Netherlands Antilles	4	1	2	1	2	3	4
Cuba	4	1	1	2	3	5	3

Sub-Group 2: Costa Rica, Surinam, Trinidad

Trinidad v Surinam 4 – 1; Costa Rica v Surinam 1 – 0; Costa Rica v Trinidad 4 – 0; Surinam v Costa Rica 1 – 3; Trinidad v Costa Rica 0 – 1; Surinam v Trinidad 6 – 1

	P	W	D	L	F	A	Pts
Costa Rica	4	4	0	0	9	1	8
Surinam	4	1	0	3	8	9	2
Trinidad	4	1	0	3	5	12	2

Sub-Group 3: Mexico, USA, Honduras

Honduras v Mexico 0 – 1; Mexico v Honduras 3 – 0; USA v Mexico 2 – 2; Mexico v USA 2 – 0; Honduras v USA 0 – 1; USA v Honduras 1 – 1

	P	W	D	L	F	A	Pts
Mexico	4	3	1	0	8	2	7
USA	4	1	2	1	4	5	4
Honduras	4	0	1	3	1	6	1

Final Round

Costa Rica v Mexico 0 – 0; Jamaica v Mexico 2 – 3; Mexico v Jamaica 8 – 0; Costa Rica v Jamaica 7 – 0; Mexico v Costa Rica 1 – 0; Jamaica v Costa Rica 1 – 1

	P	W	D	L	F	A	Pts
Mexico	4	3	1	0	12	2	7
Costa Rica	4	1	2	1	8	2	4
Jamaica	4	0	1	3	3	19	1

Mexico qualified

Asia/Africa

Group 16

Australia, North Korea, South Korea

(In Cambodia)
South Korea withdrew
North Korea v Australia 6 – 1, 3 – 1

North Korea qualified

FINAL TOURNAMENT
ENGLAND
Group 1

11.7.66 England (0) 0, Uruguay (0) 0
WEMBLEY

England: Banks, Cohen, Wilson, Stiles, Charlton J, Moore, Ball, Greaves, Hunt, Charlton R, Connelly

Uruguay: Mazurkiewicz, Troche, Manicera, Ubinas, Goncalvez, Caetano, Cortes, Viera, Silva, Rocha, Perez

Referee: Zsolt (Hungary)

13.7.66 France (0) 1, Mexico (0) 1
WEMBLEY

France: Aubour, Djorkaeff, Artelesa, Budzinski, De Michele, Bonnel, Bosquier, Combin, Herbin, Gondet, Hausser (1)

Mexico: Calderon, Chaires, Nunez, Hernandez, Pena, Mercado, Diaz, Reyes, Fragoso, Padilla, Borja (1)

Referee: Ashkenasi (Israel)

15.7.66 Uruguay (2) 2, France (1) 1
WHITE CITY

Uruguay: Mazurkiewicz, Troche, Manicera, Ubinas, Goncalvez, Caetano, Cortes (1), Viera, Sasia, Rocha (1), Perez

France: Aubour, Djorkaeff, Artelesa, Budzinski, Bosquier, Bonnel, Simon, Herbet, De Bourgoing (1 pen), Gondet, Hausser

Referee: Galba (Czechoslovakia)

16.7.66 England (1) 2, Mexico (0) 0
WEMBLEY

England: Banks, Cohen, Wilson, Stiles, Charlton J, Moore, Paine, Greaves, Hunt (1), Charlton R (1), Peters

Mexico: Calderon, Chaires, Pena, Del Muro, Juaregui, Diaz, Padilla, Borja, Nunez, Reyes, Hernandez

Referee: Lo Bello (Italy)

19.7.66 Uruguay (0) 0, Mexico (0) 0
WEMBLEY
Uruguay: Mazurkiewicz, Troche, Manicera, Ubinas, Goncalvez, Caetano, Cortes, Viera, Sasia, Rocha, Perez
Mexico: Carbajal, Chaires, Pena, Nunez, Hernandez, Diaz, Mercado, Reyes, Cisneros, Borja, Padilla
Referee: Loow (Sweden)

20.7.66 England (1) 2, France (0) 0
WEMBLEY
England: Banks, Cohen, Wilson, Stiles, Charlton J, Moore, Callaghan, Greaves, Hunt (2), Charlton R, Peters
France: Aubour, Djorkaeff, Artelesa, Budzinski, Bosquier, Bonnel, Simon, Herbet, Gondet, Herbin, Hausser
Referee: Yamasaki (Peru)

	P	W	D	L	F	A	Pts
England	3	2	1	0	4	0	5
Uruguay	3	1	2	0	2	1	4
Mexico	3	0	2	1	1	3	2
France	3	0	1	2	2	5	1

Group 2

12.7.66 West Germany (3) 5, Switzerland (0) 0
HILLSBOROUGH
West Germany: Tilkowski, Hottges, Weber, Schulz, Schnellinger, Beckenbauer (2), Haller (2, 1 pen), Brulls, Seeler, Overath, Held (1)
Switzerland: Elsener, Grobety, Schneiter, Tacchella, Fuhrer, Bani, Durr, Odermatt, Kunzli, Hosp, Schindelholz
Referee: Phillips (Scotland)

13.7.66 Argentina (0) 2, Spain (0) 1
VILLA PARK
Argentina: Roma, Ferreiro, Perfumo, Albrecht, Marzolini, Solari, Rattin, Gonzalez, Artime (2), Onega, Mas
Spain: Iribar, Sanchis, Gallego, Zoco, Eladio, Pirri (1), Suarez, Del Sol, Ufarte, Peiro, Gento
Referee: Roumentchev (Bulgaria)

15.7.66 Spain (0) 2, Switzerland (1) 1
HILLSBOROUGH
Spain: Iribar, Sanchis (1), Gallego, Zoco, Reija, Pirri, Del Sol, Amancio (1), Peiro, Suarez, Gento
Switzerland: Elsener, Fuhrer, Brodmann, Leimgruber, Stierli, Bani, Armbruster, Gottardi, Hosp, Kuhn, Quentin (1)
Referee: Bakhramov (USSR)

16.7.66 West Germany (0) 0, Argentina (0) 0
VILLA PARK
West Germany: Tilkowski, Hottges, Weber, Schulz, Schnellinger, Beckenbauer, Haller, Brulls, Seeler, Overath, Held
Argentina: Roma, Ferreiro, Perfumo, Albrecht, Marzolini, Solari, Rattin, Gonzalez, Artime, Onega, Mas
Referee: Zecevic (Yugoslavia)

19.7.66 Argentina (0) 2, Switzerland (0) 0
HILLSBOROUGH
Argentina: Roma, Ferreiro, Perfumo, Calics, Marzolini, Solari, Rattin, Gonzalez, Artime (1), Onega (1), Mas
Switzerland: Eichmann, Fuhrer, Bani, Brodmann, Stierli, Armbruster, Kuhn, Gottardi, Kunzli, Hosp, Quentin
Referee: Campos (Portugal)

20.7.66 West Germany (1) 2, Spain (1) 1
VILLA PARK
West Germany: Tilkowski, Hottges, Weber, Schulz, Schnellinger, Beckenbauer, Overath, Kramer, Seeler (1), Held, Emmerich (1)
Spain: Iribar, Sanchis, Gallego, Zoco, Reija, Glaria, Fuste (1), Amancio, Adelardo, Marcelino, Lapetra
Referee: Marques (Brazil)

	P	W	D	L	F	A	Pts
West Germany	3	2	1	0	7	1	5
Argentina	3	2	1	0	4	1	5
Spain	3	1	0	2	4	5	2
Switzerland	3	0	0	3	1	9	0

Group 3

12.7.66 Brazil (1) 2, Bulgaria (0) 0
GOODISON PARK
Brazil: Gylmar, Santos D, Bellini, Altair, Paulo Henrique, Denilson, Lima, Garrincha (1), Alcindo, Pele (1), Jairzinho
Bulgaria: Naidenov, Chalamanov, Penev, Vutzov, Gaganelov, Kitov, Jetchev, Dermendjiev, Asparoukhov, Yakimov, Kolev
Referee: Tschenscher (West Germany)

13.7.66 Portugal (1) 3, Hungary (0) 1
OLD TRAFFORD
Portugal: Carvalho, Morais, Baptista, Vicente, Hilario, Graca, Coluna, Jose Augusto (2), Eusebio, Torres (1), Simoes
Hungary: Szentmihalyi, Kaposzta, Matrai, Meszoly, Sovari, Nagy I, Sipos, Bene (1), Albert, Farkas, Rakosi
Referee: Callaghan (Wales)

15.7.66 Hungary (1) 3, Brazil (1) 1
GOODISON PARK
Hungary: Gelei, Matrai, Kaposzta, Meszoly (1 pen), Sipos, Szepesi, Mathesz, Rakosi, Bene (1), Albert, Farkas (1)
Brazil: Gylmar, Santos D, Bellini, Altair, Paulo Henrique, Gerson, Lima, Garrincha, Alcindo, Tostao (1), Jairzinho
Referee: Dagnall (England)

16.7.66 Portugal (2) 3, Bulgaria (0) 0
OLD TRAFFORD
Portugal: Pereira, Festa, Germano, Vicente, Hilario, Graca, Coluna, Jose Augusto, Eusebio (1), Torres (1), Simoes
Bulgaria: Naidenov, Chalamanov, Vutzov (o.g.), Gaganelov, Penev, Jetchev, Yakimov, Dermendjiev, Jekov, Asparoukhov, Kostov
Referee: Codesal (Uruguay)

17.7.66 Portugal (2) 3, Brazil (0) 1
GOODISON PARK
Portugal: Pereira, Morais, Baptista, Vicente, Hilario, Graca, Coluna, Jose Augusto, Eusebio (2), Torres, Simoes (1)
Brazil: Manga, Fidelis, Brito, Orlando, Rildo (1), Denilson, Lima, Jairzinho, Silva, Pele, Parana
Referee: McCabe (England)

20.7.66 Hungary (2) 3, Bulgaria (1) 1
OLD TRAFFORD
Hungary: Gelei, Matrai, Kaposzta, Meszoly (1), Sipos, Szepesi, Mathesz, Rakosi, Bene (1), Albert, Farkas
Bulgaria: Simeonov, Penev, Largov, Vutzov, Gaganelov, Jetchev, Davidov (o.g.), Yakimov, Asparoukhov (1), Kolev, Kostov
Referee: Goicoechea (Argentina)

	P	W	D	L	F	A	Pts
Portugal	3	3	0	0	9	2	6
Hungary	3	2	0	1	7	5	4
Brazil	3	1	0	2	4	6	2
Bulgaria	3	0	0	3	1	8	0

Group 4

12.7.66 USSR (2) 3, North Korea (0) 0
AYRESOME PARK
USSR: Kavazashvili, Ponomarev, Shesternev, Khurtsilava, Ostrovsky, Sabo, Sichinava, Chislenko, Banischevski (1), Khusainov, Malofeev (2)
North Korea: Chan Myung, Li Sup, Yung Kyoo, Bong Chil, Zoong Sun, Seung Hwi, Bong Zin, Doo Ik, Ryong Woon, Seung Il, Seung Zin
Referee: Gardeazabal (Spain)

13.7.66 Italy (1) 2, Chile (0) 0
ROKER PARK
Italy: Albertosi, Burgnich, Rosato, Salvadore, Facchetti, Bulgarelli, Lodetti, Perani, Mazzola (1), Rivera, Barison (1)
Chile: Olivares, Eyzaguirre, Cruz, Figueroa, Villanueva, Prieto, Marcos, Fouilloux, Araya, Tobar, Sanchez L
Referee: Dienst (Switzerland)

15.7.66 North Korea (0) 1, Chile (1) 1
AYRESOME PARK
North Korea: Chan Myung, Li Sup, Yung Kyoo, Zoong Sun, Yoon Kyung, Seung Zin (1), Seung Hwi, Bong Zin, Doo Ik, Dong Woon, Seung Il
Chile: Olivares, Valentini, Cruz, Figueroa, Villanueva, Prieto, Marcos (1 pen), Araya, Landa, Fouilloux, Sanchez L
Referee: Kandil (United Arab Republic/Egypt)

16.7.66 USSR (0) 1, Italy (0) 0
ROKER PARK
USSR: Yashin, Ponomarev, Shesternev, Khurtsilava, Danilov, Sabo, Voronin, Chislenko (1), Malofeev, Banischevski, Khusainov
Italy: Albertosi, Burgnich, Rosato, Salvadore, Facchetti, Lodetti, Leoncini, Meroni, Mazzola, Bulgarelli, Pascutti
Referee: Kreitlein (West Germany)

19.7.66 North Korea (1) 1, Italy (0) 0
AYRESOME PARK
North Korea: Chan Myung, Zoong Sun, Yung Kyoo, Yung Won, Yoon Kyung, Seung Hwi, Bong Zin, Doo Ik (1), Seung Zin, Bong Hwan, Seung Kook
Italy: Albertosi, Landini, Guarneri, Janich, Facchetti, Bulgarelli, Fogli, Perani, Mazzola, Rivera, Barison
Referee: Schwinte (France)

20.7.66 USSR (1) 2, Chile (1) 1
ROKER PARK
USSR: Kavazashvili, Getmanov, Shesternev, Kornejev, Ostrovsky, Voronin, Afonin, Metreveli, Serebrannikov, Markarov, Porkujan (2)
Chile: Olivares, Valentini, Cruz, Figueroa, Villanueva, Marcos (1), Prieto, Araya, Landa, Yavar, Sanchez L
Referee: Adair (Northern Ireland)

	P	W	D	L	F	A	Pts
USSR	3	3	0	0	6	1	6
North Korea	3	1	1	1	2	4	3
Italy	3	1	0	2	2	2	2
Chile	3	0	1	2	2	5	1

Quarter-finals

23.7.66 England (0) 1, Argentina (0) 0
WEMBLEY
England: Banks, Cohen, Wilson, Stiles, Charlton J, Moore, Ball, Hunt, Hurst (1), Charlton R, Peters
Argentina: Roma, Ferreiro, Perfumo, Albrecht, Marzolini, Solari, Rattin, Gonzalez, Artime, Onega, Mas
Referee: Kreitlein (West Germany)

23.7.66 West Germany (1) 4, Uruguay (0) 0
HILLSBOROUGH
West Germany: Tilkowski, Hottges, Weber, Schulz, Schnellinger, Haller (1), Beckenbauer (1), Overath, Seeler (1), Emmerich, Held (1)
Uruguay: Mazurkiewicz, Troche, Ubinas, Caetano, Manicera, Rocha, Goncalvez, Silva, Cortes, Silva, Perez
Referee: Finney (England)

23.7.66 Portugal (2) 5, North Korea (3) 3
GOODISON PARK
Portugal: Pereira, Morais, Baptista, Vicente, Hilario, Graca, Coluna, Jose Augusto (1), Eusebio (4, 2 pens), Torres, Simoes
North Korea: Chan Myung, Zoong Sun, Yung Kyoo, Yung Won, Yoon Kyung, Seung Zin (1), Seung Hwi, Bong Zin, Doo Ik, Dong Woon (1), Seung Kook (1)
Referee: Ashkenasi (Israel)

23.7.66 USSR (1) 2, Hungary (0) 1
ROKER PARK
USSR: Yashin, Ponomarev, Shesternev, Danilov, Voronin, Sabo, Khusainov, Chislenko (1), Banischevski, Malofeev, Porkujan (1)
Hungary: Gelei, Kaposzta, Matrai, Meszoly, Szepesi, Nagy I, Sipos, Bene (1), Albert, Farkas, Rakosi
Referee: Gardeazabal (Spain)

Semi-finals

25.7.66 West Germany (1) 2, USSR (0) 1
GOODISON PARK
West Germany: Tilkowski, Lutz, Weber, Schulz, Schnellinger, Beckenbauer (1), Overath, Seeler, Haller (1), Held, Emmerich
USSR: Yashin, Ponomarev, Shesternev, Danilov, Voronin, Sabo, Khusainov, Chislenko, Banischevski, Malofeev, Porkujan (1)
Referee: Lo Bello (Italy)

26.7.66 England (1) 2, Portugal (0) 1
WEMBLEY
England: Banks, Cohen, Wilson, Stiles, Charlton J, Moore, Ball, Hunt, Hurst, Charlton R (2), Peters
Portugal: Pereira, Festa, Baptista, Jose Carlos, Hilario, Graca, Coluna, Jose Augusto, Eusebio (1 pen), Torres, Simoes
Referee: Schwinte (France)

Match for third place

28.7.66 Portugal (1) 2, USSR (1) 1
WEMBLEY
Portugal: Pereira, Festa, Baptista, Jose Carlos, Hilario, Graca, Coluna, Jose Augusto, Eusebio (1 pen), Torres (1), Simoes
USSR: Yashin, Ponomarev, Korneev, Khurtsilava, Danilov, Voronin, Sichinava, Serebrannikov, Banischevski, Malofeev (1), Metreveli
Referee: Dagnall (England)

Final

30.7.66 England (1) 4, West Germany (1) 2
(After extra time, 2 – 2 at 90 mins)
WEMBLEY
England: Banks, Cohen, Wilson, Stiles, Charlton J, Moore, Ball, Hunt, Hurst (3), Charlton R, Peters (1)
West Germany: Tilkowski, Hottges, Weber (1), Schulz, Schnellinger, Haller (1), Beckenbauer, Overath, Seeler, Emmerich, Held
Referee: Dienst (Switzerland)

Acknowledgements

I would like to express my sincere thanks to the many friends and celebrities who kindly shared their memories of 1966 with me; to my wife Judith and our three daughters, for their love and support; to Ron Greenwood for the faith he showed in me; to Sir Alf Ramsey and the 1966 squad who all made it possible; to Michael Hart, the *Evening Standard* football correspondent who helped me write this book; to Jack Rollin for supplying the statistics; and to David Wilson, Lorraine Jerram, Sarah Kellard, Rebecca Purtell and all the magnificent team at Headline.

Picture credits

We would like to thank the following for kindly supplying material for use in the book:
Advertising Archives: 82, 102, 246
AP: 23, 55
Graham Budd: 36, 114, 210-11, 214
Neville Chadwick: 240
Corbis: 58, 112-13, 192, 198
Daily Express: 45
Hunter Davies: 63, 188
Empics: 27, 30, 33, 40-41, 53, 56-7, 59, 60, 62, 65, 69, 70, 73, 74, 75, 76, 77, 78, 79, 80, 84-5, 95, 96, 121, 122, 124, 125, 128, 129, 134-5, 136, 142, 149, 150, 161, 165, 170-71, 195, 196, 199, 205, 215, 222, 223, 226, 230, 245, 248, 249
R. Fortune: 228-9
Getty Images: 10-11, 12, 13, 14, 15, 16, 20, 28, 29, 31, 34, 39, 48, 49, 50 (right), 51, 64, 66, 89, 94, 105, 110, 118, 126, 133, 144, 154, 155, 158, 166, 167, 172, 186, 189, 190, 191, 212, 234, 239, 243, 247
Glasgow Herald: 231
Guardian: 224
Geoff Hurst Collection: 26, 44, 143, 194, 200, 202, 206, 211, 216, 217, 218, 219, 220, 233, 238
John Frost Newspapers: 19, 54, 98, 140, 146
Kobal Collection: 86, 119, 178
London Weekend Television: 232
Mirrorpix: 9, 18
National Football Museum, Preston: 210, 237
News of the World: 221
Popperfoto: 24-5, 35, 91, 92, 115, 117, 139, 148, 168, 192, 201, 204, 236, 241, 244
Redferns Music Picture Library: 101, 185
Ronald Grant Archive: 88, 103, 123, 127, 145, 177, 182
Sports Argus: 173
The Times Archive: 116, 225
Topfoto: 47, 50 (left), 61, 106, 152-3, 164, 227
Topix: 194, 213
Vinmag Archive: 21, 22, 32, 81, 87, 141, 151, 174, 175, 181, 235